Capability Brown

AND THE EIGHTEENTH-CENTURY ENGLISH LANDSCAPE

Capability Brown.

AND THE EIGHTEENTH-CENTURY ENGLISH LANDSCAPE

ROGER TURNER

WEIDENFELD AND NICOLSON
LONDON

To
those with
'a poet's feeling or a painter's eye'
this book is
DEDICATED

Designed by Joyce Chester and Yvonne Dedman
Filmset by Butler & Tanner Ltd
Colour separations by Newsele Litho S.P.A., Italy
Printed and bound in Great Britain by
Butler & Tanner Ltd, Frome and London

Contents

Synopsis of Brown's Life

1716 Lancelot Brown baptized at Kirkharle, Northumberland on 30 August.

1720 William Brown (his father) dies.

1732 Starts work with Sir William Loraine at *Kirkharle Hall*.

1739 Brown moves south. Working at *Kiddington*, Oxfordshire, for Sir Charles Browne.

1740 Working for Lord Cobham at *Stowe*, Buckinghamshire.

1742 Advising at *Wotton House*, Buckinghamshire.

1744 Marries Bridget Wayet at Stowe.

1745 *Newnham Paddox*.

1746 Bridget Brown born.

1748 Lancelot (Lance) Brown born.

1750 *Croome Court*.

1751 John Brown born.

1751 Brown family leaves Stowe for Hammersmith.

1751 *Petworth*.

1750s Thomas and Margaret (Peggy) Brown born.

1754 *Burghley*.

1757 *Bowood*.

1758 Petition for the Royal Appointment.

1760 *Chatsworth, Chillingham*.

1763 *Audley End, Blenheim*.

1764 Appointment as Master Gardener at Hampton Court, and Gardener at St James's. Moves to Wilderness House, Hampton Court.

1764 *Broadlands*.

1766 *Sandbeck*.

1767 Purchase of Fenstanton Manor, Huntingdonshire.

1767 *Wimpole*.

1769 *Claremont*.

1770 Appointment as High Sheriff of Huntingdonshire.

1771 Partnership with Henry Holland the Younger.

1771 *Coombe Abbey, Grimsthorpe*.

1773 Marriage of Bridget Brown to Henry Holland.

1774 *Harewood, Himley*.

1775 *Sherborne*.

1778 *Berrington, Nuneham Courtenay*.

1781 *Heveningham*.

1783 Death of Lancelot Brown on 13 January.

Introduction

We have discovered the point of perfection. We have given the true model of gardening to the world; let other countries mimic or corrupt our taste; but let it reign here on its verdant throne, original by its elegant simplicity, and proud of no other art than that of softening Nature's harshness and copying her graceful touch.

HORACE WALPOLE

Not many people have the chance to abandon their desks and ordinary duties and spend several months trudging round some of the most beautiful man-made landscapes in the country. It has been an experience which I have found at times uplifting, and at times depressing. Uplifting when I discovered scenes of immense and unexpected beauty: Grimsthorpe on a bright September morning, open to a wide, translucent sky; or Bowood in a November mist, an impressionistic array of autumn colours. Depressing when yet another lost landscape presented itself, a morass of reeds, nettles and brambles.

Today a survey of the work of our hero should best be called 'The Lost Landscapes of Lancelot Brown'. The number of well-preserved examples of his work is pitifully few. The 'ubiquitous Capability Brown' says one writer, and his work is generally thought to be so widespread and common that it could hardly be under threat. Yet many of his landscapes have vanished without a trace (Digswell, Fisherwick, Highcliffe, Navestock), have been built over (Benwell Tower, Caversham, Ealing Park, Testwood), or have been vitiated by Victorian alterations (Castle Ashby, Coombe Abbey, Thoresby, Trentham). The best (Highclere, Petworth) are threatened with by-passes and pylons, while the great majority are continually eroded by agriculture and forestry; many are under split ownership, a diminishing and decaying remnant, whose owners perhaps do not know what they have got or can scarcely afford to preserve. Fortunately, sufficient of Brown's work still survives to give us a fine impression of his style; indeed the maturity of the planting is such that many of his landscapes now have a richness and beauty which they never had in his lifetime.

The progress of Lancelot Brown from his obscure origins in Northumberland to fame and success is a fascinating story. Apart from his genius as a designer, we find that he was a likeable man: his clients got on well with him, and he was easy to work with and business-like in his methods. His energy was extraordinary; he thought nothing of travelling from one end of the country to the other, supervising extremely large-scale works with the utmost confidence.

If we consider the face of England and the way it has changed over the centuries, it is hard to think of many single individuals who have had an effect on the appearance of the countryside nationwide. Deforestation, the enclosure of fields, canal-building, road-making: these have all been gradual processes; and the creation of the great eighteenth-century parks was part of a general desire for improvement. Where there had been open strip farming or else a patchwork of small fields, straggling hamlets or useless marshland, a dramatic transformation took place. However, this parkland owes its splendid and effortless style to the genius of Lancelot Brown, in William Cowper's words:

> Lo he comes!
> Th'omnipotent magician, Brown, appears! . . .
> He speaks. The lake in front becomes a lawn;
> Woods vanish, hills subside, and vallies rise:
> And streams, as if created for his use,
> Pursue the track of his directing wand,
> Sinuous or straight, now rapid and now slow,
> Now murm'ring soft, now roaring in cascades –
> Ev'n as he bids!

By the time these lines were written Brown had become a somewhat controversial figure, but he had little reason to be troubled by this, so secure were his fame and reputation. Even today he tends on the one hand to be credited with laying out every piece of parkland in the country, while he is blamed, on the other, for removing all the formal gardens which preceded the Landscape Movement. As recently as 1979 the organizers of the Garden Exhibition at the Victoria and Albert Museum decided to exclude Brown, arguably Britain's most famous gardener, on the curious basis that his 'art and genius was entirely one of modulating ground, trees and water'. Maybe they were looking for exciting content, not for beauty of form.

Before we make any judgement about 'the famous Mr Brown' we must attempt to understand what his work consists of, what his intentions were, and to what extent they are represented by what survives. 'Who was this familiar but insubstantial character, alleged to have altered the appearance of much of the English countryside . . .?' This was the question that Dorothy Stroud set out to answer, just before the 1939–45 war. Thanks to her researches, a great number of facts about Brown's life and work are now known, and these have been supplemented more recently by further research by Dr Peter Willis. But there is another question we must ask, and this is: what precisely is a Capability Brown landscape? Is it a garden? Well, not exactly. Is it natural, artificial, horticultural, agricultural, aesthetic, or what is it? Certainly we must try to answer this question before we start to maintain or preserve a Brown landscape; otherwise we may do more harm than good, and impose on it our misunderstandings. If this book can do a little to create an increased appreciation of Capability Brown's work, or help to motivate someone to cut down a bramble, pull out some rushes from the water's edge, or carefully fell a dangerous tree before it falls into the lake, then it will have served some useful purpose.

The Gazetteer

The Gazetteer (p.172) attempts to provide at least a little basic information about every park where Brown is known to have worked, and those where the landscape is doubtfully attributed to him. In the event, this proved a more difficult task than was anticipated, since so few of the parks have been studied in detail. To determine even such minimal facts as the original extent and the present condition would involve a research programme of considerable length. The first edition six-inch Ordnance Survey maps are an invaluable source of information, and so is Desmond Ray's *Bibliography of British Gardens*.

A very large amount of research remains to be done, and the author would be pleased to receive further information about any of Brown's parks, especially if this leads to the correction of any errors in the Gazetteer or main text.

A harmonious and tranquil scene at Grimsthorpe, Lincolnshire: the English countryside shown to perfection. In Pope's words: 'True art is Nature to advantage dress'd . . .'

Many of Brown's landscapes have been built over or returned to agricultural use, and others are derelict. Intended views back to the house at Coombe Abbey are now virtually impossible.

Priests Sacrificing to Apollo. The paintings of Claude Lorraine (1600–82) were a constant source of inspiration to the Landscape Movement.

Overleaf: The Temple of Ancient Virtue at Stowe. Designed by William Kent, it overlooks the Elysian Fields (*c*1730), one of the earliest attempts at the natural style.

Landowners and the Landscape

L ANCELOT Brown was born in 1715, eleven years after the battle of Blenheim, nine years after Ramillies and two years after the Treaty of Utrecht. During his lifetime (1715–83) Britain enjoyed a stability and tranquillity which was not disturbed until the Napoleonic Wars at the end of the century. At home, the establishment of the House of Hanover brought an end to the conflicts between King and Parliament that had marked the Stuart period. Socially and politically the country was dominated by the great landowners, who ran Parliament and whose influence permeated every sphere of life. Yet, despite the domination of this small aristocracy, civil and personal liberties improved, toleration and wealth increased, and with the patronage of an enlightened, leisured class, literature and the arts flourished. In Trevelyan's words:

Freed from the disturbing passions of the past, and not yet troubled with anxieties about a very different future which was soon to be brought upon the scene by the Industrial and French Revolutions ... the gods mercifully gave mankind this little moment of peace between the religious fanaticisms of the past and the fanaticisms of class and race that were speedily to arise ...[1]

In place of the conflict of the seventeenth century, a desire for moderation and tolerance became increasingly evident. If the new philosophy had once 'put all in doubt', it now embraced a new faith, a faith in the reasonableness, the harmony and 'logick' of Nature. There was to be no area of study which would not succumb to the Laws of Reason. God was safe in his heaven, a comfortable non-interventionist God, busy oiling the wheels of his marvellous, almost mechanical universe: *Christianity Not Mysterious* was the title of John Toland's book, published in 1696. 'All Nature's wonders serve to excite and perfect this Idea of their Author,' wrote Lord Shaftesbury (1671–1716). 'How glorious is it to contemplate him, in this noblest of his Works apparent to us, The System of the Bigger World.' Even the landscape (a subject which specially concerns us) confirms the same 'wondrous tale':[2]

Ye fields and woods my refuge from the toilsome world of business, receive me in your quiet sanctuaries, and favour my retreat and thoughtful solitude ... O Glorious Nature, supremely fair and sovereignly good, all-loving and all-lovely, all-divine ... this solitude ... these rural meditations are sacred; whilst thus inspired with harmony of thought I sing of Nature's Order in created beings, and celebrate the beauties which resolve in Thee, the Source and Principle of all Perfection and Beauty.[3]

If a greater understanding of the natural sciences gave philosophers a belief that the universe was a harmonious and stable place, it also gave politicians a similar belief that if men behaved rationally and sociably (as Nature intended) then conflict could be resolved and stability would increase. In Christopher Hussey's words:

Where the seventeenth century had tried to impose autocratic patterns on an expanding world, the empirical English revolution found that the rational way to resolve the polarities confronting the age lay in comprehending them.[4]

Once the Protestant succession was established, and the security and stability it brought began to be enjoyed, the heat of the earlier conflicts cooled into a verbal war of tracts. The futility of these hostilities was seen by men like Jonathan Swift and Alexander Pope. Eventually, excessive enthusiasm was considered almost an indication of poor taste: 'for forms of government let fools contest',[5] declared Pope. Certainly Whigs and Tories were united when it came to comparing the liberty of the British with 'the haughty tyrants' of France.

When George I became king, the intervention of the monarchy in the running of the country declined to a merely annoying irritation. George spoke no English, and it was during his reign the role of Prime Minister appeared – in the person of Sir Robert Walpole – as if to demonstrate that some kind of recognizable leadership was required to replace what was not forthcoming (or desired) from the monarchy.

Even before George I, neither King William nor Queen Anne had kept a Court in the lively way that the monarchy had done previously. From medieval times down to Charles II, the Court had been the centre of pleasure, politics, fashion and learning, and a source of patronage for writers and artists, but from now on the great houses of the aristocracy took on this function, and royalty retired to the seclusion of Hampton Court or Windsor; even the palace at Kensington was out of town in the 1700s.

Current ideas on politics and religious toleration had been crystallized by the philosopher John Locke. Between 1689 and 1706 Locke published his four *Letters Concerning Toleration* and his two *Treatises on Civil Government*, in which he expressed his belief that it is natural for men to live peacefully together, without needing the domination of an absolute ruler. If men were naturally belligerent and ignorant (as Hobbes[6] had taught) they might need to be suppressed by an autocratic ruler who places himself beyond criticism; but Locke's belief was that men are rational creatures who desire security and justice. Furthermore, the subjects of any country must have the right to judge for themselves whether their rulers are serving the common good or not.

What makes men join together in society, according to Locke, is the desire to preserve their property. It was no accident, therefore, that the men of property now held the strings of power. The Whig theory of government was that of a 'contract' between the people and their ruler. The royal succession, for example, was not allowed to go its own way; on the contrary, George I became king at Parliament's invitation. It was said that there were fifty-seven other persons nearer in line than the Elector of Hanover. From now on laws were to be made not by the arbitrary wish of a despot, but by an elected Parliament following public debate. This was the period that saw the growth of political parties, and even saw the benefit of having an opposition. This enlightened, rational spirit, and the growing realization of the practical benefits of moderation and harmony, created a society that was stable and flexible enough to see the seeds sown of the Agrarian and Industrial Revolutions, which were to usher in the modern world.

If power had a broader base, it was now spread across those who owned property, and in general terms the greater the property the greater the power. The houses of the aristocracy became centres of political influence, and they were also centres of patronage of the arts and a source of wealth and employment for local country- and townspeople. The great landowners were dominant at local level, but at national level their influence was even stronger, owing to their overwhelming presence in Parliament. The House of

Lords, a far more powerful body than it is today, was made up almost entirely of landowning peers, and even the House of Commons was largely controlled by the aristocracy. Many members of the lower house were close relatives of the peers, and frequently elections were virtually rigged as a result of bribery and intimidation.

It has been estimated that there were about four hundred families 'who could be described as great landlords'.[7] Landownership formed a kind of pyramid, spreading out from the aristocracy down to the smallest yeoman farmer, forming three rough categories: the peers, the gentry and the freeholders. Thus landownership was not a closed social class, and the most able and ambitious were with difficulty able to break in on the established circles of the aristocracy. But to acquire a great house and several thousand acres required such a vast outlay of capital that very few indeed could do it in the course of one lifetime. Royal favour could no longer be a way of obtaining wealth and landownership in the way it had been in the past, and the only route to the top for those without inherited wealth lay in outstanding success in a military career, law or trade.

Not surprisingly the intermarriage of the established great landowners became a way of maintaining and increasing the value of the estates. The marriage connections of Lancelot Brown's clients are a study in themselves. Sometimes several small estates would be inherited, and the smallest ones would be sold off to build up the size and extent of the favourite one; such sales could also be used to fund the extension or modernization of the great house, or the improvement of the grounds under Brown's direction. At least five or six thousand pounds a year was required to support a great house, to allow for the expenses of the London season and to enable the owner to patronize the arts. More comfortably it required ten thousand a year, and the relative value of this can be appreciated when we learn that the labourers who worked on Brown's improvements at Castle Ashby earned only eight pence (3.3p) per day. To raise ten thousand pounds a year from rents between ten and twenty thousand acres of land was needed, depending on the quality of the ground and its location. From this we can calculate that the land owned by the four hundred wealthiest and most powerful families amounted to about a fifth of the cultivated area of the country. Most of this income came from agriculture but there were also profits from timber, lime-kilns, brick-kilns, quarries, and the mining of coal, iron and lead.

In Lancelot Brown's time Britain was an entirely rural country. Towns as we know them today did not exist, and even London had a population of only seventy thousand. Nevertheless it was the largest city not only in England but also in Europe. Most provincial towns were extremely small by modern standards. Norwich and Bristol were the largest at about thirty thousand, but out of eight hundred places worthy of being called a town by a contemporary writer, half had a population of less than seven hundred. Even in London one could walk out of the city into open country in a matter of minutes. Buckingham House was right on the edge of the built-up area. In every other town, the country was never far away. At the time of Brown's death in 1783, three-quarters of the population were still directly dependent on the land for their livelihood, whether as great landowners or as humble labourers. Thus the soil of the country was its main source of wealth. Food, raw materials, employment, power and prestige were all inseparably linked with the land, and there was no greater advantage for anyone, whether in economic, social or political terms, than to be a landowner.

Peace with Britain's European neighbours, though uneasy, made way for the increase of foreign trade. Products came from all over the globe, and the Thames was filled with merchant vessels. As many as fourteen hundred vessels could be seen at any one time between Limehouse and the Tower of London. Whether their wealth came from trade with the East or West Indies (both George Durant of Tong, and Edwin Lascelles of Harewood House made their money in Barbados), or whether it was inherited, it was these rich landowners who were Lancelot Brown's clients. On the whole they were relatively enlightened men despite their wealth and privilege. There were particularly arrogant exceptions, such as the Earl of Lincoln who had an apprentice boy beaten to death for gazing at him in the street,[8] or the Duke of Somerset who 'had outriders to clear the roads of plebeians lest they should see him as he passed, although one farmer refused to be stopped from looking over his own hedge, and held up a pig so that it should see him too.'[9] Generally, however, they behaved in a more reasonable manner than their Continental counterparts, and in financial terms they were better off than most of the titled nobility of Europe. It was customary for these great landowners to take a paternal interest in their tenants and in the welfare of those who had long family connections with the estate, and to make occasional charitable donations to the local poor.

Many were enthusiastic improvers of their estates: to see the countryside flourishing was a pleasure. The novelist Smollett described what he saw on his travels:

I see the country of England smiling with cultivation; the grounds exhibiting all the perfection of agriculture, parcelled out into beautiful enclosures, cornfields, hay and pasture, woodland and common ... I see her farm-houses the habitations of plenty, cleanliness and convenience: and her peasants well-fed, well-lodged, well-cloathed, tall and stout, and hale and jolly.[10]

Carried away by this vision of bucolic happiness, Smollett was blind, however, to the real – often desperate – living conditions of some of the rural poor.

Improvements were firstly agricultural and practical: visual and artistic considerations were secondary, at least if the landowner was wise. One of the reasons for Brown's success was that he was a practical man as well as a man of taste. So the buildings he suggested to ornament the grounds almost always doubled up as cottages, dairies, or dog-kennels, and were rarely purely ornamental. This approach is aptly expressed by Alexander Pope:

Who then shall grace, or who improve the soil?
Who plants like Bathurst, or who builds like Boyle.
'Tis Use alone that sanctifies Expence,
And Splendour borrows all her rays from Sense.[11]

Lord Bathurst's estate at Cirencester, Gloucestershire, still exists, as an example of so-called 'forest gardening', useful as well as ornamental, and Pope's Seat is still there. Richard Boyle, Lord Burlington, built Chiswick House, which set new standards of taste in architecture. The unspoken contrast is with contemporary French gardens, where at profligate expense grounds were laid out to be exclusively ornamental, in an 'unnatural' manner.

Naturally, these improvements required money, which only the wealthiest could spare from their own income, and many of them were carried out on money borrowed from the bank. The English banking system grew with the peace and stability of the times, creating fortunes for notable bankers such as Henry Hoare, who made his own great landscape garden at Stourhead in Wiltshire, and Robert Drummond, Brown's banker who commissioned him to landscape his estate at Cadland, near Southampton.

Agricultural improvements centred around the enclosure movement. In medieval and

Tudor times the land around villages had been tilled on the open field system, where narrow, unfenced strips of land were tended by various villagers, and any one man's strips of land would be scattered at random around the large open fields. As soon as the crops were harvested cattle would browse indiscriminately across the fields until winter, when most of them were slaughtered, for there was not enough fodder to keep them alive until the spring. The creation of large 'sheep-walks' for the wool trade had first made it necessary to enclose land into fields owned by individuals. Later, the introduction of root-crops made it possible to keep cattle over the winter, but these could not be grown in open fields where they would be eaten by other people's cattle. Once land was farmed individually in concentrated fields of reasonable size, there was much more incentive to carry out worthwhile improvements such as drainage, manuring and crop production. Improved breeds of sheep and cattle were produced, and the average weight of sheep and cattle sold at Smithfield market doubled during the course of the century.

The great landowners were advantageously placed to benefit from these agricultural improvements, and they also reaped the financial benefits. Thomas Coke ii of Holkham in Norfolk, for example, was able to increase the value of his rents from £2,200 to £20,000 between 1776 and 1816. This was another estate with a landscaped park, begun by William Kent and probably altered later by Brown.

Improvements in roads were badly needed, but there were no powers in local or national government to carry out the work. Instead, turnpike companies were given powers by Parliament to re-make and maintain the roads, in return for which they were allowed to charge tolls. In the first half of the century four hundred such Acts of Parliament were passed, increasing to sixteen hundred during the second half. During Brown's practising years, 1750–80, the time taken between London and the major towns was halved. Before these improvements bad weather and wintry conditions made travel impossible for wheeled traffic, and Defoe, writing about 1725, spoke often of 'deep, stiff roads, full of sloughs'. Lancelot Brown travelled incessantly, visiting one estate after another, in a way which would have been impossible without these improvements. He wrote to George Rice, whose estate he had visited in Cardiganshire:

> My health is not of the best kind but I assure you not the worse for my Welsh journey. The day I left you I was very ill. I found the Judges were at Hereford, which determined me to go to Lord Oxford's [Eywood in Herefordshire] and the post boys were so obliging as to take me through a river that filled my chaise with water . . .

Coaches gradually became lighter and therefore faster, but they still had no springs. Road surfaces were appalling by modern standards, overturning was commonplace and highwaymen a constant threat.

Travel became a craze, not only in this country but also abroad, and books on the subject became popular, especially as the appreciation of natural scenery grew. For appreciation of wild and dramatic scenery, however, we must wait until Wordsworth's time. In the eighteenth century most people would have agreed with Daniel Defoe's description of the Lake District, as 'the wildest, most barren and frightful of any that I have passed over in England, or even in Wales itself'. To a rural and agricultural society, barren and unproductive land is bad land, and not until the later part of the century were the educated classes able to separate in their minds the visual and the economic aspects of the countryside. There are several stories of travellers who passed through the Alps on their way to Italy and drew down the blinds of the coach because they could not bear to see the 'chaos' of 'horrid', jagged, jumbled rocks and mountains.

The kind of countryside admired by the early eighteenth century was not that of the Lake District or the Peak District, but a gentler, pastoral kind, where nymphs and shepherds and their elegant eighteenth-century counterparts could feel comfortably at home. *Windsor Forest* was an adequate subject for Pope in 1713, written to celebrate the Treaty of Utrecht:

> Here hills and vales, the woodland and the plain,
> Here earth and water seem to strive again,
> Not Chaos-like together crushed and bruised,
> But as the world, harmoniously confused:
> Where order in variety we see,
> And where, though all things differ, all agree.

The poem is a patriotic celebration of Britain and its countryside, just as Virgil had 'sung' in honour of ancient Rome. Soon Pope invokes the classical gods and goddesses of flocks and herds, of fruit, flowers and corn, and in this he emphasizes the productiveness and usefulness of the landscape:

> Here Ceres' gifts in waving prospect stand
> And nodding tempt the joyful reaper's hand,
> Rich Industry sits smiling on the plains
> And Peace and Plenty tell a Stuart reigns.

If this is England in Virgilian guise, it is also the counterpart in poetry of Poussin's splendid painting entitled *Summer*.

The nymphs and shepherds, the gods and the heroes, and all the paraphernalia of classical Arcadia became the stock-in-trade of the poets of the eighteenth century, and the countryside was portrayed mostly in these terms.

Another poet, William Shenstone, created his own small-scale landscape garden at The Leasowes, near Halesowen, which he called a *ferme ornée*. Shenstone had only a modest income and expensive garden buildings were beyond his reach. Instead he placed memorial urns and seats with mottoes and inscriptions at various strategic points, as if to ensure that the landscape would be rightly appreciated by the observer. In the same way, the landscapes described in early eighteenth-century poetry contained literary allusions which could be shared by the educated and travelled aristocracy, and along with this went instructive moral ideas of social value. The contemplation of nature was expected to produce such ideas as were described by the philosopher David Hume as being 'entitled to the general goodwill and approbation of mankind', such as 'beneficence and humanity, friendship and gratitude, natural affection, and public spirit ... and a generous concern for our kind and species.'[12] Such generalizations were often drawn out by poets, and also in man-made landscapes. Thus, the buildings in the famous gardens at Stowe, where Brown became head gardener, were called the Temple of Friendship, the Temple of British Worthies, the Temple of Ancient Virtue; and of course the Temple of Modern Virtue was in ruins. There were political implications too: the headless figure on the Temple of Modern Virtue was Sir Robert Walpole, depicted as Lord Cobham (the owner of Stowe) wished to see him; Cobham had fallen foul of Walpole in 1733.

But from the mid-century onwards a change became apparent, both in landscape poetry and in designed landscapes. To some extent it is evident in James Thomson's *The Seasons*, a poem of epic dimensions completed in 1746, which contains many landscape pictures. Sometimes they prompt reflections of a philosophical or sentimental nature, but more often Thomson is content with plain description. There is no overall narrative or argument to the poem, only the description of scenery during the seasons of the year and as many sundry incidental subjects as occur to him in passing. The important thing was to show the English countryside to advantage. And this, it could be argued, is all a Capability Brown landscape is. Lancelot Brown abandoned the idea of a landscape with literary or moral associations, and explored instead the expressive possibilities of the purely 'natural' landscape. His parks contain little in the way of architectural or literary content, of temples, urns and other trappings of Arcadia. Instead he presented an ideal picture of Nature. Not wild, uncivilized Nature, but tastefully improved Nature; in Alexander Pope's words, 'Nature to advantage dress'd'.[13]

But it is more even than that. Not only is Nature improved and made pleasing to the eye, it is also used expressively, to generate feelings and sensations in the observer. The same attitude towards Nature can be seen in the poetry of Edward Young (1683-1765) and Thomas Gray, Lancelot Brown's exact contemporary. For Gray, *A Distant Prospect of Eton College*, where 'the hoary Thames' wanders 'his silver-winding way', did not suggest a classical Arcadian scene but instead it yielded sentiments of nostalgia:

Ah, happy hills, ah pleasing shade,
Ah fields beloved in vain,
Where once my careless childhood strayed.
A stranger yet to pain!
I feel the gales that from ye blow,
A momentary bliss bestow,
As waving fresh their gladsome wing
My weary soul they seem to soothe
And, redolent of joy and youth,
To breath a second spring.

Here we find the landscape producing an emotional response in the individual, and this was something new, the discovery, in Thomas Whately's words, that 'scenes of nature have a power to affect our imagination and our sensibility',[14] whereas previously they had been regarded a useful commodity for society in general.

The landscapes of Lancelot Brown also have this capacity to create, in Whately's words:

Scenes which may be adapted to every kind of expression; ... their consequences [are] infinite: the mind is elevated, depressed or composed as gaiety, gloom or tranquility prevail in the scene.

So in spite of the classicism which is implied in the creation of an idealized landscape raised in its significance beyond the particular, there is also an element of romanticism latent in Brown's landscapes. The ability to heighten the individual character of a landscape, effects which are dramatic in quality, the element of mystery, and the subtlety of something which eludes the immediate grasp of the mind: these are all romantic concepts. But they are always fused with the search for the Ideal, the same kind of search for a moment of perfection which we see portrayed in the paintings of Claude Lorraine.

Notes

1 G. M. Trevelyan, *English Social History*.
2 Joseph Addison, 'The spacious firmament on high'.
3 Anthony Ashley Cooper, third Earl of Shaftesbury, 1671-1713, belonged to the same generation as Vanbrugh and

Jonathan Swift. He was the grandson of the first Earl, a prominent politician of the Restoration period. The third Earl had a brief political career, during which he appealed for goodwill towards Holland. Then he retired, to write 'moral philosophy'. The quotations are from *The Moralists*, 1709.

4   C. Hussey, *English Gardens and Landscapes 1700–1750.*

5   Pope, *Essay on Man*, *III*, 303–6.

6   Thomas Hobbes, 1588–1679, philosopher and political thinker, in *Leviathan* (1651).

7   G. E. Mingay, *English Landed Society in the Eighteenth Century.*

8   Mingay, op. cit.

9   C. Morris, ed., *The Journeys of Celia Fiennes* (1947), Introduction.

10   Tobias Smollett, *Travels Through France and Italy* (1766), Letter 36.

11   Pope, *Epistle to Lord Burlington.*

12   David Hume, *Enquiries Concerning the Human Understanding* (1748).

13   *Essay on Criticism*, *II*, 297

14   Thomas Whately, *Observations on Modern Gardening* (1770).

Lancelot Brown, a portrait attributed to Richard Cosway.

Below: Sir Joshua Reynolds painted portraits of many of Brown's clients. This one shows the fourth Duke and Duchess of Marlborough (Blenheim) and their family.

Opposite: The Villa Rotonda, near Vicenza, Italy, designed *c*1550 by Andrea Palladio (1508–80). The English Palladian style was derived from buildings such as this.

Above: The east front of Chiswick House, designed by its owner, Lord Burlington, in *c*1725. One of the earliest and finest examples of English Palladianism.

Below: Holkham Hall, designed *c*1734 by William Kent (1684–1748) and others for Thomas Coke, Earl of Leicester. Many features of Brown's architectural style can be traced to Holkham.

Landscape with Mercury and the Dishonest Woodman by Salvator Rosa (1615-73). Those who tired of the pursuit of perfect taste found inspiration in the sentimental and often melodramatic landscapes of Salvator Rosa.

Opposite above: Sanderson Miller's sketch for the Ruined Castle at Wimpole (1749) was an early Gothic revival design, but the castle was not built until twenty years later when Brown was carrying out improvements at Wimpole.

Opposite below: Horace Walpole's house at Strawberry Hill, Twickenham, is one of the earliest and most interesting examples of the Gothic revival. This view is by Paul Sandby.

Westbury Court the Seat of Maynard Colchester Esqr.

SVPERÆ THERAVIHCTVS

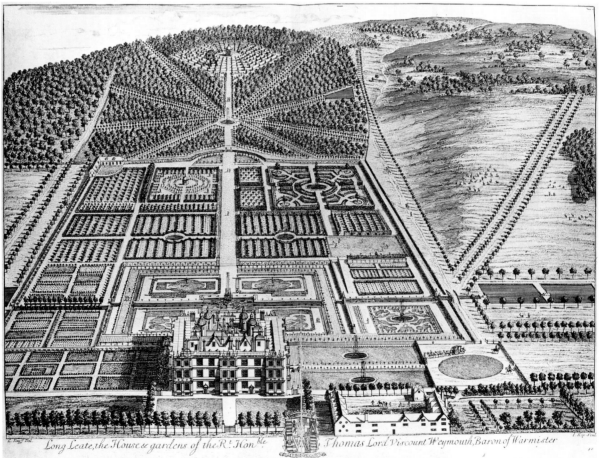

Long Leate, the House & gardens of the R^t. Honble. Thomas Lord Viscount Weymouth, Baron of Warminster.

Opposite above: One of the very few survivors of the so-called Dutch style is the garden at Westbury Court, Gloucestershire (*c*1696), an example of what Stephen Switzer scathingly described as 'those crimping, diminutive and wretched performances we everywhere meet with'. Engraving by Kip, 1720.

Opposite below: The formal gardens at Longleat before they were transformed by Brown from 1757 onwards. This engraving by Knyff and Kip shows a more coherent and larger-scale design than Westbury.

Right: Plan of Eastbury attributed to Charles Bridgeman: a vast geometrical exercise in forest gardening, covering 1200 acres, to surround a house by Sir John Vanbrugh. On the right is a paper flap which can be folded down to give an alternative design.

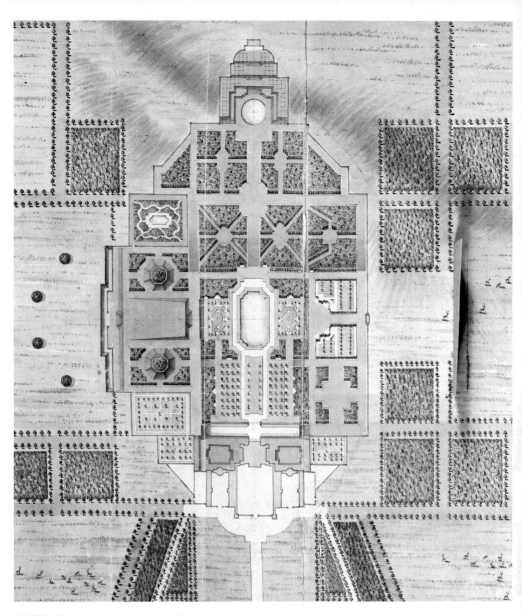

Right: A detail of the gardens at Stowe in its Bridgeman days. The formal treatment of sloping grass banks has long since vanished, replaced by gently contoured lawns in the Brown manner.

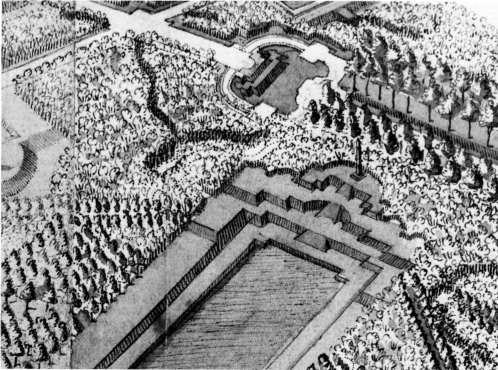

Left: One of the first signs of the new 'natural' taste in gardening was the serpenting of the 'river' in the grounds of Chiswick House in the 1730s. Painting by George Lambert.

Below: Rocque's plan of Claremont, 1738, shows Bridgeman's avenues partly replaced by Kent's scattered clumps, and the circular pool altered to an irregularly curved shape, while a bowling green is hidden among the trees.

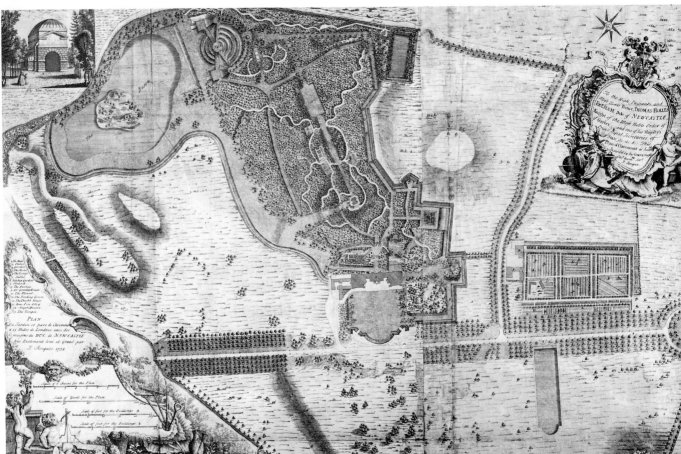

The Progress of Taste 1725–1775

T HE travellers who set off on the Grand Tour went in search of the pleasures of architecture, painting and sculpture, and to see the remains of 'the ancients', whose poetry and prose had dominated their education. The eighteenth century felt a strong kinship with the age of the Emperor Augustus, when their beloved Virgil, Horace and Ovid wrote their poetry and the first of the great buildings of ancient Rome were built. It was quite common to spend a year or more abroad, and to come home laden with paintings and sculpture to decorate the Great House.

The finest guide for travellers on the Grand Tour, which described the buildings of ancient Rome, had been written by the Italian architect Andrea Palladio (1508–80). Working mainly in Venice and Vicenza, Palladio was a generation later than those great Renaissance architects such as Michelangelo, Bramante and Raphael who had worked mostly in Florence and Rome. From 1545 onwards he studied the ancient remains, and in 1554 he published his book, *Le Antichità di Roma*. As might be expected, his own work was much closer to the original Roman buildings than any other architect had so far attempted. Those who visited Rome[1] on the Grand Tour saw the ruins, as it were, through Palladio's eyes, and this explains the amazing influence he exerted on the course of architecture in Europe, especially in England, and the best of the great houses which Lancelot Brown designed are a fine contribution to the Palladian tradition.

The only complete treatise on architecture to survive from Roman times was the *De Architectura* of Vitruvius, and naturally this too was extremely influential. Palladio prepared the illustrations for Daniele Barbaro's great edition of Vitruvius in 1556, and in 1570 published his own *Quattro libri dell' Architettura* (Four Books of Architecture). But it was not until 1730 that his drawings of the Roman Baths were published, by Lord Burlington.

The fascinating thing about British architectural history of the seventeenth to the nineteenth centuries is the way the classical style went into reverse as the works of the 'ancients' became more clearly understood. The styles of Sir Christopher Wren and James Gibbs had been derived from the work of contemporary architects working in Fance and Italy. Gibbs's church of St Mary-le-Strand, for example, built in 1714, is patterned on the work of Italian Baroque architects such as Domenico Fontana (1543–1607) and Cortona (1596–1669). The next generation, led by Colen Campbell (d. 1729) and Lord Burlington, looked back to Palladio, and through him to Vitruvius and the Romans. But after Stuart and Revett published their *Antiquities of Athens* in 1762 it was realized that the Greek style in its original form, unadulterated by the Romans and the Renaissance Italians, was an even finer model to imitate than any of the previous ones.

Richard Boyle, Lord Burlington (1694–1753), first went to Italy on his Grand Tour when he was twenty. On his return he sacked James Gibbs as architect of Burlington House, in Picadilly and in his place appointed Colen Campbell, who had just published his *Vitruvius Britannicus*.

Those who followed Palladio did not copy the Mannerist style of his *palazzi*, such as the Palazzo Thiene, with its heavily decorated surfaces. Instead they turned to the villas, where they found simple geometrical shapes and strong articulation of elements. The ancestry of English Palladian houses can be seen clearly in some of the unexecuted projects in Palladio's *Quattro Libri*, such as the house for Signor Mocenigo. Of Palladio's completed villas the Villa Rotonda at Vicenza is the most famous, and from it were derived Colen Campbell's Mereworth Castle (1722–5) and Lord Burlington's villa, Chiswick House. In 1715–1716, a Venetian called Giacomo Leoni published an English translation of Palladio's *Quattro Libri*, which helped further to establish the new style. Now the great houses of the nobility could take on a new splendour derived (as they saw it) directly from the ancients, and could be no less magnificent – a magnificence which was mostly on the inside, however: one of the most remarkable features of the new style was the contrast between the rich and complex interiors and the chaste restraint of the exterior.

Why then should this style become so dominant that it imposed a stranglehold on British architecture for more than a century? Not only did it provide the nearest thing to 'the ancients' when it first appeared, it also demonstrated the restraint and moderation of the owner, and this, of course, was a reflection of the political views of the time. No one wanted to look extravagant even if they were immensely rich: the ostentation of Versailles was something to be assiduously avoided. Blenheim Palace, designed by Sir John Vanbrugh and built between 1705 and 1720, seems to us inventive and highly imaginative in its design, but it was held in poor esteem by the Palladians. Not only did it violate the new canons of Taste which Burlington and his colleagues had established, but its vast scale dwarfed the owner:

> Who but must laugh, the master when he sees,
> A puny insect, shivering at the breeze!
> Lo, what huge heaps of littleness around!
> The whole a laboured quarry above ground . . .[2]

and, of course, it cost so much:

> Something there is more needful than expense,
> And something precious even to taste – 'tis sense.

The complicated and visually restless architecture of Blenheim contrasts with Lord Shaftesbury's call for an architecture that reflects the harmony of 'Nature', and is 'independent of fancy'.[3]

A further fascination to be found in Palladio's work was his interest in and exploration of harmonic proportions. This is the belief that pure ratios such as 1:2, or 2:3, or the golden rectangle (which is 1:618) would produce shapes and proportions pleasing to the eye. There is a parallel effect in the relationship of musical intervals,[4] hence the notion of architectural 'harmony'. The link between these ideas and the writings of Lord Shaftesbury (amongst many others) on the harmony and proportion of the natural world was not lost on the architects of the 1720s. One of its effects was the clarity with which the cubic outlines of the various blocks were articulated, the plain, undecorated surface of the exterior serving to emphasize these carefully proportioned formal elements. Not until the International Style of the twentieth century does one find architecture of comparable geometric severity.[5]

Lord Burlington was himself an amateur architect of great ability. His Chiswick House was built about 1725 and derives from a great number of sources:[6] the rusticated ground floor, for example, comes from Palladio's Villa Foscari at Malcontenta; while the capitals are from the Roman temple of Castor and Pollux, which Palladio had illustrated. The finest of English Palladian houses is Holkham Hall designed partly by Lord Burlington but mainly by William Kent, Burlington's protégé. Kent is of special interest, since he more than anyone else formed Lancelot Brown's taste both in architecture and in gardening. The articulation of the various elements of the south front at Holkham is particularly distinct, each one being marked by a step forward or a step back from the plans of elevation, and the two wings form clearly separated units. Although it is a large composition, it forms a unified but varied whole, dominated by the central portico. Brown's architectural style is entirely derived from it, and he could scarcely have chosen a finer model. It is superior both to Campbell's Houghton Hall, built for Sir Robert Walpole, and to Wentworth Woodhouse, Flitcroft's vast mansion for the Marquess of Rockingham, another important figure on the political scene.

Holkham Hall was built for Thomas Coke II, later Earl of Leicester, but it was not completed until 1761, in the time of Thomas Coke the famous agricultural improver. It was finished by Matthew Brettingham, who in the same year published *The Plans, Elevations and Sections of Holkham in Norfolk*, pointing out all the Palladian and Roman sources in detail. As one writer says, 'This is almost a classic text for illustrating the architect's claim to status not by originality but by precise identification of his learned borrowings.'[7]

Most of the travellers on the Grand Tour did not find the gardens of Italy and France to their taste. As the years passed they became increasingly of the opinion that English gardens and landscapes were better. It was all too obvious that the splendours of Versailles, for example, had been created at a price which the freedom-loving Englishman was not prepared to pay.

The poet James Thomson, who had travelled in France and Italy, as tutor to the son of the Lord Chancellor, referred (in Book Five of his poem *Liberty* of 1734) to the French gardens as those

> ... disgraceful piles of wood and stone;
> Those parks and gardens, where, his haunts betrimmed,
> And Nature by presumptuous Art oppressed,
> The woodland Genius mourns.

These travellers, educated by the paintings of Poussin and Claude Lorraine, found greater inspiration in places where the ruins could be seen in a landscape setting. John Dyer, a painter and clergyman as well as a poet, spent some time studying painting in Italy, and in his *Epistle to a Famous Painter* described a landscape obviously derived more from paintings than his own experience:

> The golden eve, or blushing dawn
> Smiling on the lovely lawn!
> And pleasing views of chequer'd glades
> And rivers, winding through the shades
> And groups of merry nymphs and swains ...
> Or some old building hid with grass,
> Rearing its sad ruin'd face.
>
> Whose columns, friezes, statues, lie
> The grief, and wonder of the eye!

Or swift adown a mountain tall
A foamy cataract's sounding fall . . .

This is the perfect Claudian landscape.

Of the landscape painters admired by the Grand Tourists none were more highly prized than Claude, Nicolas Poussin and Salvator Rosa. Claude Gellée, always known as Claude Lorraine, was a Frenchman, born in Lorraine in 1600, who went to Rome before he was twenty and stayed there until his death in 1682. The subjects of his paintings were derived from classical mythology and from the Old Testament, but the landscapes are somehow greater than their theme; they evoke the atmosphere of a lost Golden Age, moments of perfection and grandeur, caught in the golden, evening light before it fades.

Nicolas Poussin (1593–1665) was also a Frenchman, and he too worked mostly in Italy. His work is more architectural and intellectual than Claude's, his colours are more restrained and severe, and the composition of his landscapes gives the impression of being almost mathematically constructed, in contrast to the more romantic and naturalistic landscapes of Claude.

So many paintings by these artists were brought home to Britain that it was estimated at one point that there were more Claudes in Britain than in Italy.[8] Henry Hoare, of Stourhead, owned at least one, and one of the garden temples in the landscape he made there, the Pantheon, seems to have been modelled on the temple in Claude's *Coast View of Delos with Aeneas*. Further evidence of the conscious influence of these paintings on those who were laying out grounds is found in William Mason's poem *The English Garden*, first published in 1772:

> . . . your eyes entranced
> Shall catch those glowing scenes, that taught a *Claude*
> To grace his canvas with Hesperian hues:

says Mason, addressing those 'blest youths', who had been on the Grand Tour:

> And scenes like these, on memory's tablet drawn
> Bring back to Britain; there give local form
> To each Idea; and if Nature lend
> Materials fit of torrent, rock and shade,
> Produce new *Tivolis*.

A plea, in other words, to re-create the Claudian landscape on home ground.

But from the owners of the great houses there was perhaps a greater demand for portraits than for landscapes. In this field the most eminent painter was Sir Joshua Reynolds (1723–92), who was elected first President of the Royal Academy when it was formed in 1768. It is worth considering some of the ideas which Reynolds expressed in his *Discourses* and elsewhere, because these help to throw some light on Lancelot Brown's approach to his art. Reynolds had been to Rome and had studied the painters of the Italian Renaissance. Although most of his paintings are portraits, he considered that portrait painting was on a lower level than 'History Painting' – by which he meant scenes from classical mythology or the Bible.[9] He attempted to elevate the character of many of his portraits by creating a classical, idealized setting rather than a contemporary one. One of the finest examples of this is *Sarah Siddons as the Tragic Muse* (1784), where her pose is inspired by Michelangelo's prophets on the Sistine Chapel ceiling, which seems utterly appropriate for a famous actress.[10]

In the *Discourses* Reynolds compared the Dutch painters unfavourably with Claude, on the grounds that the ideal and the general must be stressed, not the particular details, for these might happen to be untypical or deformed:

... Claude Lorrain ... was convinced that taking nature as he found it seldom produced beauty. His pictures are a composition of the various draughts which he had previously made from various beautiful scenes and prospects.[11]

The painter should portray the 'general idea' of a thing, as he explained in *The Idler* in 1759:

Thus amongst the blades of grass or leaves of the same tree, though no two can be found exactly alike, the general form is invariable: a Naturalist before he chose as a sample, would examine many; since if he took the first that occurred, it might have by accident or otherwise such a form as that it would scarce be known to belong to that species; he selects as the Painter does, the most beautiful, that is, the most general form of nature.'[12]

In the same way landscape gardeners altered the particular piece of ground around a great house so that it conformed with an ideal,[13] whether Arcadian (Stowe or Stourhead) or more naturalistic. The attractive features of the estate were emphasized and the blemishes removed. It is no accident, therefore, that the great eighteenth-century parks (created artificially at great cost) seem more essentially English today than the agricultural countryside that surrounds them, with its 'accidental' asbestos barns and 'particular' hedgerows and wire fences.

During the course of the eighteenth century interest in dramatic scenery gradually increased. Thomas Gray went to the Scottish Highlands in 1765, as did Dr Johnson and James Boswell in 1773, and it was just three years after Brown's death that William Gilpin (1724–1804) wrote his *Observations on the Mountains and Lakes of Cumberland and Westmorland*. Gilpin became a kind of self-appointed connoisseur of scenery, and in a typical descriptive passage he speaks of

the mountains half-obscured by driving vapours, and mingling with the sky in awful obscurity – the trees straining in the blast – and the lake stirred from the bottom, and whitening every rocky promontory with its foam ...

But this is Romanticism, and it did not reflect the prevailing view; indeed in 1791 the poet William Cowper found even the scenery of the South Downs near Chichester rather too exciting for his taste: he was used to the gentle rolling countryside of Northamptonshire, for he lived most of his life at Olney, only a few miles from Castle Ashby, which Brown landscaped in the 1760s.

The cultivated appearance of Weston [near Olney] suits my frame of mind far better than wild hills that aspire to be mountains, covered with vast unfrequented woods, and here and there affording a peep between their summits at the distant ocean. Within doors all was hospitality, but the scenery *would* have its effect ... it was too gloomy for me.[14]

One of the sources of this interest in dramatic scenery was the work of the Italian painter, Salvator Rosa (1615–73), many of whose paintings were brought back by the Grand Tourists. His landscapes frequently depicted a group of Italian banditti in a wild ravine, usually sheltering from a melodramatic storm. Dead trees, caves and shaggy pine trees were his stock-in-trade, and his precipices and torrents added an exciting frisson to the reasonable eighteenth-century world.

In due course British painters began to depict this kind of scenery. One of the finest was Richard Wilson, whose *Destruction of Niobe's Children* (?1760) clearly shows Rosa's influence. He also painted gentler English scenery, such as *The Thames near Twickenham*, and several of Brown's landscapes, including Croome and Moor Park.

The distinction between wild and rugged scenery and gentler, pastoral landscapes was pointed up clearly in Edmund Burke's writings about 'the Sublime' and 'the Beautiful'.[15] Burke's definition of 'the Beautiful' includes such attributes as smoothness, delicacy, clarity, comprehensibility and size small enough to be understood. Smoothness is particularly relevant to the gentle contours and undulating surfaces of Brown's parkland landscapes. Burke describes smoothness as

a quality so essential to beauty, that I do not now recollect anything beautiful that is not smooth. In trees and flowers, smooth leaves are beautiful; smooth slopes of earth in gardens; smooth streams in the landscape . . .

But 'the Sublime', for Burke, implied awe and majesty, power and drama, mystery, dread, and thoughts that fill the mind with 'delightful horror'; examples include the night sky, high mountains or the uncontrollable power of storms. 'The Sublime', therefore, is something which is too great, too mysterious or confused for the mind to grasp in a rational manner; instead, the observer can only have an emotional reaction.

The recognition of this factor in life can be seen in a religious context in the rise of Methodism from 1739 onwards. John Wesley (1703-91) was Brown's contemporary, and he travelled an even greater number of miles than Brown. What moved Wesley to dedicate himself with so much energy to his cause was an experience 'in a chapel at Aldersgate' in 1738, in which his heart was 'strangely moved'. In other words, religious motivation was no longer dependent on a mental appreciation, common to all, of the rational designs of a prime-mover God, but on the feelings inside an individual.

Further connections with Burke's idea of the Sublime can be seen in the poetry of the period, in particular poetry about the night and graveyard scenes, such as Young's *Night Thoughts* or Blair's *The Grave*. The so-called 'Gothic' novels of the time fit in here too – such as Horace Walpole's *Castle of Otranto* (1764) and Ann Radcliffe's *The Mysteries of Udolpho* (1794). Poems such as Gray's *The Bard* were set in the Middle Ages, and at the same time the gloom and irrationality of Gothic architecture began to arouse some interest.

For Alexander Pope Gothicism had been the object of irony:

What beckoning ghost along the moonlight
Invites my steps, and points to yonder glade?
'Tis she! but why that bleeding bosom gored,
Why dimly gleams the visionary sword?

In this way Pope begins his *Elegy to an Unfortunate Lady*, published in 1717; what would have been serious stuff to the Gothic novelist at the end of the century is to Pope just a light-hearted pose. But in 1732 his patron Lord Bathurst, of Cirencester Park, wrote to tell Pope that his new hermitage in the wood was finished: 'All Europe cannot show such a pretty little plain work in the Brobdingnag style.'[16] The first of all mock ruins in the Gothic style, it is now known as Alfred's Hall, and it seems likely that Pope helped in the design. Another early example is the Gothic Temple at Stowe of 1741, designed by James Gibbs.

One advantage of Gothic ruins, as opposed to classical ruins, was that it was at least realistic to find a Gothic ruin on one's estate. Some landowners were lucky, like Brown's client at Sandbeck Park who inherited a splendid ruined monastery, left over from Henry VIII's Dissolution programme. A classical ruin was obviously a sham, and William

Mason, a friend of Walpole and Gray, described such ruins as 'but a splendid lie which mocks historic credence'. Even luckier was John Aislabie, Chancellor of the Exchequer, who in 1716 made one of the earliest plans to use real ruins. His grounds at Studley Royal in Yorkshire were laid out as an 'excursion' walk past formal lakes to the ruins of Fountains Abbey, one of the most picturesque sites in the country.

The 'associational' factor was another thing in favour of the Gothic style. Often in English culture artistic things are appreciated not for their own visual, plastic qualities, but for the literary, historic or poetic ideas which they stimulate. (Thus it is that in the field of conservation buildings are often saved not because they are intrinsically good, but because some obscure man of letters happened to live there.) The value of the 'association of ideas' was appreciated by Reynolds, who wrote in the *Thirteenth Discourse* of 1786:

> ... we have naturally a veneration for antiquity, whatever building brings to our remembrance ancient customs and manners, such as the castles of the Barons of ancient Chivalry, is sure to give this delight. Hence it is that *towers and battlements* are so often selected by the Painter and the Poet to make a part of their ideal Landscape.

Reynolds then has a good word to say for Vanbrugh:

> ... and it is from hence, in a great degree, that, in the buildings of Vanbrugh, who was a Poet as well as an Architect, there is a greater display of imagination than we shall find, perhaps, in any other ... Vanbrugh appears to have had recourse to some of the principles of the Gothic Architecture; which, though not so ancient as the Grecian, is more so to our imagination....

At Blenheim there were originally some brick 'bastions', or ramparts, around the formal gardens on the south side, and in a similar military vein Vanbrugh built two castle-like houses for himself, one at Claremont in Surrey and the other at Greenwich. These turreted and castellated houses are Gothic in spirit rather than in detail: they have round-arched windows, for instance, not pointed ones. Even the Gothic of the 1750s was only 'Georgian Gothick', a veneer on a Palladian base. If classical architecture was becoming increasingly correct in its imitation of Greek and Roman models, the new Gothic was naive and light-hearted, a kind of Gothic Rococo.[17]

Two of the earliest examples of the 'Gothick' were Sanderson Miller's alterations to his house at Radway, Warwickshire (c1745) and Horace Walpole's Strawberry Hill. Miller later built an ornamental 'castle' at Hagley for Lord Lyttelton, nephew of Lord Cobham of Stowe, and in 1749 designed the Ruined Castle in Capability Brown's landscape at Wimpole in Cambridgeshire (but it was not built until twenty years later).

Horace Walpole's collection of letters, of which at least 2,700 survive, provide a mirror of his age from the most serious issues to the most frivolous. He made the Grand Tour in 1739-41 accompanied by the poet Thomas Gray. His house at Strawberry Hill, near Twickenham, was built gradually and piecemeal between 1753 and 1790.[18] He used at least ten different architects, of whom the most famous were Robert Adam and James Wyatt, and although the result was certainly not the best house of its date, it was perhaps one of the most interesting and influential, and probably the most visited. Walpole was well aware of his influence: 'I give myself a Burlington-air', he wrote to Horace Mann, 'and say that as Chiswick is a model of Grecian architecture, Strawberry Hill is to be of Gothic'.[19]

Walpole travelled extensively throughout Britain, visiting country seats, and remarking on the paintings, the decorations and the grounds. He speaks eventually of 'my friend, Lancelot Brown'. In 1770 he printed the *History of the Modern Taste in Gardening*, the first attempt to trace the history of the development of the Landscape Movement; he had a unique advantage, being able to see at first-hand the transformations newly hatched, as it were, or actually in progress. 'It was fortunate for the country', says Walpole,

and [for] Mr. Kent, that he was succeeded by a very able master; and did living artists come within my plan, I should be glad to do justice to Mr. Brown; but he may be a gainer, by being reserved for some abler pen.

———

NOTES

1 The first British architect to visit Italy and make a serious study of the Roman remains with Palladio's book as his guide was Inigo Jones (1573–1652). He went twice to Italy, in 1603 and again in 1613.

2 Pope, *Epistle to Lord Burlington.*

3 Quoted by J. Summerson, *Architecture in Britain 1530–1830.*

4 For example, an octave is 1:2, as one can easily discover by halving the length of a violin string.

5 Apart from the drawings of Boullée and Ledoux in the 1790s, who were greatly influenced by the rationalism of English thought.

6 R. Wittkower, in 'British Art and the Mediterranean', section 54, and '*Diffusioni dei Modi Palladiani in Inghilterra*', *Bollettino del Centro Internazionale di Studi d'Archittetura Andrea Palladio*, Vicenza 1959, I.57, quoted by J. Burke in *English Art 1714–1800.*

7 Joseph Burke, *English Art 1714–1800.*

8 According to E. W. Manwaring, *Italian Landscape in eighteenth-century England* (1925).

9 Although Reynolds admired Hogarth's scenes of low life, he felt they could never be great art because they did not fit into any category except the lowest, because of their subject.

10 Another ambitious example is *The Daughters of Sir William Montgomery as 'The Graces adorning A Term of Hymen'* 1774, a charming picture of three distinctly English-looking nymphs, decorating a statue of the god of marriage with garlands of flowers.

11 Sir Joshua Reynolds, *Discourses IV*

12 This approach is also described by Jonathan Richardson in his *Theory of Painting*, written in 1715:

The business of painting is not only to represent Nature, but to make the best choice of it; maybe to raise, and improve it from the commonly, or even rarely seen, to what never was, or will be in fact, though we may easily conceive it might be.

13 Edmund Burke once remarked that Reynolds' portraits 'remind the spectator of the invention and the amenity of landscape'. Quoted by J. Burke, *English Art 1714–1800.*

14 Quoted in Charles Peake, *Poetry of the Landscape and the Night*, 1967.

15 Edmund Burke (1729–97) statesman, political orator and writer. His *Philosophical Enquiry into the Origin of our Ideas of the Sublime and the Beautiful* was published in 1757.

16 *Correspondence of Alexander Pope*, vol III, G. Sherburn ed., Oxford 1956.

17 It was not until Pugin (1812–52) that Gothic details were studied with earnestness and conviction, and even then he complained that the Houses of Parliament, on which he worked in collaboration with Sir Charles Barry, were 'All Grecian, Sir . . . Tudor details on a classic body'.

18 It is one of the advantages of Gothic (and picturesque) buildings that they can be added to, or taken from, at will, without any devastating effect on the design. One cannot build half a Palladian house and build phase two five years later, but one can build half a Gothic house, as Lutyens discovered at Castle Drogo. Architects who build for committees that change their minds mid-stream are well aware of this difference between the classical and picturesque approaches.

19 4 March 1753, Yale ed., xx, 361–2.

3

The Landscape Garden to 1750

NONE of Britain's many achievements in the visual arts is so original as the landscape garden. Most of the styles and traditions which have affected British artists and architects have had their origins elsewhere in Europe. But the landscape garden was an entirely English invention.

Gardens in England at the end of the seventeenth century were a mixed inheritance of Tudor, Dutch and French traditions. They consisted, as gardens always had done, of rectangular compartments with high walls and tall, clipped hedges. The word 'paradise' comes from the ancient Persian *pairidaeza*, meaning an enclosure. In many cultures Nature was originally seen as hostile, and the establishment of an ordered, external area for leisure and entertainment was in defiance of the wildness of what lay beyond the fence. In the Italian gardens of the Renaissance and Baroque period this relationship is still apparent. Each clearly shaped space is surrounded by the dark *bosco* of ilex trees, while 'inside' the garden the complex geometry of clipped box displays the rationality of the design.

But with the growth of 'natural philosophy' (which we now call science) an increased confidence began to be felt, which was expressed in an audacious way in France in the gardens of André Le Nôtre (1613–1700). Nature was no longer seen as a mysterious area where dangerous and unknown forces lurked, but rather as a subject for the rational application of the human mind. This domination of man over Nature is expressed in Le Nôtre's attempt to subsume the whole visible landscape into his scheme. Even the sky, it seems, can be trapped, reflected in his vast rectangular pools. Vast avenues disappear into the distant horizon. At a glance the logic of the whole project is revealed; all is '*claire et distincte*', in Descartes' words.

It is often forgotten that here lies one of the sources of the English landscape garden. The 'ideal of extent',[1] a wish to encompass the entire landscape, was derived from the French school, even though the way it was done was entirely different. However, this ideal was not integrated with the new 'natural' style until Lancelot Brown appeared. There are therefore two main aspects to the development of the Landscape Movement. One was the opening up of the small enclosed gardens to include more and more of the landscape. The other was the gradual abandonment of 'line and level', of T-square and set-square, in favour of the contours and features to be found already on the site. It was an increasingly empirical approach, therefore, identifying 'the genius of the place' (a phrase taken from the fifth book of Virgil's *Aeneid*) and building on this, rather than imposing on the ground the Euclidean projections of the mind. The important thing now was not that I can think (Descartes) but what my senses tell me about the world (Locke).

There were three phases in this development: the Arcadian landscape, the Ideal landscape and the Romantic landscape. In the Arcadian landscape, of which Stowe and Stourhead are perhaps the finest examples, the atmosphere of classical antiquity is evoked by the presence of temples, urns and statuary, combining a literary and didactic purpose with a visual one. The Ideal landscape abandoned these trappings: by common consent there were just too many buildings at Stowe (many were deliberately removed in the late eighteenth century). If there must be buildings let them be English Gothic, but for the Ideal landscape the main thing was to concentrate on the pure elements: ground, water and trees. The landscape of nymphs and shepherds was replaced by an improved version of the English countryside, a landscape conformed to an ideal. It was no coincidence that, when *le jardin anglais* went abroad, not only to France but to America, Scandinavia and Russia, it took the English countryside with it: the deciduous trees, the green lawns, soft contours and medium scale. The Russian Empress Catherine II (the Great) wrote to Voltaire in 1772:

> I passionately love gardens in the English style, the curved lines, the gentle slopes, the ponds pretending to be lakes, the archipelagos on solid ground, and I deeply disdain straight lines.... I should say my anglomania gets the better of planimetry.[2]

For the third phase, the Romantic landscape, and the advocates of the Picturesque, we must wait for Chapter 7 (p. 159).

At first the small enclosed gardens of the late 1600s were opened up only hesitantly. The 'Dutch' garden at Westbury Court in Gloucestershire is almost the sole survivor of its period. It shuts out the humdrum agricultural landscape that surrounds it, and the railings of the *clairvoyée* at the front are there, one suspects, so that passers-by will see in, not for those in the garden to look out. Another garden which survives from the reign of the 'Dutch' king, William III, is at Powis Castle. Here a strictly architectural series of terraces was created on the slopes below the castle. They overlook splendid views of Welsh Border country, showing a definite appreciation of the landscape; but the garden itself is an architectural creation quite separate from it.

An engraving of about 1700 by Kip and Knyff of Longleat in Wiltshire, shows how a garden at this date, on less dramatic terrain, could now be less inward-looking and grander in scale. Influenced by '*La Grand Manier*', as Stephen Switzer (1682–1745) described the French style, Longleat at this date was still enclosed, but the overall pattern is given much greater significance: the scheme has been considered as a whole and was meant to be seen as a whole. It is no longer a collection of separate spaces which have accumulated additively over the years. Long axes run through it, un-obstructed by obstacles, even penetrating the distant wood. An opening or *clairvoyée* on the right-hand side gives views of formal ponds which are right outside the enclosed gardens, and from here one can also look down a double avenue of trees stretching into the distance.

The master of the grand scale was Charles Bridgeman (1680?–1738). Bridgeman became Master Gardener in 1728, but despite this achievement the details of his life remain obscure. Among his many projects were Blenheim, Stowe, Claremont, Rousham and Wimpole, all of which were later re-worked by either William Kent or Lancelot Brown, or both. According to Switzer, who was a writer and nurseryman as well as a gardener, it was Bridgeman's belief that 'true greatness consists of size and dimension':

> This aiming at an incomprehensible vastness, and attempting at things beyond the reach of Nature is due in a great measure to a late eminent designer and gardener whose fancy could not be bounded.

says Switzer, in his *Ichnographia Rustica* (1742 edition). He tells us in a footnote that he means Bridgeman:

and this notion has been in many places carried so far, that no parterre or lawn that was not less than 50 or 60 acres, some of them 80, 90 or 100, were by him esteemed capacious enough, though sometimes it took up the whole area of ground, and made the building or mansion-house in the middle look very small, and by no means proportionable to it.

A reference to the boldness of scale at which Bridgeman worked can be seen in Alexander Pope's reference to his habit of substituting water for the intricacy of parterres:

> The vast parterres a thousand hands shall make,
> Lo! Bridgeman comes, and floats them with a lake:[3]

The plan of the grounds at Eastbury in Dorset is a striking example of Bridgeman's work. The house was by Vanburgh, but it only survived until 1762 when Earl Temple (who had already inherited Stowe) decided to blow it up with gunpowder. The area covered by the plan is about twelve hundred acres, showing the scale on which he worked. In contrast, the Dutch garden at Westbury covers only four acres. The uncompromising geometry of the design is everywhere apparent, and this is done mostly with trees, which reach right up to the house. The number of parterres is small: one each side of the central pool, and three near the house. Elsewhere the design consists either of avenues of trees or of solid blocks of planting. Although the front of the house is open to the countryside the rest of the grounds are surrounded by a continuous belt of planting which excludes the outside world. In places where some of the avenues reach the perimeter, the belt is broken, making those avenues open-ended; but all the views from the house would have been contained by the large-scale geometry of the design. Any difference in levels in the more detailed central area was taken up by steep and straight banks between levelled areas.

Where the paths of the central area line up with the avenues in the outer area there may well have been a sunk fence, or 'ha-ha'. Bridgeman certainly used this famous device, and Horace Walpole credited him with inventing it, although it had in fact been used earlier at Versailles and elsewhere. Walpole says:

> The capital stroke, the leading step to all that has followed, was (I believe the first thought was Bridgman's) the destruction of walls for boundaries, and the invention of fosses – an attempt then deemed so astonishing, that the common people called them Ha! Ha!s to express their surprise at finding a sudden and unperceived check to their walk.[4]

At first the sunk fence was used in short lengths at the end of an avenue, and an example of a short sunk fence can be seen at Wimpole where Bridgeman (and later Brown) worked. The effect of the sunk fence on the 'ideal of extent' is clear. Now the park and the garden could be united visually, in Walpole's words:

> the contiguous outlying parts come to be included in a kind of general design: and when nature was taken into the plan, under improvements, every step that was made pointed out new beauties and inspired new ideas.

A sunk fence dating from about 1720 exists at Duncombe Park in Yorkshire.[5] Here there is another of Vanbrugh's houses, placed scenically where views may be obtained across the valley. Although there is a straight walk parallel with the front of the house, the main feature of the design is the walk along the edge of the hill. This is of interest for two reasons. Firstly it was made specifically to provide views over the countryside – 'to call in the country', as it was described at the time. Secondly, it makes no pretence at geometry, but merely follows the contours. Eventually the walks were extended to include views of Rievaulx Abbey nestling in the valley below; but originally they were terminated by small classical temples, one of which was a rotunda by Vanbrugh. At Duncombe, therefore, Vanbrugh carefully positioned the house so that the owner was able, as it were, to take possession of the whole valley, thereby increasing the scale and grandeur of the whole setting.

Instead of the small-scale 'Dutch manner' which Switzer called 'those crimping, diminutive and wretched performances we everywhere meet with', Duncombe exemplifies his recommendation that 'all the adjacent country be laid open to view, and that the eye should not be bounded with high walls, woods misplaced, and several obstructions, that one sees in too many places, by which the eye is, as it were, imprisoned.' Switzer himself laid out a terrace at Grimsthorpe (where Vanbrugh extended the house and Brown later worked on the grounds) and this too overlooked the countryside. The 'prospect' here is shallower though more extensive, and it probably contained the fishponds which later became Brown's lake.

Vanbrugh's association with these schemes is no accident, since his appreciation of scenic values was certainly ahead of its time. The house he built for himself at Claremont in Surrey was sited there because the situation was 'singularly romantick'. Similarly, the siting of Castle Howard (from 1699) impressed even Horace Walpole, who was anti-Vanbrugh. Instead of being approached frontally in the traditional way the house faces panoramic views which were made possible by the demolition of Henderskelfe Castle, village and church, at Vanbrugh's suggestion. The route to Vanbrugh's scenically placed Belvedere of 1724, inspired by Palladio's Villa Rotonda, followed an old track along the contours of the land. Switzer remarked that the gardens at Castle Howard reached 'the highest pitch that natural and polite gardening can possibly ever arrive to', but Vanbrugh more modestly said,

I may commend them because Nature made them; I pretend to no more merit in them than a midwife, who helps to bring a fine child into the world, out of bushes, bogs and briars.[6]

In an article in the *Spectator* in 1712, Joseph Addison observed:

that there is generally in Nature something more grand and august than what we meet with in the curiosities of Art. When, therefore, we see this imitated in any measure, it gives us a nobler and more exalted kind of pleasure than what we receive from the nicer and more accurate productions of Art.

After noting that it would be 'of ill consequence to the public, as well as unprofitable to private persons' to create gardens as large and diverse as the French and Italian ones, he suggests:

Why may not a whole Estate be thrown into a kind of garden by frequent plantations, that may turn as much to the profit, as the pleasure of the owner? ... if the natural embroidery of the meadows were helped and improved by some small additions of Art, and the several rows of hedges set off by trees and flowers, that the soil might be capable of, a man might make a pretty landskip of his own possessions.

Addison's next paragraph leads us directly to the second aspect of the development of the Landscape Movement – the gradual abandonment of geometry in favour of natural contours, serpentine lines and informal planting. Searching for some authority for his suggestions, and not being able to find it in classical antiquity, he turns to the Chinese. The influence of chinoiserie on gardening is doubtful: fifty years later Thomas Gray remarked, 'it is very certain, we copied nothing from them';[7] nevertheless, travellers on the Grand Tour might well have been affected by the current vogue for chinoiserie in

Italy. Lord Burlington in fact owned a series of thirty-four engravings of the Imperial Gardens at Jehol published in Italy in 1713, and also various books by travellers to China.[8] It would seem best to conclude that the eighteenth century saw in the Chinese gardens something it was already looking for. Addison continues:

> Writers, who have given us an account of China, tell us, the inhabitants of that country laugh at the plantations of our Europeans, which are laid out by the rule and the line, because, they say, anyone may place trees in equal rows and uniform figures.... They have a word, it seems, in their language ...

Addison is referring to the word *sharawadgi*,[9]

> by which they express the particular beauty of a plantation that thus strikes the imagination at sight.... Our British gardeners, on the contrary, instead of humouring Nature, love to deviate from it as much as possible. Our Trees rise in Cones, Globes and Pyramids. We see the marks of the scissors upon every plant and bush. I do not know whether I am singular in my opinion, but, for my own part, I would rather look upon a tree in all its luxuriancy and diffusion of boughs and branches, than when it is thus cut and trimmed into a mathematical figure; and cannot but fancy that an orchard in flower looks infinitely more delightful, than all the little labyrinths of the most finished parterre.

Alexander Pope made his opinion of topiary clear in an article in the *Guardian* the following year (1713), when he produced a comical 'catalogue of greens' supposed to be for sale. These included:

> Adam and Eve in Yew; Adam a little shattered by the fall of the Tree of Knowledge in the great storm; Eve and the Serpent very flourishing ...
> The Tower of Babel, not yet finished ...
> A pair of Giants, stunted, to be sold cheap ...
> An old Maid of Honour in Wormwood ...
> A Lavender Pig, with sage growing in his belly.

Lord Shaftesbury had already spoken of the 'mockery of princely gardens' in *The Moralists* (1709):

> I shall no longer resist the passion growing in me for things of a natural kind; where neither art, nor the conceit or caprice of man has spoiled their genuine order, breaking in upon that primitive state. Even the rude rocks, the mossy caverns, the irregular unwrought grottoes, and broken falls of waters ... as representing Nature more, will be the more engaging, and appear with a magnificence beyond the formal mockery of princely gardens.

It seems that formality was abandoned on paper before it was abandoned on the ground. Several of the plans published by Stephen Switzer in his *Ichnographia Rustica* show both serpentine paths and winding water-courses. However, these plans do not have a practical look to them: the crazy, intestinal meanderings of his paths do not recommend themselves, and do not seem to have won him many clients at the time. Most of his designs appear to come into the category of what he called 'forest gardening'. Compared with Brown's plans, his are a mass of trees with no open spaces of any great consequence: they are merely the areas left in between the many tree-lined walks. However, even they compare favourably with the absurd, wiggling and maze-like paths shown by Batty Langley in his *New Principles of Gardening* (1728).

Robert Castell (d. 1729), a member of Lord Burlington's circle, published *The Villas of the Ancients* in 1728 and dedicated it to Burlington. The book was partly based on Pliny and other classical writers, partly on Italian villas of the Renaissance and Baroque period, and partly his own ideas, with a dash of chinoiserie thrown in. His plans show estates with a combination of formal areas and informal parts which were meant to demonstrate what Pliny called *imitatio ruris*. In drawing such areas Castell seems to have had half an eye on Matteo Ripa's drawings of the Chinese gardens at Jehol. They certainly look far more realistic and capable of execution than Batty Langley's or Switzer's published drawings.

If Lord Burlington's villa at Chiswick was the seminal building of the new English Palladianism, it was also in the grounds of the villa that the seeds of the new style of gardening first bore fruit. In fact the gardens had already been laid out before the villa was built. By 1730 the villa was complete, set amongst formal walks and avenues terminating in temples, with statuary, clipped hedges and, in some of the wooded areas, rather tortuous serpentine walks. But in 1733 Lord Burlington began to reshape the gardens with the aid of William Kent.

Burlington had met Kent in Rome in 1716, where Kent was already the companion of the young Thomas Coke (later Earl of Leicester and builder of Holkham House) and John Talman, the son of the architect William Talman, designer of Kimberley House, Norfolk, later landscaped by Brown. Kent had gone to Italy in 1710 to study painting, some Yorkshire gentlemen having 'raised a contribution', since 'his parents' or friends' circumstances were not in a condition to forward his practice and the expense of a profession'.[10] In 1713 the *British Mercury* reported that 'Mr. W. Kent ... is said this year to have gained the annual prize given by the Pope for painting'. After his return to England in 1719 he worked as a painter and designer of interiors and furniture, executing several ceiling paintings at Kensington Palace in 1724 and 1725, and was appointed Master Carpenter to the Board of Works in 1725.

The important change made at Chiswick in the 1730s, which shows the advance of the new 'natural' taste, was the serpentining of the 'river'. It was formed by deliberately altering an existing regularly shaped and straight-sided 'river', and this seems to have been one of the first pieces of water whose shape was purposely designed to be irregular. Whether it was Kent's idea or Burlington's is impossible to say; but in the same decade Kent was also working at Stowe on the buildings in the Elysian Fields, where there was another new serpentine river. By 1738 he had enlarged and irregularized Bridgeman's circular pond at Claremont and designed a temple for the irregularly shaped island in it.

But the project that established Kent's reputation was the garden at Carlton House for Frederick, Prince of Wales, begun soon after 1733. As one letter-writer put it in the following year:[11]

There is a new taste in gardening just arisen, which has been practised with so great success at the Prince's garden in Town, that a general alteration of some of the most considerable gardens in the Kingdom is begun, after Mr. Kent's notion of gardening, viz., to lay them out, and work without either level or line ... when finished, it has the appearance of beautiful nature, and without being told, one would imagine art had no part in the finishing, and is, according to what one hears of the Chinese, entirely after their models for works of this nature, where they never plant straight lines or make regular designs. The celebrated gardens of Claremont, Chiswick and Stowe are now full of labourers, to modernise the extensive work finished in them, even since everyone's memory.

It is significant that no plans by Kent have survived, in view of the empirical approach suggested by the use of 'no line or level'. Instead, we have a large number of sketches which show that his proposals were based on a visual and pictorial approach, which is hardly surprising considering he was a painter. Most of his sketches show garden buildings set amongst trees, and the way these are placed is quite formal on plan. The semicircular ending of the exedra which terminates the main lawn at Chiswick is a typical arrangement, and this is repeated at Stowe in both the Temple of the British Worthies and the Temple of Venus. The drawings show that almost all the buildings were meant to be viewed axially, and the plans by John Rocque of his garden show that many of his spaces are still conceived architecturally, as being of distinct shape. What has gone is the old stiff outline with all the little clipped hedges: the parterres have vanished and everywhere there are the soft outlines of Claudian trees – in all their 'luxuriancy', as Addison had remarked, 'and diffusion of boughs and branches'. One of the practical advantages of the new style was that it was labour-saving: once the parterres were removed many hours' work involved in hedge-clipping and training was eliminated. According to Horace Walpole, Kent's 'ruling principle was that nature abhors a straight line':

> The pencil of his imagination bestowed all the arts of landscape on the scenes he handled. The great principles on which he worked were perspective and light and shade.... Thus selecting favourite objects and veiling deformities ... he realised the compositions of the greatest masters in painting.

The care that he took to make a naturalistic effect was noted by the writer and conversationalist Joseph Spence (1699–1768), who remarked that:

> Mr. Kent always used to stake out his grovettes before they planted, and to view the stakes every way, to see that no three of them stand in line ...[12]

Although some of the sketches show shrubs or bushes, most of the trees have bare trunks so that one can see through from one 'set-piece' to the next,[13] an effect already used by Alexander Pope in his 'groves' at Twickenham. Pope's garden was very influential in spite of its size (Pope compared his efforts with those of a man who carved the twelve apostles out of one cherry stone). Walpole remarks that Kent was not 'without assistance':

> Mr. Pope undoubtedly contributed to form his taste. The design of the Prince of Wales' garden at Carlton House was evidently borrowed from the poet's at Twickenham. There was little of affected modesty in the latter, when he said, of all his works he was most proud of his garden. And yet it was a singular effort of art and taste to impress so much variety on a spot of five acres.

On the plan prepared by Pope's gardener of the garden as it was when Pope died, two kinds of planted areas are apparent: solid *bosco*, and the areas labelled in the key as 'The Grove'. These are shown as a series of dots, presumably indicating the trunks of the trees. To reach the main space of the garden from the house one had to pass through this grove, between the trees. Suddenly, therefore, the clear-cut distinction between 'path' or 'space' on one hand and solid 'planted area' or *bosco* on the other is seen as artificial, and the gradual, softer merging of one into the other, as found in nature, is now seen as more desirable. In Horace Walpole's words:

> Where ... an ancient wood extended wide its undulating canopy ... Kent thinned the foremost ranks, and left but so many detached and scattered trees as softened the approach of gloom and blended a chequered light with the thus lengthened shadows of the remaining columns.

Walpole also confirms the feeling that Kent's vision was small-scale. A study of the plans of Rousham, Claremont and Stowe leads one to believe that his ideas related to the setting of particular buildings or groups of statuary, and to make a larger garden he simply created a series of these, like a sequence of contrasting stage sets, each one a fresh 'discovery'. There is interest, variety and contrast but no grand conception; the 'ideal of extent' is not fulfilled. The difference may be illustrated by an analogy from contemporary developments in the musical world: whereas Handel (Kent's contemporary) composed orchestral suites and oratorios, constructed of a series of items (aria-recitative-chorus-aria-recitative and so on), Haydn (Lancelot Brown's contemporary) created the sonata form, a larger overall structure into which contrasting sections could be integrated, and it was this creation which earned him the title 'father of modern music'. Similarly, Brown's contribution was to construct large schemes covering hundreds of acres as a whole, in which there were variety and contrast within an overall unity.

Some of the landscapes shown in Kent's book illustrations (to Spenser's *Faerie Queen* and Thomson's *The Seasons* for instance) are broad in scale, and have a Claudian air. But when he attempts a larger-scale sketch for a designed landscape, as at Euston Hall in Suffolk, he reverts to symmetry – albeit with naturalistic elements matching each other on either side.

The artificial 'stage-set' character of Kent's gardens is seen clearly in the best-preserved of his landscapes, Rousham in Oxfordshire, designed for General Dormer. The 'rill', a serpentine streamlet which runs through part of the garden in a narrow stone channel, is curiously artificial and faintly ridiculous. The alterations to the old mill cottage, too, have an obvious falseness, and the Eye-Catcher, a sham ruin on the horizon, is a most strange creature.

Rousham is the best preserved of Kent's works, for few alterations took place after General Dormer's death in 1741. In the same year Henry Hoare II inherited Stourhead in Wiltshire, and he spent the next fourteen years creating the most successful of all the eighteenth-century Arcadian landscapes (by coincidence, its development was exactly contemporary with Brown's career). What makes Stourhead so perfect for the visitor is its 'circuit-walk' around the irregular lake, which winds gently in and out of the planting, giving fresh views at every turn. Such a circuit-walk had already been made at William Shenstone's garden, The Leasowes, which no longer survives.

There are no compartments at Stourhead. Everything is blended into a unity and the whole is contained by a backcloth of tree-planting. The lake has narrow creeks and its plan shape cannot be conceived by the visitor. In contrast to Kent's more rounded and obvious lakes, this one, like many of Brown's, is mysterious and romantic in conception. There is no political symbolism, but rather a poetic invocation of Elysium, modelled on Aeneas' journey to the underworld, described by Virgil in the sixth book of the *Aeneid*.

On the indirect route to the lake from the house one sees first a distant glimpse of the Pantheon, designed by Flitcroft; then one passes along a wooded walk called The Shades, and on reaching the lake the first 'building' we encounter is the grotto. '*Facilis descensus Averno*' (or 'the road to Hell is easy'), wrote Henry Hoare in one of his letters, quoting from Virgil and referring to the steps down to the grotto. A remarkable jagged opening in the side of it gives a view across the lake, and inside is a statue of the Nymph of the Grot lying across the source of the River Stour. The grotto is similar to the one in Alexander Pope's garden, and a quotation from Pope is carved on a nearby marble bath.

After passing a Gothick cottage we reach the Pantheon. Then passing across an iron bridge we come eventually to a rock bridge which leads up to the Temple of Apollo. From this appropriately Claudian height we can look back across the whole scene,

William Kent's drawing of the cascade in Venus's Vale at Rousham, with the surrounding trees growing (in Addison's words) in all their 'luxuriancy and diffusion of boughs and branches'.

Kent's design for an exedra at Chiswick. Here an architectural set-piece is framed by naturalistic planting.

The most famous of the Arcadian landscapes is Stourhead in Wiltshire, made by its owner Henry Hoare between 1741 and 1785, a period almost exactly contemporary with Brown's professional career. A view by Bampfylde.

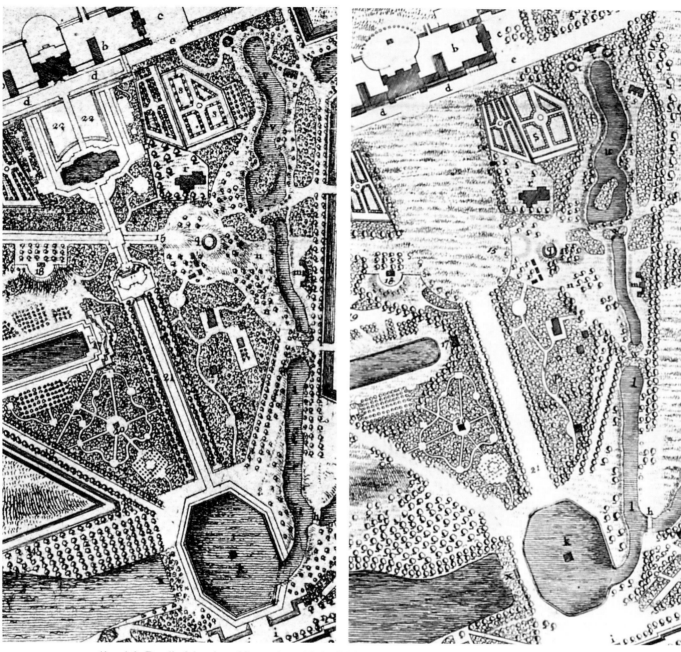

Above left: Detail of the plan of Stowe (1739) in its Bridgeman years, showing the gardens between the house and the lake (now covered by a large lawn) and the Elysian Fields on the right-hand side.

Above right: The same area on the 1753 plan, several years after Brown had left, showing the simplifying and softening process that had gone on in the meantime.

Opposite above: Rocque's plan (1746) of the Royal Gardens and Little Park, Richmond, showing many small-scale formal areas and the remains of the original field pattern.

Opposite below: Brown's plan for the Royal Gardens, covering the same area (north is towards the bottom left-hand corner): a total transformation owing nothing to what preceded it.

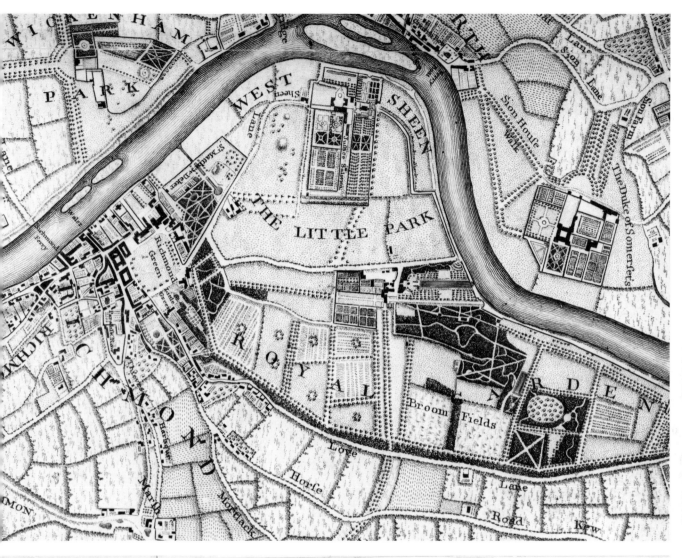

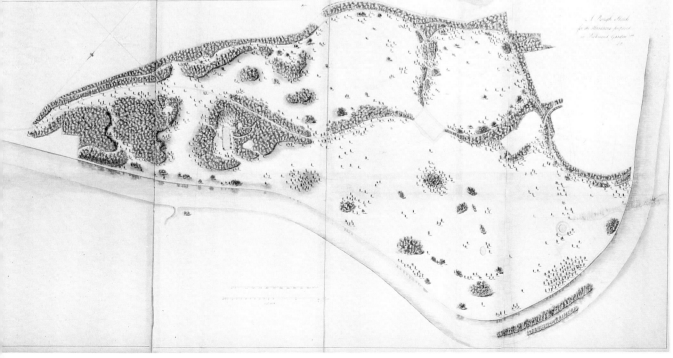

Above: Lancelot Brown, by Nathaniel Dance.

Opposite above: Fenstanton Manor, which Brown purchased from the Earl of Northampton in 1767.

Opposite below: A detail from John Spyers' 'Survey of the Manor of Fenstanton', prepared for Brown and dated 1777.

A PLAN OF THE MANOR
OF FENSTANTON.
in the COUNTY of HUNTINGDON.
1777.

The Stanch

also four able Horses with Harness during the Execution of the Work.

The Times of Payment.

	£	s	d
In June 1763	200	0	0
In September	200	0	0
In Ja.~~~~~~	140	0	0
on Finishing the Works	120	0	0
	660	0	0

Lancelot Brown

Left: Brown's signature, from his contract for Audley End.

Below: Brown's memorial in Fenstanton Church. This fine tribute was written by the Reverend William Mason.

LANCELOT BROWN Esq. died Feb. 6.th 1783. Aged 67 Years.

LANCELOT BROWN Esq
Son of
LANCELOT & BRIDGET
BROWN
he died the 28.th of Feb.y 1802
in the 54 Year of his
AGE.

Ye Sons of Elegance, who truly taste
The Simple charms that genuine Art supplies,
Come from the sylvan Scenes His Genius grac'd,
And offer here your tributary Sigh's.
But know that more than Genius slumbers here,
Virtues were his which Arts best powers transcend
Come, ye Superior train who these revere
And weep the Christian Husband Father Friend

Sacred
to the Memory of JOHN BROWN Esq.
Second Son of
LANCELOT & BRIDGET BROWN
An ADMIRAL in the British NAVY
He died the 3.d of May 1808
AGED 57 YEARS.

Also Sacred
to the Memory of
MARY tho WIDOW of
ADMIRAL BROWN
who died March 21.st 1834
AGED 71 YEARS

framed by trees. The inspiration for the next stage of the circuit-walk is given in one of Henry Hoare's letters: 'the bridge, village and church altogether will be a charming Gaspard picture at the end of that water.'[14]

The size and dominance of the lake at Stourhead give the scheme an overall unity possessed by no earlier garden: even at Stowe one is aware that the gardens were created by accumulation. At Stourhead, however, the additions were made to a basic framework that could be loaded even with nineteenth-century exotic planting without being totally compromised. Though some rightly say the rhododendrons are extrinsic to the original intention, others feel that this garden now has everything. I suppose exotics are less damaging to an Arcadian landscape than to the idealized Nature of a Brownian landscape.

NOTES

1 Christopher Hussey's expression, *English Gardens and Landscapes 1700–1750*.

2 'Russian Parks of the Eighteenth Century', in M. Iljin, *Architectural Review*, February 1964, pp. 100–111.

3 *Epistle to Lord Burlington*. In later editions Pope replaced Bridgeman with Cobham, the owner of Stowe.

4 Horace Walpole, *The History of the Modern Taste in Gardening* (1771–80).

5 For a detailed discussion see C. Hussey, *English Gardens and Landscapes 1700–1750*.

6 *The Complete Works of Sir John Vanbrugh, Vol IV The Letters*, ed. Geoffrey Webb, 1928. Letter, 8 August 1721, to the Duke of Newcastle.

7 Letter to William Taylor How, 10 September 1763, quoted in full in the notes to William Mason's poem *The English Garden*.

8 According to P. Willis, *Charles Bridgeman*.

9 For discussion of *sharawadgi* see N. Pevsner and S. Long, 'A Note on Sharawaggi' in Pevsner, *Studies in Art, Architecture and Design*, Vol I. It appears that it derives from the Chinese *sa-ro-kwai-chi*, and means the art of being impressive or surprising through careless or disorderly grace. However, I am inclined to think that the 'wadgi' part is *wu-shih* 'lack of affectation, or simplicity'. For the Chinese ideograms and discussion see Alan W. Watts, *The Way of Zen*.

10 According to Vertue, quoted in M. Jourdain, *The Work of William Kent*.

11 Sir Thomas Robinson to Lord Carlisle, 1734. Historical Manuscripts Commission Report, 42 Carlisle MSS, pp. 143–4.

12 Letter to Revd Wheeler, 1751, in *Observations, Anecdotes and Characters of Books and Men* (1820).

13 This provides a kind of interpenetration reminiscent of the use of pilotis in modern architecture.

14 Hoare to Lady Bruce, 1762, quoted in K. Woodbridge, *Landscape and Antiquity* (1971). He is referring to Gaspard Poussin (1615–75), whose real name was Dughet, but who adopted the name of his brother-in-law Nicolas Poussin.

4

Lancelot Brown 1715–1783

———

Lancelot Brown was born in the small Northumberland village of Kirkharle, which lies in rugged country about twenty miles north-west of Newcastle on the Jedburgh road. The exact date of his birth is not known – it was either in 1715 or the first few weeks of 1716[1] – and he was baptized on 30 August 1716 in the tiny church of St Wilfrid. In the parish register his name was spelt as Lancelote and the name of his father William Browne was also spelt with an 'e'.[2]

Only four years later William Browne died, leaving his wife with six children of which Lancelot was the fifth. The family was 'of yeoman farming stock' and had come from Ravenscleugh in Redesdale,[3] in the Scottish Borders. There are few records to enable us to picture the village of Kirkharle in those days. In about 1740 the village was moved as part of the improvements to the local estate of Kirkharle Hall, and some time later it had only two hundred inhabitants, thirty-three houses and a small school. Young Lancelot went to school at Cambo,[4] a village three miles away, where, as a local historian, the Reverend John Hodgson (writing in 1827) remarked,

the fertile and ingenious mind of *Capability Brown* underwent the first processes of cultivation and had those seeds of useful learning sown upon it, which enabled him to rise to the head of a new and elegant profession, to become the companion of the most celebrated men of his time, and to leave his family in honourable affluence.[5]

In 1732, when he was about sixteen, Lancelot left school and started work at Kirkharle Hall, owned at that time by Sir William Loraine, formerly a barrister in London and a Member of Parliament. Since inheriting the estate in 1718 at the age of sixty, Sir William had employed much of his time and energy in the improvement of it, and had built, according to the Reverend Hodgson, 'a new mansion-house of his own plan and contrivance, with all the offices, out-houses, gardens, fountains, fishponds etc.' He was 'exemplary in planting and enclosure', and between 1694 and 1738 had planted 24,000 trees, and according to another writer[6] he 'drained the morasses and cleared the land of "ponderous, massy and hard stones" to prepare it for tillage.'

Lancelot Brown worked for Sir William for seven years. No doubt he learned at Kirkharle all the basic practicalities of estate improvement, and began to acquire the technical ability which later enabled him to undertake large-scale projects with confidence. A plan of improvements at Kirkharle has recently come to light, prepared by Brown, but not signed or dated,[7] and the maturity of the drawing style suggests that it was done much later, during one of Brown's periodical visits to his family, or when he was working at Wallington and Rothley some year later.

Brown may well have learned much from Sir William in the architectural field, and also in the appreciation of scenic values, for he was (according to Reverend Hodgson) 'skilled in architecture and physic'. The outstanding architect in the north country had been Sir John Vanbrugh, who had died in 1726. Seaton Delaval was not far away[8] and even closer was Morpeth Town Hall which Vanbrugh designed in 1714. Whether Sir William actually met him is not known, but he may have done so through a family connection with the Howards of Castle Howard, or through the owner of Seaton Delaval, Admiral Delaval, who owned another estate called Great Bevington about three miles south of Kirkharle. So it is possible that he was conversant with Vanbrugh's work at Castle Howard, and could have passed on to Brown ideas about the 'natural taste' in improvements, of which Castle Howard is an early example.

In 1743 Lancelot's older brother, John, married Sir William's youngest daughter, and several years later he acted as Steward for the Kirkharle estate. This may be an indication that the Browns were not of quite such humble origin as is often assumed.

During this period young Lancelot must have observed the improvements being carried out at the Wallington estate, almost next door to Kirkharle, formerly owned by Sir William Loraine's mother, Grace Fenwick, but by the 1730s the property of Sir Walter Calverley Blackett. Reverend Hodgson also tells us that Brown was 'for some time employed as a gardener to Mr Robert Shafto, of Benwell', which is on the outskirts of Newcastle. Today Benwell Tower is surrounded by suburban development, leaving only some 'scraggy planting'.[9] This Robert Shafto was probably uncle to his more famous heir of the same name, who 'went to sea', and became a Member of Parliament. A contemporary drawing shows the younger Bobby Shafto with Brown and Lord Craven of Coombe Abbey. He married Anne Duncombe of Duncombe Park.[10]

In 1739[11] Brown left Northumberland. The immediate reasons for this move are unknown. The milder climate of the south would have been beneficial to his health, for he suffered from chronic asthma, but in addition it is easy to see that the remote corner of England into which he had been born would have held nothing further for a talented, ambitious young man. No doubt the energy, perseverance and self-confidence which marked Brown throughout his career were the driving force. A year earlier the two outstanding gardeners of the time, Charles Bridgeman and Henry Wise, had both died, and in 1739 Bridgeman's widow published a splendid folio volume entitled *Views of Stowe*, illustrating the gardens (already the most famous in the country) as Bridgeman made them. It was no accident, therefore, that Brown was next at work at a garden only a few miles from Stowe.

The former High Sheriff of Buckinghamshire, one Richard Smith, was Sir William Loraine's father-in-law. Aged almost ninety, he was living at Preston Bissett, a few miles south of Buckingham on the Oxfordshire border. He could well have recommended Brown to the owner of Kiddington Hall,[12] Sir Charles Browne. Kiddington still has an attractive lake, made by damming the tiny River Glyme: serpentine in shape, it widens out to contain a tree-planted island.

After working here for a while, Brown came to the attention of Lord Cobham, perhaps on the recommendation of a nurseryman. Lord Cobham apparently required someone 'who could continue with him at Stowe, able to converse instructively on his favourite pursuit, but free from the vanity and conceit which had rendered his former assistants disinclined to alterations which he had determined upon.'[13] In 1741 the head gardener at Stowe, William Love, left after fifteen years, and Lancelot Brown took his place. His wages were £25 a year plus £9 in board.[14] There is no basis for the legend that initially he was in charge of the kitchen garden; on the contrary he was already recognized as a competent 'improver' of gardens[15] before he began at Stowe.

Thus at the age of twenty-four Brown became head gardener at the most famous garden in the country. Alexander Pope had already singled out Stowe as the finest example of what can be achieved in gardening:

> Nature shall join you; time shall make it grow,
> A work to wonder at – perhaps a *Stowe*.[16]

As early as 1724 Lord Percival had written in a letter to his brother-in-law, 'Yesterday we saw Lord Cobham's house, which within these five years has gained the reputation of being the finest seat in England.'[17] To be in charge of grounds such as these at such a comparatively young age was an achievement in itself. At least two hundred acres were within the area enclosed by the sunk fence, and the Stowe Ridings extended over a much vaster area.[18] There were many lakes, the largest being of eleven acres, and Lord Cobham's enthusiasm and determination for constant improvement meant that the gardens had always been in the forefront of taste as styles had changed over the years.

A succession of famous designers had worked there, but the main contribution was Bridgeman's. A plan of the gardens, published in *Views of Stowe*, shows that at that time they were significantly different from what we now see. The influence of Brown can be seen everywhere, even though the changes mostly took place after Brown himself left. In 1739 there was no overall concept such as at Eastbury. The scale was smaller than it is now, partly because the planting had not matured, and the plan contained a large number of geometrically conceived compartments and long straight avenues.

Today the green lawn in front of the house sweeps uninterrupted down to the lake. In 1739 there was first the House Terrace and then the parterre, which included a lake of complex geometrical outline, all surrounded by a clipped hedge with arched indentations. A narrow path through trees and past a junction with other paths led to a formal arrangement of banking,[19] after which an avenue – the Abele (Poplar) Walk – led to the Octagon Lake.[20]

The only non-geometrical part was the Elysian Fields, startlingly different in those days from the rest of the park. The water here (the Alder River) has a slightly irregular outline, and is probably the work of Kent, since he also designed the buildings nearby. He may have ceased work at Stowe by the time Brown arrived, but his ideas remained, influencing Lord Cobham's approach from then on.

Brown soon mastered the Kent style. The ability to learn quickly from experience and to recognize those from whom more may be learned is a feature of men of outstanding ability. The way Brown rose from obscurity to become the dominating figure in the national craze for 'improvements' is something which Humphry Repton considered:

> But of this art, painting and gardening are not the only foundations. The artist must possess a competent knowledge of surveying, mechanics, hydraulics, agriculture, botany, and the general principles of architecture. It can hardly be expected that a man bred and constantly living in the kitchen garden should possess all these requisites; ... It may be asked from whence Mr. Brown derived his knowledge? – the answer is obvious: that being at first patronised by a few persons of rank and acknowledged good taste, he acquired by degrees the faculty of prejudging effects, partly from repeated trials and partly from the experience of those to whose conversation and intimacy his genius had introduced him.

A general plan of Stowe published in 1753,[21] two years after Brown left, illustrates the changes which had been taking place. The sharp lines have gone and many of the paths have been grassed over, as has the parterre, with its lake, in front of the house. The Grecian Valley has appeared, of naturalistic outline, and the Hawkwell Field has acquired scatterings of isolated trees. The eleven-acre lake has lost its straight sides, and has gained a soft outline and two tree-covered islands. In addition to overseeing the practical side of such work, Brown had considerable financial and managemental responsibilities, which evidently included work on the buildings as well as the grounds, since he supervized the payment of carpenters, carters, sawyers, plasterers and masons as well as under-gardeners.

While he was at Stowe Lancelot met Bridget Wayet. Little is known of her family or background, except that she belonged to 'a very respectable county family of Boston and Tumby-in-Bain, Lincolnshire'.[22] They were married on 22 November 1744, at St Mary's Church, Stowe. Bridgeman had 'screened out' this church with trees, and the village that originally surrounded it had been removed when it got in the way of improvements. The Browns' first child, born in 1746, was called Bridget, and parish records tell us that their next child, Lancelot, was christened on 13 January 1748.

After a few years at Stowe Brown was asked to give advice at other estates, and it seems that Lord Cobham was happy with this arrangement. One of the first, naturally enough, was the neighbouring estate of Wakefield, owned by the Duke of Grafton.[23] William Kent had recently designed a new mansion for the Duke and it is easy to imagine that either he or Lord Cobham recommended Brown. Another project of interest in this period was Wotton, near Brill in Buckinghamshire, which was owned by Richard Grenville, Lord Cobham's nephew and heir. In 1746 Brown was advising the Earl of Denbigh at Newnham Paddox (about ten miles east of Coventry). A 'building book'[24] records:

Begun the alteration of this great canal and carrying it on to the head of the pond in the park by a plan and the direction of Mr. Brown, gardener to Lord Cobham ...

This cost £194 6s 1d. Work on the grounds continued, with payments to Brown recorded until 1754.

In 1749 Cobham died, and after this Brown stayed on only for a further eighteen months. During this period two more children were born into the Brown family: William, born in 1750, who survived only a month, and John, who was born the following year.

Meanwhile Brown's independent practice was growing. One of his early projects was Packington Hall in Warwickshire, and some sketches for quite elaborate garden buildings which were never carried out have survived.

The death of his patron and the increasing number of large commissions no doubt combined to persuade Brown to move away from Stowe. In 1751 the family left for Hammersmith, which at that time was a hamlet favoured by nurserymen on the outskirts of the village of Fulham near London. For the next fourteen years he lived in a house on the Mall, a building which has since disappeared. At about this time he did some work at Warwick Castle for Lord Brooke and by 1751 the work was sufficiently mature to win the praise of Horace Walpole in a letter to George Montagu. Obviously Brown was as yet an unknown name:

On my return I saw Warwick, a pretty old town, small and thinly inhabited, in the form of a cross. The castle is enchanting; the view pleased me more than I can express; the river Avon tumbles down a cascade at the foot of it. It is well laid out by one Brown who has set up on a few ideas of Kent and Mr. Southcote.

In 1753 Brown began to alter the buildings at Warwick Castle, including rebuilding the porch and stairs to the Great Hall and altering the internal arrangements to create larger rooms for the use of Lord Brooke's family. Brown executed a remarkable number of architectural projects, which in view of his lack of formal training is surprising. It may seem natural for the art of landscape to extend to the design of small garden buildings, but at Croome, Redgrave and Claremont, to list only a few, Brown built large, comfortable mansions which were also the central feature of the surrounding landscape. No doubt he would have agreed with William Mason's comments in a letter to Humphry Repton in 1792:

> I am uniformly of the opinion that where a place is to be formed, he who disposes the ground and arranges the plantations ought to fix the situation at least, if not to determine the shape and size of the ornamental buildings.[25]

He adds that

> Brown ... was ridiculed for turning architect, but I always thought he did it from a kind of necessity having found the great difficulty which must frequently have occurred to him in forming a picturesque whole, where the previous building had been ill-placed, or of improper dimensions.

After Brown's death Repton became England's leading landscape designer, and his comments on Brown's work are therefore of particular interest. Of his architectural work he said:

> Mr. Brown's fame as an architect seems to have been eclipsed by his celebrity as a landscape gardener, he being the only professor of the one art, while he had many jealous competitors in the other. But when I consider the number of excellent works in architecture, designed and executed by him, it becomes an act of justice to his memory to record that, if he was superior to all in what related to his own particular profession, he was inferior to none in what related to the comfort, convenience, taste and propriety of design in the several mansions and other buildings which he planned.[26]

Repton's remarks about 'convenience' were confirmed by Henry Holland, Brown's son-in-law:

> No man that I ever met with understood so well what was necessary for the habitation of all ranks and degrees of society; no one disposed his offices so well, set his buildings on such good levels, designed such good rooms, or so well provided for the approach, for the drainage, and for the comfort and conveniences of every part of a place he was concerned in.[27]

Brown always aimed to provide a building which was appropriate to its position, even if this meant simply repeating what was there already, as at Corsham, where he doubled the size of the Elizabethan wings on the south front. Few architects of recent years would be content with such anonymity.

A glance at Brown's portrait, painted several years after this by Sir Nathaniel Dance, will give some idea of his temperament. The kindly eyes and the lines around the mouth are the marks of a man who is easy to get on with, who is good company and whose keen vision misses nothing, while the firm mouth and unlined brow show determination and self-confidence. Contemporary descriptions of his character confirm this picture. François de la Rochefoucauld, in *Mélanges sur L'Angleterre*, says that 'Le Brun' 'had so quick and sure an eye for the country that after riding for an hour he would conceive the design for a whole park, and that afterwards half a day was enough for him to mark it out on the ground.' Although Brown's correspondence shows, superficially, the required deference to his social superiors, the underlying tone is of one who is at ease with his clients, for his manner is not distant or flattering, but conversational and straightforward. 'Lancelot Brown', wrote Lord Chatham, 'shares the private hours of the King, dines familiarly with his neighbour at Sion [The Duke of Northumberland's estate] and sits down at the tables of all the House of Lords, and ... he is deserving of the regard shown to him, for I know him, upon very long acquaintance, to be an honest man, and of sentiments much above his birth.'

Lord Chatham, William Pitt the Elder, was only one of his many famous clients, a list of whom, it has been said,[28] reads like Debrett. Chatham was perhaps the greatest politician of his day, but not much liked by George III; Brown, however, was on good terms with both men. Chatham is supposed to have turned to Brown on one occasion after they had dined together and said: 'Go you and adorn England', to which Brown replied, 'Go you, and preserve it'.[29] Chatham was married to Hester Grenville, niece of Lord Cobham of Stowe, and when in the 1760s he inherited Burton Pynsent in Somerset, he asked Brown to design a commemorative pillar there. Two letters from Brown to Lord Chatham on this subject survive:[30] 'I have sent you by your steward a design for the pillar which I hope will merit your approbation', he writes, and in a later letter to Lady Chatham[31] he enquires after her husband's health (he was subject to intense depression):

I was most heartily rejoiced to find that Lord Chatham was well enough to move from North End, and that his Lordship and family were set out for Pynsent. I hope in God that his Lordship mended every day, and that you have all had a good journey.

Pardon my zeal! Pardon my vanity, but I wish above all things to know [how] my Lord does, and how the pillar pleases his Lordship!

His Lordship was apparently happy enough since the pillar was duly built, and still stands on the hillside opposite the house.

Some of Brown's projects lasted for many years, and speak of good client relationships which were able to survive all the upheavals involved in alterations to houses and estates. His work for Lord Exeter on various projects at Burghley House, near Stamford, lasted for thirty years and was only terminated by his death. Brown's portrait by Dance still hangs in the Pagoda Room at Burghley. The friendliness between client and designer can be seen in little notes in their correspondence, such as that from Lord Exeter on 4 January 1773: 'May happy new years ever attend the family at Hampton is the sincere wish of yours, Exeter.'

Another note about the family comes in a letter from Lord Bruce, of Tottenham House in Wiltshire: 'I hope your family are well as mine, Thank God.' Lord Bruce received a letter from his agent in March 1765 which gives a typical picture of Brown on one of his periodic visits. Bad weather was obviously no deterrent:

Mr. Brown came here on Sunday to dinner. In the afternoon he took a view of the gardens in a storm of snow. Early this morning, which proved tolerably favourable, he allowed lining out and finally settled the serpentine walk all round the garden, marked such trees as were proposed to be taken away and gave general directions to Winckles [Lord Bruce's steward] upon everything that occurred. He thinks it best to keep house a fortnight or three weeks longer to get the levelling business forward. In general he approves of what has been done except the taking away [of] a few large trees in one or two places. If the high bank and trees had been taken down, great would have been the fall indeed, Brown would have excommunicated us all ...

Lord Bruce wrote to Brown in 1772 in terms which reveal the way his clients relied on his judgement during the course of the work:

Upon our arrival here last night, we found what has been done ... much to our satisfaction, but we shall scarce venture to go a step further to complete it without your advice upon the spot, which we wish to have as soon as conveniently can be to yourself...

One particularly well-pleased client was Lord Coventry, whose estate at Croome Court in Worcestershire was transformed by Brown's work. After Brown's death he erected a memorial to him overlooking the lake, with the inscription:

> *To the Memory of*
> *Lancelot Brown*
> *who by the powers of*
> *his inimitable*
> *and creative genius*
> *formed this garden scene*
> *out of a morass.*

The memorial has recently been restored after tree-damage; but the sad state of the lake and landscape surrounding the memorial today can more accurately be described as a 'morass' than anything else. The house is also by Brown, his first major architectural work. In a letter to Humphry Repton, Lord Coventry said:

I write from a house which he built for me which ... is, perhaps, a model for every internal and domestic convenience. I may be partial to my place at Croome, which was entirely his creation, and, I believe, originally as hopeless a spot as any in the island.[32]

Earlier in the letter he remarked, 'I certainly held him very high as an artist, and esteemed him as a most sincere friend'.

It begins to become quite clear that Brown was not just an original designer and a skilful practitioner; he was also a likeable man. 'He left [his clients] pleased', Henry Holland[33] said later 'and they remained so as long as he lived.' After pointing out in some detail Brown's proficiency in practical architectural matters, Holland adds, 'This he did without ever having had one single difference with any of his employers.'

Whether of buildings or of landscapes, Brown's drawings have a neat, careful style. Some of the plans were extremely large: one of his plans for Heveningham, for example, is more than ten feet long. Details and drawings of small garden buildings were usually on smaller sheets, and occasionally the drawings were bound together in a book.[34] Some of the plans were left for the owner to execute himself, but many of Brown's best-known works were carried out under his own supervision, in which case a contract would be drawn up giving details about who would provide materials, men, horses, and so on. Brown would then put the work in charge of an overseer, such as Benjamin Read, who worked at Croome Court and Blenheim. At a relatively small estate such as Ingestre, Lord Chetwynd had seventy men working for two years under 'an overseer sent by Mr Brown'. The amounts that the owners of these estates were prepared to pay is astonishing: over £21,500 was spent at Blenheim, for instance. For surveys Brown charged per acre – sixpence or eightpence, though at Byram he charged a shilling, probably because it was a relatively small estate of only 373 acres.

Brown's care with the financial side of his work was a feature which strongly recommended him to clients. Horace Walpole remarked that he 'had great integrity in his dealings with those for whom he laid out ground, and returned money he had received on account if more than the expense he had incurred.' At Cadland in Hampshire, the owner (and Brown's own banker), Robert Drummond, was so pleased that he added £200 to the account that Brown had rendered. To this Brown replied:

Dear Sir,

On looking over the Accounts, I find you added for my trouble on the Out of Doors work, two hundred pounds, which is more than I can possibly accept of from you, by one hundred pounds, I having a reasonable profit in the Building, on which Account I have annexed a Receipt to you for one hundred pounds on that of what is now doing at Cadlands.

At Branches Park in Suffolk, Brown recorded a rare confrontation with one of his clients. It was over a bill for additional work which had been done at the client's request, and for which Brown charged an additional £58 1s 8d. The client, Ambrose Dickens, refused to pay, and Brown wrote in his account book, 'Mr. Brown could not get the money for the extra work and tore the account before Mr. Dickens's face and had his say upon that business to him.'

While Brown was living at Hammersmith with his family, he met Henry Holland (the Elder). Holland came from a successful family of builders, and had himself built many mansions for well-known architects, and designed and built several large houses in the Fulham area. Brown's daughter Bridget was later to marry the younger Henry Holland. In the early 1760s the two men were both involved in a commission at Ashridge, Hertfordshire, the seat of the Duke of Bridgewater. This is one of the first entries in an account book which is the only surviving item of all Brown's business papers. Many of his projects have been identified from it.

Apart from Croome Court, one of the chief projects which Brown worked on during the early 1750s was Belhus in Essex, an estate belonging to Lord Dacre. Lord Dacre's correspondence shows the considerable fame which Brown had already achieved, but it also reveals for the first time the chronic ill-health from which he suffered. Attacks of asthma were to hinder Brown in moving about the country throughout his career. Apparently he was prevented from preparing a scheme for Lord Dacre as soon as he would have liked: in October 1753 Dacre wrote to Sanderson Miller,

Brown has been here and by what I find has really been very ill; he made me a great many very serious professions how ready he was to serve me and while he stayed here slaved at setting out the road and rest of the shrubbery all day and drew Plans all evening and was in the best humour imaginable . . .

Among the large projects started in the 1750s were Bowood, Burghley and Petworth, which we shall look at later. Another was Moor Park for Lord Anson in Hertfordshire, where earth-moving on a vast scale was undertaken to improve the setting of the main front of the house. Anson had been the fortunate victor of the battle of Cape Finisterre, where he had captured the Spanish plate fleet, and he spent at least £80,000 of his prize money on the house and grounds.

In 1756 Brown was forty, and his fame was complete. The nickname 'Capability' was already established and he was a national figure, and it is not surprising to find him applying for the post of royal gardener. William Kent had laid out Kensington Gardens for George II and Queen Caroline, and no doubt Brown looked on himself as Kent's successor.

A petition was laid before the Treasury in 1757, sponsored by an impressive number of the nobility, most of whom had been his clients. The First Lord of the Treasury was the Duke of Newcastle, who was also 'Patronage Secretary', and who unfortunately would have considered Brown's patrons his political enemies; although he gave some vague verbal promises, nothing happened. But Brown's loyal supporters did not intend their petition to be forgotten. In March 1758 they wrote again to the Treasury:

We whose Names are underwritten, being well-wishers of Mr. Browne, whose Abilities and Merit we are fully acquainted with, do most earnestly request the Duke of Newcastle to promote his speedy appointment to the care of Kensington Garden agreeable to his Grace's very obliging promises in that respect, the delay having already occasion'd great loss to Mr. Browne in his Business and great inconvenience to many Persons for whom he is Employ'd.

Anson	[Moor Park]
Temple	[Stowe]
Ashburnham	[Ashburnham]
Egremont	[Petworth]
Holdernesse	[Syon Hill]
Midleton	[Peper Harow]
Stamford	[Enville]
Ancaster	[Grimsthorpe]
Exeter	[Burghley]
Coventry	[Croome Court]
Brooke	[Warwick Castle]
George Grenville	[Wotton]
Hertford	[Ragley]
Northumberland	[Syon House and Alnwick]

But even this was not successful. It was not until seven years later that Brown obtained his appointment, after the accession of George III.

In 1764 the *Gentleman's Magazine* announced that Lancelot Brown had been made 'Surveyor to His Majesty's Gardens and Waters at Hampton Court'. This was not strictly correct, since Brown's post was 'Master Gardener', in succession to James Greening. He was appointed Gardener at St James's in the same year. In the documents it is stated that he was to receive £1,107 6s, plus £100 for 'raising pineapples', and £100 for 'parcel fruits'. However, Brown's own account book shows that he received £2,000 a year from 1765 onwards, in quarterly amounts of £500. From this he had to pay the cost of replacing trees, plants and gravel and also pay the under-gardeners, but no doubt it was still quite profitable.

In addition, a house was provided for the Master Gardener, a comfortable residence called Wilderness House. This red-brick building lies a few hundred yards west of Lion Gate at Hampton Court, and has scarcely changed since the time when the Brown family lived in it. It contains four pleasant panelled rooms on the ground floor, with a wide flight of shallow stairs leading to the upper floors, and has a small garden of its own at the rear within the palace grounds. Here Lancelot Brown lived with his family, and even after he bought his own private residence he continued to use Wilderness House for much of the year. By this date the Browns' fifth child, Margaret, had been born and their youngest son Thomas was born in 1761. In the same year the young Lancelot, now aged thirteen, was sent to be educated at Eton, where the poor child was nicknamed 'Capey' after his father.

Few changes were made at Hampton Court while Brown was royal gardener. It has been said that George III suggested that he should alter the formal walks and avenues, but that Brown 'had the good sense and honesty to decline'.[35] He is said to have grassed over some of the paths, and is also credited with planting the famous Great Vine, which still bears fruit.

The tone of some of the letters which have survived from clients and would-be clients tells us something about Brown's prestige. A letter from Lord Lisburne[36] of Mamhead in Devon, for example, reads as follows:

I should esteem myself much obliged to you if I might hope for the favour of seeing you here any time during the autumn when it may best suit your other engagements ... I am encouraged to hope from you what you said [to] me when we met accidentally last winter, that, notwithstanding the distance, you may find an opportunity to come here, as I should be glad to make what improvements the scene is capable of under the direction of a genius whose taste is so superior and unrivalled ...[37]

Little has survived of Rycote in Oxfordshire, where the Earl of Abingdon spent £2,400. He sounds like the ideal client: 'I pay so great deference to your taste, prudence and judgement, that I never make the least inquiry concerning the improvements at Rycote, but shall always be happy to meet you there.'

If Brown's reputation was great, he did not despise projects smaller than the grandiose ones for which he was famous. One of these was for a certain Frederic Nicolay, who lived not far from him, in Richmond, at a house in Hill Street. He appealed to Brown in 1770:

Sir, If you have five minutes to spare when you come to Richmond, I should take it as a great favour if you would give yourself the trouble to call at my house. I am in very great distress and trouble, which one coup d'oeuil of yours into a large piece of ground of mine would soon relieve me from. I hope it is no offence to wish for a miniature picture from a Raphael.[38]

Elizabeth Montagu, of Sandleford Priory, was another of Brown's clients. She confessed that she could not compare with some of Brown's immensely rich clients:

I ... make a very paltry figure to him as an employer. He is narrowly circumscribed, both in space and expense; but he really gives the poor widow and her paltry plans as great attention as he could bestow on an unlimited commission and an unbounded space. He has made a plan ... and will execute as much of it every year as I choose ...[39]

She too found Brown congenial as well as capable: 'He is an agreeable, pleasant, companion, as well as a great genius in his profession.' Not all clients were as careful as Mrs Montagu, however. No expense was spared at Lord Donegall's magnificent house and park at Fisherwick near Lichfield, both by Brown. But the estate only survived for forty years. When Lord Donegall died in 1799 he left debts of £100,000 (including £44,000 owed to Hoare's Bank): the whole estate was sold off in forty-two lots, the mansion was demolished, and scarcely a trace remains today.

Spencer Compton, eighth Earl of Northampton also ran into 'grave financial difficulties' while work was being carried out on his estate at Castle Ashby. Henry Drummond, of Drummond's Bank, was his brother-in-law and acted as trustee when he teetered on the edge of bankruptcy in 1766.[40] When Lord Northampton offered another of his estates, Fenstanton Manor in Huntingdonshire, to Drummond for £13,000, Brown somehow got to hear about it and expressed an interest in purchasing it. Eventually Lord Northampton agreed to sell it to him for the same amount. Brown was no doubt thinking ahead to his retirement when he would have to leave Wilderness House, which was Crown property, but it is difficult to see what attracted him to this piece of ground in flat, uninteresting countryside with few 'capabilities', or to the house, which is not at all grand in style. One is tempted to think that he spotted a bargain and took advantage of an opportunity when it came. It is also possible that Lord Northampton owed him some money: on the document dealing with transfer of ownership Lord Northampton added in his own handwriting, 'I take the Manor of Fen Standon to belong to Lawrence [sic] Brown Taste Esq., who gave Lord Northampton Taste in exchange for it.' In 1770

Brown was made High Sherriff of Huntingdonshire, so presumably he used to spend some of his time at Fenstanton.

From 1760 onwards Brown was extremely busy, and the list of projects starting in this period is very long. Apart from Tottenham Park, Castle Ashby and Fisherwick, other schemes which he worked on between 1759 and 1765 include Blenheim, Chillington, Corsham, Dodington (Avon), Kimberley, Lowther Castle, Milton Abbey, Temple Newsam, Ugbrooke and two schemes for 'his neighbour' the Duke of Northumberland, at Alnwick Castle and Syon House. Syon is opposite the Royal Gardens, which at that time were called Richmond Gardens, but which are now Kew Gardens and the Old Deer Park.

By now Brown had position, fame, friends and wealth enough to relax, and it is almost as if a sense of mission drove him to work so untiringly. The miles he covered must have been exceptional for a man of his time. 'I have so much to do', he wrote to Lord Bruce of Tottenham Park. It is the only time there is a hint of a complaining note: 'when I am galloping in one part of the world my men are making blunders and neglects which [make] it very unpleasant.'

The alterations made at Richmond were drastic. All the small compartmented areas, formal and semi-formal,[41] which had developed from the old field pattern, were altered in favour of a comprehensive development.[42] 'Merlin's Cave', a grotto designed by Kent, was removed, and the kitchen garden moved much further from the King's Lodge. Two parallel roadways, separated by planting, are shown in one detailed plan of part of the grounds; one private road for 'their Majesties', leading to the Lodge, and the other, leading unseen to the 'Offices', for tradespeople.[43]

Brown's assistant at Richmond was Michael Milliken, who had earlier worked on the improvements at Chatsworth. Several delightful letters have survived[44] from Milliken to his wife Polly before she moved down to Hampton to join him. His spelling was none too good. In January 1765 he wrote:

> The King and Quen come 2 or 3 days a week here and talkes as free and ... is as bent on the work as ever the Duke of Devonshire was. The Princ of Walls was all over the garden esterday in a chise drawn by a mare and the other princ in the nurses armes for two hours, notwithstanding the cooldness of the day indeed they are fine lusty boys and do not fear the coold.

We learn of Brown's own frequent contact and familiarity with George III from some correspondence he had with Lord and Lady Chatham. Lord Chatham was firmly opposed to the continuation of the war in America, and Brown had acted as a kind of intermediary between him and the King. In 1777 he reported to Chatham:

> In a conversation I havè lately had [with George III] I was heard with attention. I went as far as I durst, upon such tender ground. My reason for troubling your Lordship with this, is owing to a conversation I had with the Duke of Northumberland ... There was a meeting yesterday amongst the Lords Rockingham, Camden, Shelburne, Grafton, Abingdon, Craven etc. [Lord Shelburne, of Bowood; Lord Grafton of Euston, Suffolk; Lord Abingdon of Rycote; all of them clients of Brown.][45]

Later the same year he reported:

> Today, and indeed many opportunities have occurred of late, in which I have had very favourable conversations ... I said ... that I was very sure what [Lord Chatham] advanced was meant for ... the happiness of his Majesty and the royal family, and the lustre of the whole empire ...

In her reply, Lady Chatham sends Brown 'sincerest thanks' for his 'kind friendship':

It is impossible not to feel sensibly the animation of your conversation, in support of my Lord's principles, and of his zeal for the prosperity of the whole empire … The sentiments of esteem and friendship which my Lord and myself have for you are of the most unfeigned sort …

William Mason reported the story[46] that when George III heard that Brown had died he said to Michael Milliken, 'Brown is dead. Now Mellicant [sic] you and I can do here what we please.'

Although Brown's sympathies lay with the Whigs, he was able to be on equally good terms with the Tory aristocracy. Lord Bute, for example, who had been George III's tutor and later briefly Prime Minister, employed Brown at Luton Hoo and Highcliffe.

To cope with his enormous workload Brown had two men who worked as surveyors and draughtsmen. One was Samuel Lapidge; the other, by the name of John Spyers, was first recorded as being at Tottenham in 1764, where he spent '3 weeks 2 days' taking measurements. Other estates where Spyers is known to have helped Brown are Castle Ashby, Cardiff Castle, Berrington, and Sandleford Priory (for Mrs Montagu). At Fisherwick he painted the delightful set of six watercolours which is all that survives of Fisherwick today.

Amongst the projects that occupied Brown in the later 1760s were Audley End, Broadlands, Sandbeck, Weston Park and Wimpole. To ease the architectural workload Brown entered into some kind of partnership with Henry Holland the Younger in 1770, when Holland was twenty-five. The first project on which they worked together was Claremont, near Esher in Surrey, where Brown had designed a new house for Clive of India.

Brown's son, Lance, had by now left Eton and was studying law at Lincoln's Inn. His second son, John, was in the Navy, and Thomas was still at school. In 1772, John received 'a firm commission' in the *Savage*, thanks to Lord Sandwich, who was Brown's neighbour at Fenstanton and also First Lord of the Admiralty. Three years later John Brown was on the *Nautilus*, and involved in the American War of Independence, which his father, like many others, thought was an 'unfortunate and disgraceful' war. Eventually John was to rise to the rank of Admiral of the Blue.

Brown continued to be as busy as ever in the early 1770s. His current projects included Brocklesby, Coombe Abbey, Grimsthorpe, Paultons, Benham, Harewood and Himley. Meanwhile Henry Holland's architectural practice was flourishing, and before long he was employing a young assistant called John Soane, who was to become one of Britain's most famous and original architects. In 1773 Holland married Brown's daughter Bridget, at St George's, Hanover Square, and a gift of £5,000 from Brown, in addition to a dowry, is recorded by Drummond's Bank. Brown's affection for his daughter is indicated in his will, where he says, 'I wish her to believe I love her with unchangeable affection'.

Several letters from Brown to his wife have survived. In one, written from Coombe Abbey in 1775, he tells her he had been 'very much upon the phylosophick strain', having been alone most of the day. But:

a day so spent is not one of the worst we spend, and just to conclude it, I have entered into a conversation with you, which has every charm except your company which will ever be the sincere and the principal delight, my dear Biddy, of your affectionate husband.[47]

Another letter, to his daughter Margaret, or Peggy, tells her that he had sent her some plovers' eggs. Margaret kept the letters he sent her and also collected some of his other letters; known as the Pakenham correspondence, these have proved invaluable in piecing together her father's life.

Brown's eldest son was anxious to get into politics. At first he sought the help of Sir James Lowther of Lowther Park in Cumbria, for which Brown had prepared plans in 1763. Sir James, who was described as 'a madman too influential to be locked up', did not prove at all helpful to poor Lance, who nevertheless eventually became Member of Parliament for Totnes in 1780, and in 1792 was Member for Huntingdon. In one election he was unfortunate enough to be described in a handbill produced by his opponents as 'a mere mushroom sprung from a Dung-hill in Stowe gardens' who 'can never have the slightest *Capability* to render ... even the slightest service.' Later he applied for the Stewardship of the Chiltern Hundreds, and became Gentleman of the King's Privy Chamber in 1795.

Some of the projects that occupied Brown in the last four years of his life included Cadland, Sherborne, Sheffield Park (Sussex), Berrington, Nuneham Courtenay, Heveningham, and Sandleford Priory (for Mrs Montagu).

In 1779 Brown made his will; and in February 1783 he made various small alterations to it. Whether he had been ill at this time is not known, but on the day after putting his signature to the codicil he collapsed and died, presumably from a heart attack. Horace Walpole pasted the following obituary notice in his notebook:

February 6, 1783, about nine o'clock, died Lancelot Brown, Esq., of Hampton-court, aged 67. His death was probably occasioned by a violent blow he received falling in a fit in the street as he was returning from a visit at Lord Coventry's house in Piccadilly to the house of his son-in-law [Henry Holland] in Hertford Street. For above thirty years he had laboured under a very troublesome asthma, and though he bore it with an uncommon degree of fortitude and good spirits, yet at times it reduced his life to alarming situations, and had lately prevailed so as to make him consider himself as drawing near that period, which he believed (with great strength of mind and resignation) as the price of a future state of perfect happiness. His great and fine genius stood unrivalled, and it was the peculiar felicity of it that it was allowed by all ranks and degrees of society in this country, and by many noble and great personages in other countries. Those who knew him best, or practised near him, were not able to determine whether the quickness of his eye, or its correctness, were most to be admired. It was comprehensive and elegant, and perhaps it may be said never to have failed him. Such, however, was the effect of his genius that when he was the happiest man, he will be least remembered; so closely did he copy nature that his works will be mistaken.

His truth, his integrity, and his good humour, were very effectual, and will hold a place in the memory of his friends, more likely to continue, though not less to be esteemed.

Walpole himself wrote to the poet William Mason, saying, 'Are you not concerned for the death of Brown?' But in a letter to Lady Ossory he wrote on a more flippant note, 'Your Dryads must go into black gloves, Madam. Their father-in-law, Lady Nature's second husband, is dead!'

It was William Mason who wrote the epitaph which can be seen in Fenstanton Church:

Ye Sons of Elegance, who truly taste
The Simple charms that genuine Art supplies,
Come from the sylvan Scenes His Genius grac'd,
And offer here your tributary Sighs.
But know that more than Genius slumbers here,
Virtues were his which Arts best powers transcend.
Come, ye Superior train who these revere
And weep the Christian, Husband, Father, Friend.

NOTES

1 According to Reverend John Hodgson in Part 1 of his unpublished *Biographical Dictionary of Northumberland* (1820), it was 1715. John Hodgson, 1779-1845, had for several years been vicar at Kirkwhelpington, only three miles from Kirkharle. Later he was Secretary to the Society of Antiquaries of Newcastle upon Tyne.

2 Kirkharle Parish Baptismal Register 1695-1751, Northumberland CRO, EP 127/1, unnumbered folio. Quoted by Peter Willis in 'Capability Brown in Northumberland', *Garden History* Vol IX, No. 2.

3 According to Hodgson.

4 A plaque was unveiled there in May 1977 commemorating Brown, see *Garden History* Vol V, No. 3, 22-24.

5 Op. cit.

6 Sir Lambton Loraine, 11th Bt., quoted by P. Willis, op. cit.

7 See Willis, op. cit., pp. 163-5 for discussion, and illustration of the drawings.

8 About twenty-five miles.

9 According to Willis. See also Gazetteer, p. 189.

10 See p. 31.

11 The date given by Rev. Hodgson.

12 John Penn, in his *History and Descriptive Account of Stoke Park* (1813), says that 'the first piece of water which he formed was at Lady Mostyn's in Oxfordshire', Lady Mostyn being Sir Charles Browne's grand-daughter. John Penn had lived most of his life at Stoke House, the adjoining estate to Stoke Park, his father having bought the house from Lady Cobham's executors. Lady Cobham retired there after the death of Lord Cobham in 1749. Regarding Lancelot Brown, Penn says that he found 'uncommonly few notices concerning him in books of reference [which could] furnish materials to the biographer'.

13 According to John Penn.

14 P. Willis, *Charles Bridgeman*.

15 According to John Penn.

16 *Epistle to Lord Burlington.*

17 British Library. Egmont Papers quoted by P. Willis, op. cit.

18 Which now includes the Silverstone race-track.

19 A grander example of this kind of thing has survived in the amphitheatre at Claremont.

20 For a detailed discussion of Stowe in its Bridgeman phase see P. Willis, *Charles Bridgeman*, Chapter 5.

21 Engraving by Bickham and Chatelain from Bickham, pub., *Views of Stowe*, 1753, illustrated in P. Willis, op. cit., pl. 146.

22 Quoted by Stroud. For the Wayet family, see Sir George Gilbert Scott, *Recollections*.

23 Attributed by Alicia Amherst, *A History of Gardening in England* (1895), and by family tradition. Brown's client here was the second Duke of Grafton, father of the third Duke who became Prime Minister in 1768.

24 Now at Warwickshire County Record Office.

25 Quoted in Repton's *Sketches and Hints on Landscape Gardening* (1795).

26 Humphry Repton, *The Theory and Practice of Landscape Gardening* (1803), p. 266.

27 Quoted in Repton, op. cit. pp. 168-9.

28 By Stroud.

29 Pakenham correspondence, PRO Chatham MSS. Bundle 24; and *Thraliana, The Diary of Mrs Hester Lynch Thrale*, K. C. Balderston (1942).

30 PRO Chatham MSS. Bundle 24.

31 10 September 1767.

32 Quoted by Repton in his *Theory and Practice of Landscape Gardening* (1803).

33 Henry Holland the Younger.

34 Such as those for Belvoir, a scheme not carried out.

35 According to E. Law, *The History of Hampton Court Palace* (1885-91), quoted by Stroud.

36 Lady Lisburne was a sister of Robert (Bobby) Shafto of Benwell Tower where Brown once worked.

37 Quoted by Stroud.

38 Pakenham correspondence, quoted by Stroud.

39 Letter to Mrs Robinson, quoted by Stroud.

40 See P. Willis, 'Capability Brown's account with Drummond's Bank 1753-83', *Architectural History*, Vol. 27, 1984.

41 For a plan of Richmond Gardens pre-Brown see Rocque, *An Exact Survey of the City's of London, Westminster ... and the Country Near Ten Miles Round* (1746).

42 See *Survey of the Royal Gardens of Kew and Richmond*, Thomas Richardson, 1771.

43 See Plan P.R.O. Works 32/96, illustrated in P. Willis, *Charles Bridgeman*; this drawing is clearly in Brown's drawing style.

44 Stroud, pp. 126-8.

45 Stroud, p. 186.

46 *Correspondence of H. Walpole and W. Mason*, Rev. J. Mitford 1851, quoted by Stroud.

47 Pakenham correspondence, Stroud p. 177.

48 Pakenham correspondence, Stroud, p. 161.

Capability Brown's Style and Techniques

———

THE creation of a Brown landscape involved the removal of all the accidental defects left behind by history, and the restoration of the landscape that is felt to be truly characteristic of the locality: it aims, moreover, to construct scenes which will evoke 'the Poet's feeling' and please 'the Painter's eye'. 'The business of a gardener', said Thomas Whately,[1]

is to select and to apply whatever is great, elegant or characteristic . . . to shew all the advantages of the place upon which he is employed; to supply its defects, to correct its faults, and to improve its beauties. For all these operations the objects of nature are still his only materials.

But to do this requires taste and imagination. Joseph Spence (1699-1768)[2], who was Professor of Poetry at Oxford, explained in exactly what way Nature should be copied:

The chief aim of our best designers . ·, is to imitate Nature. Not like the Dutch painters, who often choose to copy Nature in her lowest and most disagreeable works, nor like . . . Caravaggio who takes to her indifferently as he finds her, nor like Guido Reni who often hides or disguises her with a profusion of grace and beauty, but like Raphael, who follows her always with a careful judgement and a happiness of choice.

As we have seen, there is a close parallel between this and the way Sir Joshua Reynolds approached the painting of his portraits.

Brown had a unique ability to exploit his medium to the full and bring out of it something which his clients could never have imagined. When he carried out his improvements the potential of the particular estate to provide varied and surprising scenes of seemingly natural beauty was realized. It required his imagination to see the possibilities that each site possessed.

It is important to understand what the ideal of Brown's landscapes is, for this in itself was new. Having spent several years as Lord Cobham's head gardener at Stowe, Brown was as familiar as anyone with the landscape of classical associations. Yet he rejected this tradition, feeling that such allusions were extraneous. In this he was not alone: Horace Walpole remarked after a visit to Stowe in 1753, referring to the political aspects, 'I have no patience at building and planting a satire.'[3] A Brown landscape is pure landscape; the layer of Arcadian associations has been stripped away. Brown's approach, therefore, could be called purist, in the sense that he worked with the elements of nature as his sole medium. Within the given situation he was able to create landscapes that were beautiful in themselves: they did not have to acquire borrowed beauty by making reference to the landscapes of antiquity. Such classical associations can be likened to the programme in programme music. Berlioz's *Symphonie Fantastique*, for example, is built on and inspired by complex story, but many other composers have felt that their music did not need such extra-musical interest to give it validity.

In spite of Brown's immense success his work was misunderstood even in his lifetime. Sir William Chambers (Architect to the King 1760, Surveyor General 1782) described

Above: No amount of labour was spared to create lawns of a perfectly smooth, gently undulating surface. These men are scything the grass at West Wycombe, Buckinghamshire. Engraving by Woollett, 1760.

Right: A selection of gardeners' tools, an engraving by Liger, 1723. With such primitive-looking tools as these Brown undertook large-scale projects and gave them a most refined finish.

Opposite below: Grimsthorpe; the gently rolling contours of the south Lincolnshire countryside show off the Brown style to perfection.

Opposite above: A Brown landscape of quite a different character can be seen at Ugbrooke, set in a romantic valley in south Devon.

Above: The ha-ha, or sunk fence, at Weston Park, Staffordshire. This device enabled designers to link the house and the landscape visually, and yet keep animals out of the ornamental gardens.

Right: Brown's plan for Castle Ashby: a large-scale design which was only partly carried out. The ride round the perimeter of the grounds was designed to offer a sequence of contrasting views.

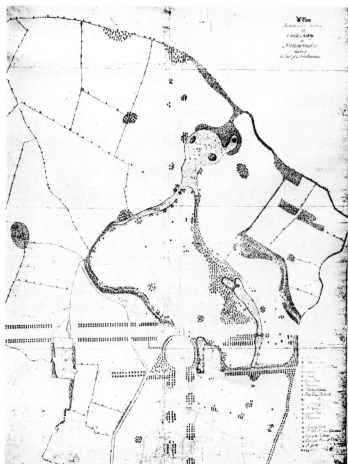

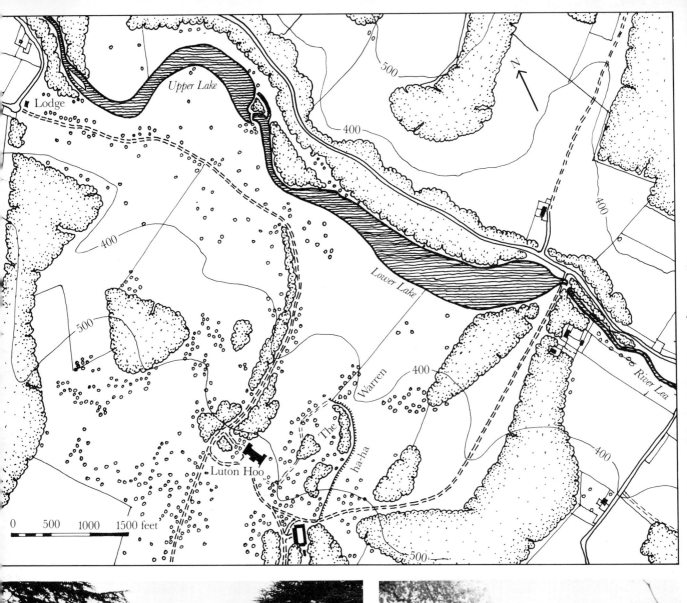

Upper Lake

Lodge

400

500

400

Lower Lake

500

The Warren

ha-ha

Luton Hoo

River Lea

400

400

500

N

0   500   1000   1500 feet

The three-arched classical bridge at Compton Verney, Warwickshire. The waterside plants would not have been allowed in Brown's day.

Opposite above: The shape of the lakes at Luton Hoo is a perfect example of Brown's treatment of water. There are no straight banks, no intricate or jagged shapes, but instead a smoothly curving outline.

Opposite below left: The Warren at Luton Hoo, Bedfordshire, is an example of Brown's use of dells. The view down to the lake has been blocked by Victorian planting.

Opposite below right: The overflow at Weston Park, one of the devices that enabled Brown to control the water level of his lakes very accurately.

Above: The lake at Blenheim, looking vast and apparently endless, exactly as Brown intended.

Left: Brown's plan of Wimpole (detail). He deliberately made the extent of the lake vague and uncertain by curving it at the top end, and by carefully positioning a tree-planted island.

These 'before and after' sketches, done by Humphry Repton, demonstrate clearly the benefit of selective felling of avenues of trees, making longer and wider views possible. Langley Park, Kent.

Clumps of trees at Petworth, West Sussex. Brown's clumps were sometimes much larger than these.

Brown's subtle treatment of planting between the curving lines of woodland and the lake can be seen in his plan of Trentham, dated 1759.

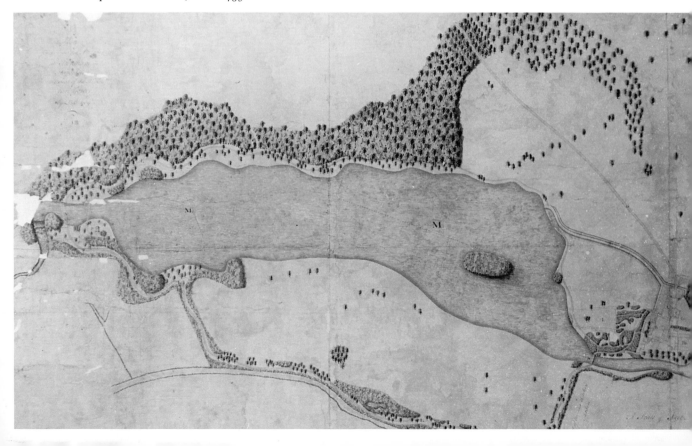

his landscapes as 'gardens differing very little from common fields, so closely is vulgar nature copied in most of them.' In other words, Chambers 'found the Nymph a Drab',[4] or in plain language he found nature dull as a medium because he expected to find literary associations or other excitements and was disappointed. But when they retired to the country from business or politics Brown's clients sought peace of mind, not excitement.

Brown's ideal was the middle position between the two extremes of a utilitarian landscape which has accommodated itself entirely to man's needs (which Defoe admired), and a hostile landscape of rocks and mountains (admired by the Romantics). Thus the utilitarian kitchen garden was banished to a walled enclosure screened by trees, and any sign of the ploughed fields and hedgerows of Agriculture was moved out of sight of the great house. But most of the great landlords had more sense than to devote a vast number of acres to a purely aesthetic purpose, and so herds of deer or sheep were allowed to 'wander wild and free' in the parks. A fine balance was achieved, therefore, in this partnership with Nature. Insofar as the park was useless it displayed the wealth and the taste of the owner; insofar as it was useful, it showed his good sense and lack of ostentation. As for a desire to emulate the rugged landscape of which Wordsworth wrote in the last years of the century, any such thing was inconceivable in 1750 when Brown began his independent career. Dr Johnson showed a similar disdain for wild prospects. Having visited Scotland he remarked, 'the noblest prospect which a Scotchman ever sees is the high road that leads him to England!'[5]

Southern England lends itself perfectly to the accomplishment of the Brownian ideal, with its gently rolling contours, the soft outlines of the natural vegetation and the mildness of the climate. This kind of ideal landscape corresponds very closely with what Christian Norberg-Schulz calls a classical landscape in his book *Genius Loci*,[8] though I have not adopted his terminology since his is a far more general term. He identifies three basic kinds of natural landscape – romantic, cosmic and classical – but there are also more complex landscapes where elements of these are combined. As a typical example of the romantic landscape he describes the Nordic forests, where the strong relief and dense vegetation produce an environment which is almost overpowering, on which it is hard for man to impose any order. Instead, man has to find a way to live with the dominating presence of Nature. The cosmic landscape, on the other hand, is typified by the desert, which offers no refuge, and unlike the romantic landscape, no corners in which to hide. The desert presents only the infinitely extending barren surface of the earth and the immense and cloudless sky. To live here is either to take shelter in an oasis, or else, as the Romans did, to impose order arbitrarily on a neutral ground.

The classical landscape, however, is neither overpowering nor a monotonous blank; instead it appears as something intelligible, human in scale, amenable to agricultural use. 'How then does "classical man" dwell in the landscape?' asks Norberg-Schulz. 'Basically, we may say that he places himself in front of nature as an equal "partner". He is where he is, and looks at nature as a friendly complement to his own being.' It is this partnership which is beautifully expressed in the parks of Capability Brown. There is no question of man's domination of Nature; instead there is a splendid and harmonious ease. The order which is achieved in them, though artificial, seems to be quite natural. 'Wherever art appears, the gardener has failed in his execution,'[7] said Philip Southcote, and William Shenstone remarked that 'art should never be allowed to set foot in the province of nature, other than clandestinely and by night.'[8] The art of the artless, then, is to create scenes where the designer's hand is nowhere apparent. Brown worked on a much larger scale than William Kent had done, and instead of a series of enclosed scenes, what we are presented with in a Brown park is, apparently, a whole 'world'. This world is Utopian in concept, offering a kind of perfection to the senses, where every alien or untoward element has been gracefully banished.

Horace Walpole reported that the Duke of Leinster once invited Brown to Ireland, and offered him a thousand pounds on landing in addition to the cost of the work he required. But Brown refused, explaining that he had not yet finished England! He evidently realized that his art of improvement could be applied to the entire country.

One feature of the English countryside is the variation from one area to another, and Brown's style is remarkable for the way it builds on the special character of each locality. In this way he fulfilled, in a way none of his predecessors had, Alexander Pope's advice to 'Consult the Genius of the Place in all'.[11] So it is, for example, that Ugbrooke, deep in a Devon coombe, is dark and romantic, while Grimsthorpe is bright and cool, open to a wide Lincolnshire sky.

To complain that Brown worked to a formula is as foolish as complaining that Haydn symphonies always have four movements. It is easier to argue that formal gardens conform to a formula: you take a rectangular piece of ground and make it absolutely level, then you take another piece of ground next to it and you level that, and so on, irrespective of contours, views and natural surroundings. But a landscape such as Petworth is unique because it is dependent on the local topography.

Just as some writers have misguidedly accused Brown of being formulaic[10], so it has been claimed that his approach was literary.[11] A conversation Brown had with Hannah More shortly before his death is sometimes produced as proof of the second claim. She reported it as follows:

> I passed two hours in the garden the other day ... with my friend Mr. Brown. I took a very agreeable lecture from him in his art, and he promised to give me taste by inoculation. He illustrates everything he says about gardening by some literary or grammatical allusion. He told me he compared his art to literary composition. 'Now *there*,' said he, pointing his finger, 'I make a comma, and there,' pointing to another spot, 'where a more decided turn is proper, I make a colon; at another part, where an interruption is desirable to break the view, a parenthesis; now a full stop, and then I begin another subject.'

What Brown is describing here is what happens to the viewer as he passes through a park, translated, for the sake of his listener, into literary terms; how a variety of impressions is gained along a path that may turn first towards a view and then turn away from it; or how a change, from one space or area to another, can be made – either suddenly, as a surprise, or gradually, in stages. These effects are well known to designers and architects, but to explain them to a writer Brown chose to use a literary analogy. What he was referring to were visual and three-dimensional effects.

Unfortunately Brown did not put down on paper, as Repton did, an explanation of the secrets of his art, no doubt feeling that his work could speak for itself. One letter does survive which summarizes in a general way his main intentions and preoccupations in 'gardening and place-making'. In 1775 he was asked by a friend, the Reverend Thomas Dyer, to provide a plan for a Frenchman who wished to improve his estate in the English manner. In his reply Brown wrote:

> I have made a Plan ... as well as I could, from the survey and description you sent me ... In France they do not exactly comprehend our ideas on Gardening and Place-making which when rightly understood will supply all the elegance and all the comforts which Mankind wants in the Country and (I will add) if right, be exactly fit for the owner, the Poet and the Painter. To

produce these effects there wants a good plan, good execution, a perfect knowledge of the country and the objects in it, whether natural or artificial, and infinite delicacy in the planting, etc., so much Beauty depending on the size of the trees and the colour of their leaves to produce the effect of light and shade so very essential to the perfecting of a good plan: as also the hideing of what is disagreeable and shewing what is beautifull, getting shade from the large trees and sweets [i.e. perfumes] from the smaller sorts of shrubs etc. I hope they will soon find out in France that Place-making, and a good English Garden, depend entirely upon principle and have very little to do with fashion; for it is a word that in my opinion disgraces Science wherever it is found.

It is interesting to find Brown remarking that 'our ideas ... will ... be exactly fit' not only for 'the owner' but also 'the Poet and the Painter'. He makes an even clearer allusion to visual considerations when he refers to the colours of leaves, as related to 'the effect of light and shade'. The need for 'a perfect knowledge of the country and the objects in it' is, of course, plain language for a need to consult the genius of the place.

The way the house is approached through a Brown park is an example of the art involved in creating a succession of interesting effects and contrasting views. In his *Observations on Modern Gardening* (1770), the politician and writer Thomas Whately describes in great detail the approach to the house at Caversham Park near Reading, which Brown had landscaped a few years earlier. (This has recently been built over.) It was a mile long, and Whately's account runs for several pages, almost a yard by yard description. In a typical passage he describes the contrasting characters of the landscape along the way:

To these succeeds an open space, diversified with only a few scattered trees; and in the midst of it, some magnificent beeches crowding together, overshadow the road, which is carried through a narrow, darksome passage between them: soon after it rises under a thick wood in the garden up to the house, where it suddenly bursts out upon a rich, and extensive prospect, with the town and churches of Reading in full sight, and the hills of Windsor Forest in the horizon.

Then Whately explains the ways in which this variety is achieved. Of the 'several scenes':

one is characterised by a grove; the next by clumps; and others by little groups or single trees: ... The ground ... is cast into an infinite number of elegant shapes, in every gradation from the most gentle slope, to a very precipitate fall: the trees also are of several kinds, and their shadows of various tints ...

The various parts of a Brown landscape, as Whately points out, provide not only spatial variety but also areas of contrasting mood or character: often we forget that when we walk out of a dark, shadowy, 'gloomy' space into a brightly lit, open, 'cheerful' space that this is a carefully designed effect. In many ways, effects such as these have proved more lasting than those created by Brown's predecessors. The 'associational' and intellectual elements at Stowe in its Bridgeman phase, for example, depended on a knowledge of classical studies, which then formed the basis of formal education, and on current political and philosophical ideas. The effects of contrasting mood or character can still be appreciated, however, and experienced, and so have proved more lasting and universal in their appeal.

Needless to say, the roads in a Brown park are never straight; they always follow a gentle flowing route, as examples of the serpentine line. The same kind of line occurs in the perimeter rides around the parks and in the outlines of the lakes. In his book *The Analysis of Beauty* (1753), William Hogarth called this kind of serpentine line the Line of

Beauty, and he had even higher praise for a three-dimensional curved line, which waves and winds at the same time, and which he called the Line of Grace. There are many examples in Brown's work of this effect: his approach roads do not rigidly hug the contours, they rise or fall slightly as they go. This line, Hogarth said, he found in Nature, which is always 'simple, plain and true in all her works'. The curving lines of Brown's landscapes also fulfil Hogarth's recommendation that they should not curve too much: they are gradual, quite unlike the ones proposed by Stephen Switzer or Batty Langley. William Mason was possibly thinking of the latter when he advises us to 'scorn/ Those quick, acute perplex'd and tangled paths,/ That .../ Writhe in convulsive torture.'[12] It is also noticeable that in a Brown landscape a curving drive never copies a parallel curve at the edge of a lake, for example, nor do the edges of a planted area ever run exactly parallel with the water's edge or with a road. Such an arrangement would soon be seen as artificial, and so had to be avoided.

The key device which opened up the park to the whole landscape was the sunk fence, or ha-ha. Many skilful examples may be seen in Brown's parks: the one at Sandbeck, for example, is particularly difficult to detect. As William Mason put it:

> The wand'ring flocks that browse between the shades,
> Seem oft to pass their bounds; the dubious eye
> Decides not if they crop the mead or lawn.

Brown's sunk fences are normally placed so that they lie at right-angles to the line of sight; in this way one looks straight over the ditch and not along it. Furthermore, these sunk fences always run along the contours; never against them which would look most awkward. The sloping side of the ditch must be gradual so that the animals can browse right to the base of the wall and keep the ditch free of weeds, which would interrupt the smoothness of the surface.

Hedges and fences formed no part of Brown's parks, except at some outer boundary, as they interrupt the smooth 'flow' of the ground and are a sign of agricultural use. William Shenstone is categorical:

> Hedges, appearing as such, are universally bad. They discover art in Nature's province.
>
> Trees in hedges partake of their artificiality, and become part of them. There is no more sudden, and obvious improvement, than a hedge removed, and the trees remaining; yet not in such manner as to mark out the former hedge.

When we consider the art of contouring, or of grading large areas of ground, there is no doubt that Brown was its greatest master. There was never such an attempt before, and probably has not been since, to alter the surface of the land so extensively for purely aesthetic purposes. The scale of such operations was astounding. His earth-moving equipment consisted only of spades, barrows and carts, and yet recent excavations at Heveningham in Suffolk, for example, have revealed that the original soil level was as much as twelve feet below the present level. The result of Brown's work everywhere was an almost perfectly smooth surface: every irregularity and blemish has been manicured out of existence. Contemporary engravings show the care that was taken to maintain this smooth surface: not only was the grass scythed frequently, brushed and swept, it was also rolled by large and heavy rollers that needed two men or even a horse to pull them.

It was customary for the lawn to sweep right up to the house without any intervening boundary or interruption. Brown's parks were criticized for this later on, and even Repton said he thought it was inappropriate for deer or sheep to come right up to the windows. But any kind of terrace or fenced area introduces a kind of artificiality which

Brown was strenuously trying to avoid. He and his contemporaries appear to have enjoyed the complete contrast of artifact and Nature which occurs when the house rises suddenly out of the surface of the park – though the contrast was often softened by trees which framed the house as seen from the park, as at Burton Constable. In the case of ornate buildings such as Burton Constable or Audley End the plain surface of the lawn also makes an effective foil to the intricate surface of the façade of the building. However, some of Brown's followers overdid it and left the building isolated and exposed, so that Horace Walpole remarked:

> In other places the total banishment of all particular neatness immediately about a house, which is frequently left grazing by itself in the middle of a park, is a defect. Sheltered and close walks in so very uncertain climate as ours, are comforts ill-exchanged for the few picturesque days that we enjoy ...

Brown always avoided creating a completely flat area of lawn, and he even avoided large areas of evenly sloping ground, preferring to make some areas gently concave and others gently convex, and blending the two together. When a slope met a more level area this was achieved with a gentle tangential curve which was called a 'concave scoop'.

When a relatively flat area, or one which is slightly dished in profile, has higher ground on each side of it, it is then framed or 'contained', and this helps to concentrate the eye on whatever lies straight ahead. In Brown parks the main view from the house often fits this description. If the ground in front of a house slips sideways it gives an awkward effect, and often earth-moving was undertaken to correct it. In many parks Brown used a similar 'dell' effect, created by making a shallow valley with undulating sides. His first use of this effect must have been the Grecian Valley at Stowe which leads north-east from the Temple of Concord and Victory, and similar valleys can be seen, for example, at Bowood, Luton Hoo and Moor Park, running more or less parallel with the main vista from the front of the house. Unfortunately the effect at Luton Hoo (which is called the Warren) has been destroyed by insensitive nineteenth-century planting which blocks the view to the lakes. Higher ground was sometimes crowned with trees, and the ground itself never forms a peak, which would look false, but instead is always tapered to a flatter area on top.

Included in his improvements there was often a drainage scheme, designed to eliminate any boggy ground in the surrounding parkland, and to make the park suitable for both walking and grazing. In many parks, large and carefully constructed drains have been discovered, apparently to carry springs to the lake, to keep up the water level. At Petworth, for example, there is no convenient stream and the lake is dependent on an arrangement such as this. Care needs to be taken in the use of heavy machinery in these parks, so that the drains are not broken.

Where the ground meets water Brown took particular care to create a pleasing result, often with very subtle effects. As the level of the water could be controlled exactly, he was able to bring the ground down in a concave scoop to meet the water within an inch or two of the same level. This arrangement emphasizes the water's reflectiveness because one tends to look across its surface rather than down into it. Even where the banks are quite steep, such as at Blenheim, Brown allowed himself enough room for a concave scoop at the bottom, so avoiding that artificial flooded effect that is often seen in reservoirs.

It goes without saying that Brown meant his lakes to be neatly edged by lawns. A messy line of reeds, brambles, nettles, and bushes was never his intention, though this is what we find surrounding so many of them now. It is important either to mow or else to let cattle browse right up to the water's edge. A fence not only looks unsightly in itself, it also encourages weeds.

If the smooth surface of Brown's parks reveals Brown at his most classical, his use of water displays what is perhaps the most romantic aspect of his work. There is always a slight element of mystery about a Capability Brown lake. A geometrical shape can be appreciated immediately by the mind; but the curved, irregularly shaped lakes such as Brown made can give no exact impression of their size or form. Brown made the shape of his lakes deliberately obscure by curving the farthest end of the lake out of sight of the main area of water, and by the creation of shadows to mask the points where it terminates. The plans almost always show an area of dense planting which clusters around the farthest point, making the water dark and its edge indefinite, and frequently an island, densely planted, further masks the extent of the lake.

The influence of Kent can be seen in Brown's early work, such as at Ingestre in Staffordshire and at Petworth, where he originally suggested a grotto beside the lake. But the way Brown used water in his mature landscapes demonstrates clearly the fundamental difference between his approach and Kent's. A glance at Kent's sketch of Venus's Vale at Rousham reveals a different world from Brown's. Although Rousham was the most naturalistic thing in gardening when it was created, when we return to the scene at Venus's Vale from a Capability Brown lake, its rounded ponds seem static, contrived and artificial, like a stage set. The only kind of ornamentation that Brown brought to his lakes was the practical one of a bridge over the water. There are several fine examples of three-arched classical bridges in his work, such as at Audley End, Blenheim, Burghley, Compton Verney, Sherborne and Shortgrove, to take a random selection.

It was Kent's usual practice to terminate his lakes with a feature such as a shell bridge or a grotto, which gives an air of finality to the scene. Brown's lakes, on the other hand, invite exploration from the observer. Interestingly, amongst Kent's surviving drawings is a pair of sketches in the Chatsworth collection which do show the end of a lake terminating in the Brown manner: it is not known, however, whether these relate to a particular site or whether they are purely imaginary.

The sheer size of many of Brown's lakes also contrasts with Kent's work. Clients were apparently quite happy to put sixty or eighty acres of fertile ground under water, and Brown was obviously capable of arranging it for them. Often these lakes were quite shallow, and several can be waded across without difficulty, but they nevertheless represent a considerable technical achievement, considering the resources available at the time. Blenheim is by far the largest, and illustrates some of the effects Brown was able to create. Apart from creating the main lake, which is splendid in itself, he widened the little River Glyme beyond the Cascade, and gave it the proportions and curved outline of a large river. It was here that Brown was supposed to have said, 'Thames, Thames, you will never forgive me!' and seen from the classical New Bridge, it really does seem to rival the Thames in gracefulness. A 'river' effect can often be found in Brown's parks though not usually on so grand a scale. They always look more effective if there is some illusion of 'flow', and it helps if they are curved on plan (as is almost always the case), and if the surface reflects the light, because this means that any effect of wind on the surface can be easily seen. If the banks become overgrown on both sides, sheltering and overshadowing the water, the water will look still and black, and the illusion Brown tried to create will be lost.

Blenheim also contains an example of a 'creek', which branches westwards off the main body of water towards Park Farm. This feature not only adds interest and length to a walk round a lake, but also increases the irregularity of the water's outline, helping to heighten the illusion of naturalness. This illusion was also fostered by the use of 'headlands', flattish pieces of land projecting into the lake like promontories which, by varying the relationship of the land contours to the water, again help to avoid the 'drowned' reservoir effect.

Brown's lakes were constructed using puddled clay, the same technique as was used in canal-building from the 1760s. Although it sounds primitive and was highly labour intensive, this process is highly effective, and enduring. Where the ground is subject to stress, such as against a dam, a stone lining might be added, but an additional thickness of clay up to eighteen inches deep was just as effective. The overflow arrangements to the lakes were carefully built in stone or brick, and in some cases a plug-like device was provided so that the water could be let out and the lake emptied. Several of the lakes have weirs, and others have a circular device more like a standing-waste. But more research is needed before any definite information can be given about the technical aspects of Brown's lakes; so many lakes have been altered since his time and it is hard to tell in many cases how much is his own work.

Many of Brown's cascades have also been altered, and again some additional research is needed before a pattern can be established. However, it seems that early examples, such as the one at Charlecote (1757), tended to be architectural, while the later ones were more rocky and romantic, such as at Blenheim, which was functioning by 1768. His approach no doubt varied according to what he thought was appropriate to the character of the landscape. Many of the cascades are quite simple, such as at Kimberley and originally at Ugbrooke, consisting of a simple level lip, curved on its front edge, over which the water pours in a sheet.

The trees which Lancelot Brown used in his parks were almost all native species. Once we understand Brown's overall aim of an improved version of Britain's natural scenery we can appreciate that there is nothing horticultural about his landscape gardens. His use of ornamental planting was limited to the 'close walks' near the house. Legal agreements drawn up between Brown and his clients show that they often provided the trees. A surviving 'Nursery Book'[13] at Tottenham in Wiltshire, shows the kind of material that was in use at the end of Brown's life. The deciduous trees being 'grown on' included several thousand oaks, beeches, chestnuts, birches, and elms.[14] There were also smaller quantities of ash, sycamore, plane, Spanish chestnut (*Castanea sativa*), mountain ash (*Sorbus aucuparia*) and bird cherries, and fewer than a hundred each of whitebeams (*Sorbus aria*), scarlet oaks (*Quercus coccinea*) Balm of Gilead (probably *Populus balsamifera*) and limes. Unlike other parks (such as Caversham) there were no maples, but there were several thousand 'hazels' which may have been intended as 'nurse' plants, to protect the young trees until they became established.

Of course some of these are not strictly natives. The horse chestnut, for instance, was only introduced in about 1640, but it blends well enough with the landscape and is attractive in itself. The important thing was whether the colour, size and shape of the tree would be in harmony with the English scene. Brown would never have used purple foliage, nor yellow-leafed trees, for these are completely incongruous in the English landscape: they belong to horticulture, not to Nature. Sweet chestnuts and plane trees were sometimes planted near the house, and more recent introductions (such as

Liriodendron), could also be used if their overall appearance is sympathetic. But it is noticeable that the further out into the landscape Brown went, the more of a purist he became, sticking to true natives such as oak or beech.

In addition to deciduous species Brown also used evergreen trees extensively: the native yew, holly and Scots pine and also two other trees which have the same dark green colour, ilex, or holm oak (introduced in about 1500) and the cedar of Lebanon (introduced in 1638). Most of the pointed coniferous trees which are most common today had not been introduced in Brown's time, and the major impact of 'plant-hunters' did not occur until after his death. But Brown, as we know, was not looking for novelty, and no doubt his opinion of pointed conifers was similar to Horace Walpole's, who remarked, 'In general, except as a screen to conceal some deformity, or as shelter in winter, I am not fond of total plantations of evergreens. Firs, in particular, form a very ungraceful summit all broken into angles.'

The value of evergreen trees is that they give winter colour, and for the rest of the year provide a contrast to the paler colours of deciduous trees. Brown often planted yews as a kind of 'second line', irregularly along the edges of plantations, so that the dark colour would appear as dense shadows. This gave young plantations increased solidity and also heightened the effects of light and shade. The evergreen trees he used are extremely dark in colour, almost black. He never used conifers with a bluish colour, for they are out of place in the English countryside. The dark green colours he chose are very effective in contrast with stonework, and he frequently used ilex trees as a background or to frame a house. The more sculptural shapes of cedars, however, are shown to better effect in isolation.

The different character of each kind of tree was duly appreciated by the 'men of taste' as they planted their estates. William Shenstone remarks that 'a large, branching, aged oak, is perhaps the most venerable of all inanimate objects':

All trees have a character analogous to that of men: Oaks are in all respects the perfect image of the manly character ... As a brave man is not suddenly either elated by prosperity, or depressed by adversity, so the oak displays not its verdure on the sun's first approach; nor drops it on his first departure. Add to this its majestic appearance, the rough grandeur of its bark, and the wide protection of its branches.[15]

But there were also economic and patriotic reasons for planting oaks. Every good ship in Britain's navy required vast quantities of oak: according to William Marshall, who wrote a book called *Planting and Rural Ornament* in 1785, a naval vessel of seventy-four guns required two thousand oak trees each weighing two tons.

Along with the awareness of a plant's character goes a feeling for its suitability for various locations. For example, willows belong by the water's edge and Scots pines on a windswept hill, and not *vice versa*.

Near the house, Brown often made a close walk through a sheltered area of planting, suitable when the weather was not favourable enough to explore the rest of the park. The walk would usually provide views of the park or of the wider landscape, with a foreground of varied planting. It was within the confines of these 'close walks' (or 'pleasure grounds') that Brown used his horticultural material. Petworth has one of these areas, and a list of some of the plants used there has survived, on a bill from a nurseryman called John Williamson. Amongst the trees there were ten ilex, six bird cherries (*Prunus padus*), six double cherries (probably *Prunus avium* 'Plena') ten double thorns (*Crataegus oxyacantha* 'Plena' or 'Rosea Flore Pleno'), ten 'Virginia Schumachs' (*Rhus glabra*), seven American maples (*Acer rubrum* or *saccharum*), twenty 'Laburnhams'

Right: Croome Court, by Richard Wilson. Here the owner erected a monument commemorating how Brown 'by the powers of his inimitable and creative genius formed this garden scene out of a morass'.

Below: Moor Park, by Richard Wilson. This landscape, made at great cost for Admiral Lord Anson, has been severely damaged during its conversion to a golf course.

Wimpole, Cambridgeshire.
The perimeter belts of tree-
planting on the horizon
show the large scale of
Brown's operations. He
built the Ruined Castle to
Sanderson Miller's design
in 1769.

Brown's landscape at Paultons contained a U-shaped lake surrounding the house on three sides. The house is now demolished and the landscape virtually lost. A view from Hewetson's *Architectural and Picturesque Views of Noble Mansions in Hampshire*, 1830.

and fifty lilacs. The shrubs included five 'Oriental Colluteas' (*Colutea orientalis*), a form of the bladder senna with copper-coloured flowers which is unusual even today, six 'Cockgyreas' (*Cotinus coggygria*), six butcher's broom (*Ruscus aculeatus*), eight candleberries (probably *Myrica cerifera*, a North American shrub whose fruits are covered with a wax which can be used for candle-making), eight Persian jasmine (*Syringa persica*, a charming species lilac), four tamarisks, four sea buckthorns (*Hippophae rhamnoides*) and six Portugal laurels (*Prunus lusitanica*). In addition there were eighty roses, including 'Rosa Mundi', 'Maiden's Blush' and 'York and Lancaster'. (This of course is an arbitrary list which happens to have survived on a particular estate, but it gives an indication of the variety of worthwhile plant material that was available in Brown's time.)

Brown's planting schemes depended, naturally, on the scale at which he was working. Whereas great attention to detail can be given to plants in the foreground of a view near the house, the planting of a distant hill must be done in a bold and generous manner. Here he would use only one, or at most two, types of tree. On flat ground it is necessary to plant sparingly in order to maintain long views in various directions, but hilly ground obstructs the view in any case, and there the trees serve to 'clothe' and heighten the hill.

In the matter of planting Brown's practical background gave him an advantage over William Kent, and enabled him to work on a much bolder scale. Horace Walpole in his *Essay on Modern Gardening*, suggests that, 'owing to the novelty of his art', which was still a new fashion, 'Kent's landscapes were seldom majestic. His clumps were puny, he aimed at immediate effect, and planted not for futurity. One sees no large woods sketched out by his direction. Nor are we yet entirely risen above a too great frequency of small clumps ... How common to see three or four beeches, then as many larches, a third knot of cypresses, and a revolution of all three.'

The right way to plant was 'without any seeming order, or the visible interference of art'[16] (William Mason suggested that trees should be planted as if the seeds had been dropped by a bird pursued by a hawk), but of course it was never quite so random. Attempts have been made to classify Brown's planting into belts, clumps and specimen trees, but a study of his plans shows that it was not as simple as that. He frequently planted a belt of trees around the perimeter of his parks, partly in order to screen them from unenclosed strips of agricultural land,[17] and partly to shelter the ride that often encircled the park at its greatest extent. (It was often a matter of pride for the owner to be able to say just how many miles it was round his estate.) But its chief function was to ensure that all the land visible from the house was the owner's domain, as if the house were in a world of its own with the outside world screened out of existence. The area of land owned by Brown's clients was often so large, however, that one is quite unaware of the existence of these belts, which are far away over some horizon. Usually the shape is so irregular, with contours adding a further complication, that one is not aware of the exact limits to the estate. In front of the belt he usually placed clusters of trees, scattered clumps, and odd specimen trees, all of which soften the outlines so that any idea of a hard edge was removed.

The idea of the perimeter ride was not new. A circuit-walk had been a celebrated feature of Philip Southcote's garden at Woburn Farm, but this was on a much smaller scale; something closer to Brown's perimeter ride was done by Bridgeman at Eastbury, but as it consisted of extremely long and straight avenues which opened only occasionally onto the park or the surrounding country it was rather monotonous. Stephen Switzer explained the idea in his 'Proemial Essay' to the 1742 edition of *Ichnographia Rustica*:

I have one thing more to add, as to design which has been generally omitted by all that have wrote ... and that is the Ambit, Circuit or Tour of a Design, such as in all large designs can be only done on horseback, or in a chaise or coach: and is by the French called *Anfilade*, probably *Unum Filum*, a clue or continuation of thread, of which this *Anfilade* or Circuit is composed.

This *Anfilade* ... should be carried over the tops of the highest hills that lie within the compass of any nobleman's or gentleman's design ... and from those eminencies (whereon ... building[s] or clumps of trees ought to be placed) it is that you are to view the whole design ...

Brown's plans show that his large areas of planting were of two kinds: solid 'wood', and looser and more open 'groves' (an effect derived from Kent and Pope), where the trees, rather than forming an impenetrable mass, stand each in their own space, with no underplanting to obscure views. On his plan for Ashburnham, for example, are two large clumps placed side by side; one is a dense mass, but in the other every tree is separately drawn, each with its own shadow.

Brown treated the edges of his planted areas with great skill. A good example of this can be seen in his plan of Trentham: the main part of the planting terminates in a serpentine line which does not follow the nearby curving line of the lake-edge. Groups of trees are dotted irregularly between the two, giving a soft edge to the planting and providing variety along the path that runs between the wood and the lake.

Needless to say, avenues formed no part of Brown's designs (though he did not always remove them). Although they have a certain fascination, avenues are an obvious feature in a landscape and cannot produce many subtle effects. They also have the disadvantage of blocking any views at ninety degrees to the line of the avenue. As William Shenstone remarks: 'It is not easy to account for the fondness of former times for straight-lined avenues.' Brown always preferred to arrange clumps so that 'when a building, or other object has been onced viewed from its proper point, the foot should never travel to it by the same path, which the eye has travelled over before.' It is much more effective to 'lose the object and draw nigh obliquely'. Shenstone felt that 'to move on continually and find no change of scene in the least attendant on our change of place, must give actual pain to a person of taste. For such a one to be condemned to pass along the famous vista from Moscow to Petersburg, or that other from Agra to Lahore in India, must be as disagreeable a sentence as to be condemned to labour at the galleys.' Brown would frequently break an avenue into groups and clusters of trees so that views across the line of the avenue were opened up.

The planting of 'clumps' was criticized in later years, but the plans of Brown's parks show considerable variety in the way he used them. Most are extremely large, appearing on nineteenth-century Ordnance Maps as 'Fourteen-acre Clumps', for example, and are many times the size of the clumps in Repton's sketches. The rounded shape of these clumps gives them a soft, naturalistic outline from whichever angle they are viewed, and this effect is enhanced by the specimen trees Brown dotted around them. A good example of this can be seen in his plan of the Royal Gardens at Richmond.

A further dimension of Brown's planting is time. In many cases Brown never saw the full effect of his designs, but he was associated with some of his clients for many years: at Burghley, for example, he would have seen thirty years' growth, which would have reached maturity of a sort. In those estates where he did not start entirely from scratch he may have been able to move a few of the trees around to increase the apparent maturity of the park. The planting of an estate is never a once-and-for-all thing. At every stage of development care is required to plant, to prune, to thin out, to plant replacements, and to maintain the overall visual effect. Although Brown would be appalled if he could see some of his parks today, time has given many of them a magnificence which he could never have known. These parks were planted for posterity, and need to be maintained in the same spirit.

———

NOTES

1 *Observations on Modern Gardening* (1770).
2 Letter to Mr Wheeler, 1751, published in *Observations, Anecdotes and Characters of Books and Men* (1820).
3 Walpole to Chute, quoted by P. Willis, *Charles Bridgeman.*
4 William Mason.
5 Boswell, *Life of Johnson*, 6 July 1763.
6 Christian Norberg-Schulz, *Genius Loci: Towards a Phenomenology of Architecture* (1980).
7 This was a note which Southcote added to Joseph Spence's letter to Mr Wheeler, op. cit.
8 William Shenstone, *Unconnected Thoughts on Gardening* (1764).
9 From *An Epistle to Lord Burlington 'Of the Use of Riches'*, 1731.
   The whole passage is as follows:

   Consult the Genius of the Place in all
   That tells the waters or to rise or fall;
   Or helps the ambitious hill the heavens to scale,
   Or scoops in circling theatres the vale;
   Calls in the country, catches opening glades,
   Joins willing woods, and varies shades from shades;
   Now breaks, or now directs, the intending lines;
   Paints as you plant, and, as you work, designs.

10 Christopher Hussey, for example, in *The Picturesque*, judges Brown by the standards of Uvedale Price rather than those of Brown's own period. David Watkin, in *The English Vision*, chose to use Basildon Park in Berkshire as 'a standard example of Brown's unvarying manner', but there is no evidence that Brown advised on anything except the kitchen garden at Basildon.
11 See Hussey's introduction to Stroud.
12 *The English Garden*, II, 41–3.
13 At Wiltshire County Record Office, 17 January 1785 onwards.
14 The approximate numbers at Tottenham were:

21,000 oaks	200 'plains'
14,000 beech	300 Spanish chestnut
4,800 chestnut	200 mountain ash
3,200 birch	100 bird cherries
2,300 elms	50 whitebeams
700 ash	12 scarlet oaks
450 sycamore	10 Balm of Gilead
	30 limes

15 William Shenstone, *Unconnected Thoughts on Gardening* (1764).
16 *Ibid.*
17 The strips of common fields can be clearly seen on a 1783 map of the Audley End estate, duly screened by a belt of trees. See J.D. Williams, *Audley End, the Restoration of 1762–1797*, Plate XVI(b).

The Landscapes

═══

Audley End

═══

AUDLEY End House was built during the reign of James I by Baron Howard de Walden, Earl of Suffolk, who decided 'to erect a mansion which should surpass in size and magnificence all the private residences of the kingdom.'[1] Unfortunately the family did not have the resources to maintain such a vast palace, much less live there in style. At one stage it was sold to the Crown, but by 1747 it was virtually a ruin: the outer court had been demolished, the glass had gone from the windows, and 'the cupola, in the centre of the building, rocked about in every high wind and seemed likely to fall.'

In 1762 Sir John Griffin Griffin inherited the property, and began its restoration. In a letter to him in 1765, Lord Chatham says, 'As you are at Audley End, I imagine you deeply engaged in the amusing cares of building, planting, decorating, etc.'[2]

Records show that Griffin spent £100,000 on the property between 1762 and 1792, and that he involved himself tirelessly – almost obsessively – in the work. In 1762 a new brickworks was opened on the estate, and produced one and three-quarter million bricks over a period of thirty years; stone was brought in by barge and wagon from as far away as Rutlandshire, while Griffin's carpenters were sent off to King's Lynn to acquire various kinds of timber imported from the Baltic states. Some of the best craftsmen of the day worked in the house, including Rose (the plasterer) and Hobcroft (the joiner), both of whom worked for Brown at Broadlands.

To improve the estate Griffin spent £30,000 on additional land (he had only inherited half the estate), and by a private Act of Parliament he moved several roads further away from the house, and removed altogether part of Audley End village.

He was not one of those clients who were prepared to leave Brown alone to get on with the work: on the contrary, he watched his every move. When Brown was creating the lake Griffin's involvement become too close for comfort; a surviving document records his feeling on the matter:

I allow Mr B his own charges for his trouble, of £150, and take no notice of the injury done to the work, by giving a wrong bend to the river, and contrary to his own plans, which was agreed to be executed by a contract and which would have run to a much greater expense, on account of working against the hill and the levels that must have followed in consequence, and this part of the river was finished where I let him off his contract.

Eventually Griffin paid Brown £800, although the contracted price was £660. Brown, however still maintained that he had not been 'honourably treated', but concluded that he would not 'labour more to convince Sir John as he knows there is none so blind as him that will not see.'

Today the peaceful scene at Audley End betrays no hint of such acrimony. The house makes a dramatic impact when it comes suddenly into view from the London-Cambridge road. The clusters of green-tipped turrets, the restless stepped façade and the great mullioned bay-windows are seen framed by enormous trees. In front of the house are many of the hallmarks of Brown's handiwork: the subtly curved outline of the widened River Cam, the smooth lawns sweep down to the water's edge with perfect precision, the gently curving approach roads, and the mature cedars of Lebanon. There is also a fine view from the Robert Adam bridge on the Saffron Walden road. On this side the house and landscape are immaculately maintained by English Heritage, but unfortunately when we look in the opposite direction, towards the part of the landscape still owned by Griffin's descendants, there is nothing but a morass of nettles, weeds and undergrowth. Inside the house a set of six slightly naive views of the house in its setting, commissioned by Griffin from William Tomkins as the work neared completion, can still be seen on display.

Some records of the trees planted on the estate survive. At one stage 10,000 Scots pine seedlings were bought; other records show purchases of 1,300 larches, and limes, silver firs (*Abies* species), Portuguese laurels, Carolina poplars and birches. From Rotterdam came 3000 Dutch alders, at a cost of £4 2s. By 1790 there were fifty gardeners working at Audley End, and it took twelve of them more than a week to mow the seven miles of grass walks. The Elysian Garden was made in 1782, after Brown had finished his work, and the Palladian Bridge further down the river was designed by Robert Adam. A mid-nineteenth century writer summed up the landscape's qualities:

its internal grandeur and external beauties, replete with all the varieties of hill and vale, wood and water, are rarely to be combined in such limits ... Its palatial character, with its trees and gardens, is there very imposing, and resting in quiet splendour amidst such agreeable scenery, it cannot fail to awaken admiration.[3]

NOTES

1 Lord Braybrooke, *History of Audley End* (1836), quoted in *Audley End, the Restoration of 1762–97* by J. D. Williams.
2 Essex County Record Office, quoted by J. D. Williams, op. cit.
3 John Player, *Sketches of Saffron Walden* 1845. This information and much else is taken from J. D. Williams, op. cit.

Blenheim

A CELEBRATED example of the design effect known as 'surprise' can be found at the Triumphal Gate into Blenheim Park. At one moment we are in a small urban situation in a Woodstock street, with high stone walls all round us; the next, after stepping through the archway, an astonishing picture lies before us: the lake, the palace and the Grand Bridge. 'A transition' says one writer, 'from nothing to everything.'[1]

Nowhere does Brown's lake look wider than from this point, and there is no doubt that this view is a deliberate effect planned with the greatest skill. Even the position of the island seems to play an important part in the picture, providing a centre of interest which resolves the dual attractions of the palace on one side and the bridge on the other. In the background is a continuous dark band of trees, while in the foreground the bright surface of the lake reflects the changing colours of the sky.

Blenheim Palace was built for the Duke of Marlborough as a gift from the nation after his sensational victory against the French at Blenheim, near the River Danube. It was designed by Vanbrugh as a monument rather than as a house to be lived in, and this led to endless conflicts with the strong-minded Duchess. The palace is Vanbrugh's greatest achievement, romantic in outline, strong and dramatic in style and highly inventive in detail. The gardens to match it were laid out by Henry Wise, the Master Gardener of the time, and a plan dating from 1710 survives. It shows the avenue of trees (recently replanted), which leads directly to the bridge and the Great Court. On the south side (the other side from the bridge) there was a 'Military Garden', framed by mock fortifications or bastions built by Vanbrugh (something similar can still be seen at Vanbrugh's Castle Howard). Within this setting, Henry Wise created a series of formal parterres leading to the 'Woodwork', a plantation of trees dissected by straight avenues and containing thirteen criss-crossing and curving paths. It is a curious plan, very fussy and somehow out of scale with the palace, and the site is now covered by Brown's simple, sweeping south lawn.

The plan also in *Vitruvius Britannicus* (vol III) shows two large lakes separated by the Grand Bridge, and their naturalistic outline would seem to be in accord with Vanbrugh's appreciation of natural scenery and its picturesque possibilities. However, like many other things at Blenheim, it did not suit the Duchess, and a later engraving shows the more formal canal and a circular lake which were made for her by an engineer called Colonel Armstrong.

Vanbrugh's famous bridge was never finished; the arcaded superstructure shown in his drawing was not built. Originally funds for Blenheim were virtually unlimited, but in 1710 the Duchess was foolish enough to quarrel with Queen Anne, and after a change of government, funds stopped, and the Marlboroughs went into exile until after Queen Anne's death. When work was resumed in 1716 it was mostly at the Marlboroughs' own expense. The Duchess, now the dominant figure since her husband's stroke, thought the Grand Bridge was the height of extravagance, and before long she quarrelled so violently with Vanbrugh that he resigned from the work. He never saw the final picture. When he called a few years later with the Lord Carlisle (of Castle Howard) he was refused entry.

Vanbrugh was overruled on another issue of great interest. The grounds of Blenheim contained the remains of old Woodstock Manor, a small Elizabethan palace which had fallen into disrepair during the Civil War. Vanbrugh himself had lived there, 'altho' in the middle of rubbish'. He sent the Marlboroughs a memorandum in June 1709, recommending that it should be preserved for its picturesque and associational value, noting also that a saving of £1,000 would be made, and sending a painting to illustrate his idea. The ruins should be maintained, Vanbrugh argued (in the first recorded instance of anyone wishing to preserve a ruin for its own sake) because:

they move more lively and pleasing reflections than history without their aid can do, on the persons who have inhabited them; on the remarkable things which have been transacted in them, or the extraordinary occasions of erecting them.

He pointed out that the view from Blenheim:

has little variety of objects, nor does the country beyond it afford of any value. It therefore stands in need of all the helps that can be given, which are ... buildings and plantations. These, rightly disposed, will indeed supply all the wants of Nature in that place. And the most agreeable disposition is to mix them. ... The building left ... would make one of the most agreeable objects that the best landscape painters can invent. If, on the contrary, the building is taken away, there then remains nothing but an irregular, rugged, ungovernable hill, the deformities of which are not to be cured but by a vast expense.[2]

The Duchess would have none of it, and in 1723 'the manner house' (her own spelling) was removed and grassed over. She did not realize that Vanbrugh had anticipated a shift in taste: less than ten years later the first mock ruin was built for the first Earl Bathurst at Cirencester Park.

It was left to a later generation to 'cure by a vast expense ... the deformities' at Blenheim. It was for the fourth Duke of Marlborough that Brown prepared plans for improving the grounds, and work began in 1764 and took ten years to complete. Payments to Brown during that period amounted to more than £21,000.

The first Duchess's opinion of the original landscape was that it was 'a chaos which only God Almighty could finish'. Brown, however, was prepared to try. His masterstroke was to raise the level of the water in the lakes by fifteen feet, and although this obscured part of the base of Vanbrugh's bridge it created a great sheet of water worthy of the bridge. It is Brown's largest lake and it is perhaps unique in the steepness of its banks. The lakes at Compton Verney or Chillington are set in flatter country where only the height of the trees contains the water, but here the gracefully contoured and carefully graded banks are in scale with the water. With Brown's characteristic accuracy, the water reaches exactly to the springing of the arch: if it had been lower the lake would have been too small; if higher the appearance of Vanbrugh's bridge would have been spoilt.

Magnificent mature beech trees match the grandeur of the setting, and clearly the paths have been positioned to give the walker every opportunity of seeing the park to best advantage. In the words of the 1789 Blenheim guide:

The water, the Palace, the gardens, the Grand Bridge, the Pillar, Woodstock, and other remote and near objects, open and shut upon the eye like enchantment, and at one point, every change of a few paces furnishes a new scene which forms a subject worthy of the sublimest pencil.

Is is possible to walk round most of the lake, but the Grand Cascade can only be reached, unfortunately, by making a special trip through the Pleasure Gardens. The cascade is a romantic creation, natural-looking and quite different from Brown's earlier cascade at Charlecote, which is architectural and controlled, or his simple falls at Ashburnham and Kimberley.

There is a high standard of maintenance throughout most of the park, but sadly this area does not seem to get the attention it deserves at the moment, partly because of its isolation. There is a tatty modern pump house which is rather an eyesore, and the 'river' beyond the cascade is badly silted up. Part way down from the palace to the cascade is the Temple of Diana, which, like the New Bridge, was designed by Sir William Chambers. He meant it to look out across the lake, but young trees now block the view, nor can the temple be seen from the lake.

Most of the features of the Vanbrugh/Wise landscape were retained by Brown, including the mile-long avenue leading from the Column of Victory northwards to the

Ditchley Gate and the avenue from the main Hensington Gate on the east side. An extensive area of 'forest gardening' was also kept to the south of the avenue to the Hensington Gate (on the opposite side of the park road from the Garden Centre), but was removed after Brown's time, probably in the late nineteenth century.

One of the changes Brown did make was to grass over the Great Court on the north side (facing the bridge), a wise move since the gold-coloured stone contrasts perfectly with green lawns. Unfortunately the ninth Duke thought he knew better and had the court paved over again between 1900 and 1910, which gives it a dreary, monochrome effect, exaggerated by the fact that the court is north-facing.

The park is so large that to explore it thoroughly is more than a day's task. In the words of the 1789 guide:

> The Park is one continued galaxy of charming prospects, and agreeably diversified scenes. Its circumference is upwards of twelve miles; its area about two thousand seven hundred acres, round which are the most enchanting rides, chiefly shaded towards the boundary with a deep belt of various trees, evergreens, and deciduous shrubs, whose mingled foliage exhibits the different gradations of tints from the most faint to the most obfuscate green.

Nothing on this scale had been attempted before. Even the gardens at Stowe were a mere 200 acres – less than one tenth of the size of Blenheim. The Stowe Ridings, it is true, covered about 800 acres and Eastbury about 1,200, but these were 'forest gardening', consisting of straight rides through trees.

On the north-west side is Park Farm, where there was a menagerie in the fourth Duke's time, which contained amongst other things a tiger sent to him by Lord Clive in 1771. For these buildings Brown designed a Gothick façade with a castellated parapet and some pointed and some quatrefoil windows, all symmetrical with a central ogee-headed archway. Part of this has survived, though it was remodelled in the 1850s. Further to the west is High Lodge, another essay in the Gothick style with a castle-like appearance and pointed windows. Although the palace is in the classical baroque style, it has, like much of Vanbrugh's work, something of a castle air; in fact the drawings published in *Vitruvius Britannicus* Vol. 1 in 1717 are titled Blenheim Castle. Brown's Gothick somehow seems more suitable here than the anaemic classicism of Sir William Chambers' Temple of Diana.

Brown also made proposals for castellating the portion of the park walls that ran in front of Woodstock village as seen from the palace. This was a most advanced and original idea which would have given Woodstock the appearance of being a walled medieval town, with square towers and round bastions at intervals along the wall, a romantic concept, and a worthy successor to Vanbrugh's scheme for the preservation of Woodstock Manor. By wrapping the wall around the village Brown was effectively uniting it into a single, picturesque object in the landscape. This proposal at Blenheim probably dates from the 1760s, about a decade before Brown's involvement in village planning at Milton Abbas in Dorset, and thirty years before Sir Uvedale Price wrote about the picturesque possibilities of villages in his *Essay on the Picturesque* (1794), claimed by some as a pioneering work. Brown's idea, however, met with as little enthusiasm as Vanbrugh's, and the scheme was never built. Another unbuilt project was a bathing house at Rosamund's Well, a spring on the far side of the lake (on the left after crossing the Grand Bridge).

The landscape was famous from the start. Even Brown was pleased. 'The Provost of Eton,' wrote one visitor, 'who converses with Brown, told us that he himself cries it up

The curving line of the widened River Cam at Audley End.

Brown's plan for Audley End, prepared c1753.

Lancelot Brown's contract for Audley End.

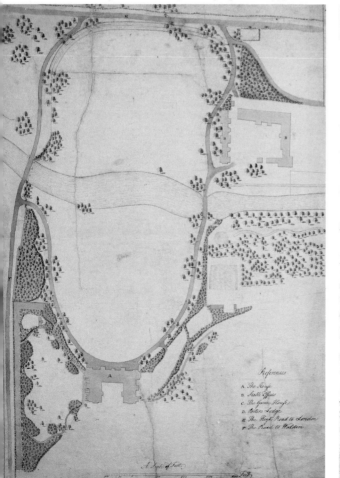

References

A The House
b Stable Offices
c The Green House
d Porters Lodge
E The High Road to London
F The Road to Walden

A Scale of Feet

Article the 5th To make all the necessary preparations for as well as to plant all the Trees and Shrubbs
that shall be thought Necessary for the adorning of the Ground
according to the Plan and Ideas agreed of with Sr John, as
also to sow with Grass seeds and Dutch Clover or Lay
with Turff all the Parts of the Ground which is to be altered
And any that Grass or Turff fail to make it good
Article the 6th To take down all the Walls which fall
within the Work, the Court Wall excepted, to make what
drains may be wanted to keep the Ground dry.

Article the 7th To make the new Road at both ends
or on each Side of Chalk Pit, with Foot Path,
of the Bridge, raising it to a proper height, as also to fill
up the Old Course of the River below the Old Bridge which
was damaged by the Floods, To make such alterations
in the shape and make of the side Gravel walks or
Roads to the House as shall be thought Necessary.

The said Lancelot Brown does promise for himself
his Heirs Administrators or Assignes to finish the above
seven Articles in the best manner in his or their power
between the date hereof and May one Thousand Seven
Hundred and Sixty four.

For the due performance of the above written seven
Articles, Sr John Griffin Griffin does covenant and agree
for himself his Heirs Administrators, and Assigns to
pay or cause to be paid to the said Lancelot Brown
his Heirs Administrators or Assigns if good and lawfull
money of England, at the under written times of payment
the summ of Sea Hundred and Sixty Pounds, Sr John to
find Trees and Shrubs, Boats, and Wheelbarrows, as also

Brown's landscape provides
the perfect foil for Vanbrugh's
architecture at Blenheim.

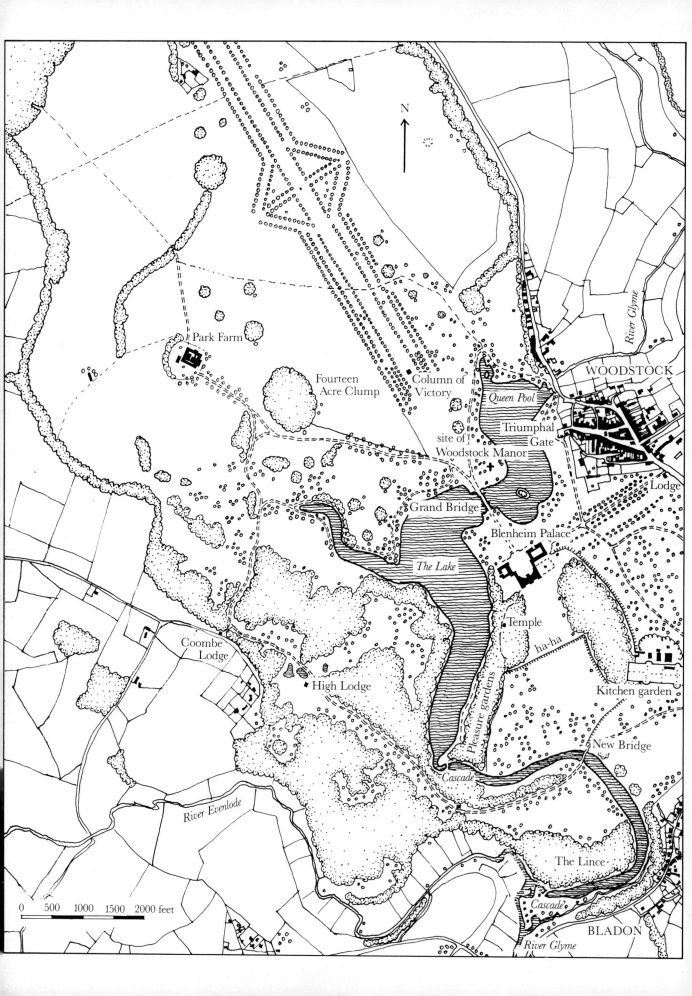

N

Park Farm

Fourteen
Acre Clump

Column of
Victory

Queen Pool

Triumphal
Gate

WOODSTOCK

site of
Woodstock Manor

Grand Bridge

Blenheim Palace

Lodge

The Lake

Temple

ha-ha

Coombe
Lodge

High Lodge

Pleasure gardens

Kitchen garden

New Bridge

Cascade

River Evenlode

The Lince

Cascade

BLADON

River Glyme

0   500   1000   1500   2000 feet

Above: An idyllic corner of Blenheim Park.

Opposite: Plan of Blenheim Park, probably Brown's largest project.

Right: Brown's sketch of Blenheim showing his proposals (not carried out) for castellating the walls around Woodstock town, as seen from the palace, making it a picturesque feature in the landscape.

Opposite: The Doric Temple seen across the lake at Bowood.

Above: Broadlands, seen from the River Test. Brown's west front.

Below: Brown's design for the south elevation of Broadlands (*c*1771).

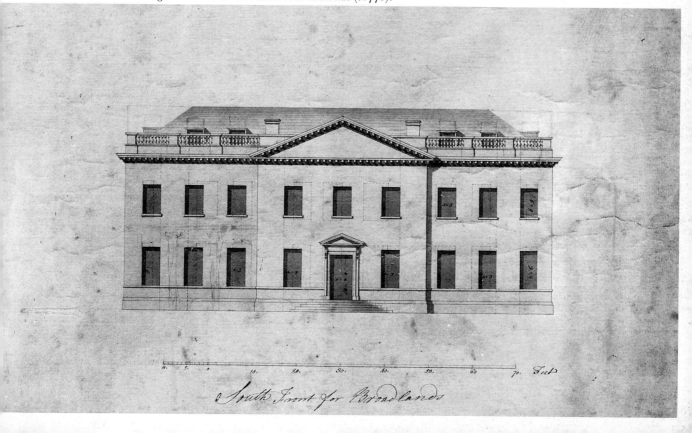

South Front for Broadlands

Above: Burghley House, seen from the western end of Brown's lake.

Left: The Bath House at Burghley, designed by Brown in the Jacobean revival style.

as the master-piece of his genius'.[3] In 1776 Dr Johnson and James Boswell came to Blenheim, and Boswell remarked, 'You and I, Sir, have, I think, seen together the extremes of what can be seen in Britain: the wild rough island of Mull, and Blenheim Park.' In 1786, George III visited Blenheim, at short notice, and his verdict was blunt: 'We have nothing equal to this'.[4]

When the ninth Duke inherited the estate in 1892 he made several changes besides removing the grass from the Great Court. He was in America when he learned of his accession, and he immediately cabled his agent at Blenheim: HAVE THE LAKE DREDGED. And it was, at great expense. He also added the impressive formal gardens on the west side of the palace, which fortunately make no impact on the park, as they are screened by the surrounding planting.

The Duke's other contribution was the replanting of the avenue on the north side with elms, which unfortunately succumbed to Dutch elm disease and were replaced by limes in the 1970s. Altogether he planted 465,000 trees in the park, and much of its beauty today is due to him. He did not, though, fully appreciate the nature of a Capability Brown park, and introduced large areas of blue Atlantic cedar and copper beech, which Brown would never have used, as their coloured foliage appears artificial in his 'natural' landscapes. Now that these trees are reaching maturity it becomes more obvious that it was a mistake to impose on Blenheim these extraneous blocks of colour. So many of Brown's parks are irretrievably lost, and the few which survive deserve to be maintained with as much authenticity as possible.

To the present owners' credit, a long term plan for the future of Blenheim has been commissioned,[5] which envisages that the key plantings around the lake and on the perimeter of the park will be conserved by continuous and gradual replacement, while other areas will be replanted in sequence every other century. The individual qualities and characteristics of the various parts of the park have been identified and an appropriate approach for each is proposed, and the 'centrepiece' of Brown's lakeside landscape has been given greatest priority for 'exact preservation'. The varying needs of those things which contribute to the funding of the park's maintenance have been identified: the 400,000 visitors; agricultural production; forestry and the estate sawmill; pheasant shooting; nature reserves, and nature trails for schoolchildren; sports, charity events and promotional days. In the words of Hal Moggridge, who was deeply involved in this plan:

The passage of time, the additions and subtractions of succeeding generations, have not diminished the emotional impact of this great landscape.[6]

NOTES

1 Boydell, quoted in the Blenheim Guide.
2 *The Complete Works of Sir John Vanbrugh*, IV, *The Letters* (1928), G. Webb ed.
3 J. Nicholls, *Literary Illustrations*, 1817, quoted by Stroud.
4 Letter to the Archbishop of Canterbury, quoted in *Blenheim Palace*, D. Green.
5 Reports on the plan by Hal Moggridge can be read in *The Garden*, November 1983, p. 432, and in *Landscape Design*, op. cit.
6 Moggridge, op. cit.

Bowood

BOWOOD was the home of the Marquess of Lansdowne, an outstanding and controversial figure in eighteenth-century politics and a man of wide interests in the arts and sciences. After distinguishing himself in military service he was made an aide-de-camp to George III, and went on to hold many important government posts, including responsibility for the British Colonies during the American War of Independence. In 1782–3 he was First Lord of the Treasury, and he was Prime Minister when the United States' independence was finally conceded. His income was about £25,000, but after various expenses, he explained, he had only £7,000 to spend on his estate. (However, he told Dr Johnson that 'a man of rank who looks into his own affairs may have all that he ought to have ... for £5,000 a year.')

Bowood House in Brown's time consisted of the Big House, mainly by Henry Keene, who also designed two courts to the north-west, which were service buildings and domestic rooms, known as the Little House. In 1768–70 Robert Adam altered the Big House, and closed off the courtyards on the south side with the so-called Diocletian Wing and connected them to the Big House.

In 1955 the eighth Marquess felt he could not maintain the Big House any longer and pulled it down, hoping this would better safeguard what remained. So now Bowood lacks a strong central feature. Adam's Diocletian façade is splendid but only one storey high, and therefore lacks the scale to dominate its setting in the way the Big House did, a failing which is especially apparent from the lake. The mainly two-storey front of the Little House is a quiet design, intended to be subservient to the more strongly articulated Big House. Another effect of the demolition is that both the Keene and the Adam fronts are set too far back from the top of the slope which runs down to the lake, and this, too, weakens their impact.

The upper terrace in front of the Adam wing was made in 1817–18, by Sir Robert Smirke (architect of the British Museum), and the lower one in 1851 by George Kennedy. Looking down to the southern end of the lake today one has to remember that the lake was designed to be viewed not from here but from the Big House, which stood at the southern corner of the East Terrace.

Brown was first asked to visit Bowood in 1757, by the first Earl of Shelburne:

Mr. Brown ... passed two days with me ... and twenty times assured me that he does not know a finer place in England than Bowood Park ... I am persuaded that the man means to present me at some future time with a well-digested plan for this place.

But work did not begin until 1761, a few months before the Earl's death, and Brown's plan for Bowood was not done until 1763. One of the problems he faced was that the boundary on the east side was too close, and moreover contained a hamlet which had to be moved. Just one cottage from it remains, picturesquely placed on the far side of the lake, and presumably its reprieve was a conscious design decision, a Reptonian touch to provide signs of life and movement in the valley. On old plans it is called the Boat House. The boundary is also awkwardly close on the north-east side, where Brown built the dam and cascade, but there is no hint of this as one looks across the lake today to the belt of fine trees that forms the backdrop to the scene.

There was already a small pool in the valley when Brown arrived, but the rest of the land consisted of small agricultural fields and hedgerows. Two streams joined in the valley: the Washway, from a spring in the park to the east, and the Wetham brook from the south. Flooding this valley created a long sinuous lake running north-south with an 'arm' or creek leading eastwards up the Washway valley. To increase the apparent length of this water Brown made a second lake, linked to the first by a pathway which crosses the dam between them. At one stage it was intended to make this the main approach, and Robert Adam prepared an imposing scheme for a 'Roman aqueduct bridge' which was never built. From this direction the first sight of the lake would have been of a narrow creek at the southern end of the lake near Pond Tail Lodge. Today this creek no longer reaches the road because the last hundred yards of the lake have silted up, but an exploration of the lake from this end yields, nonetheless, one of the best views of the house and the lake together. From here, framed by the narrow valley, the house still looks a match for the lake.

Adam's first commission was to design a Mausoleum in memory of the first Earl of Shelburne. Completed in 1765, it stands on high ground looking down the Washway valley across the parkland and the Wiltshire landscape. Today it is surrounded by rhododendron walks. The 1773 estate map shows an additional lake below the Mausoleum, as planned by Brown in his plan of 1763, but this has long since gone; not even the second edition Ordnance Survey map of the 1880s shows it.

On the north side of the house are the splendid Pleasure Grounds, which since the mid-nineteenth century have been an arboretum. The *Gardener's Chronicle* of 1845 said:

The gardens and an extensive lawn are managed superbly, and it will give some idea of the extent of the place when we mention that 60 acres are devoted to flower garden and pleasure ground, on which the scythe and the rake keep a continual polish ... Hundreds of Cedars of Lebanon are everywhere profusely grouped and these were planted in 1775 ... There is no place within our recollecting where such a large number of cedars of this age exist.

The majority of these cedars have now gone. Most arboreta are of nineteenth-century origin and are planted on natural ground; Bowood must be unique in having a carefully graded eighteenth-century base on which to work. One of the 'dells' gives a long vista, stretching from the estate road, now used as the public entrance, down to the lake and the Doric Temple. Until 1864 the temple stood in the Pleasure Grounds, and this confirms the evidence that Brown intended a natural landscape, rather than an Arcadian one.

Bowood looks especially good in the autumn; the bronze tints of the beech trees, the apricot of the limes, the oaks still dark green and shadowy, the lime-green of the ash trees and the red stems of the dogwood on the margins of the lake all contrast with one another and with the yews, dark in the shadows beneath the trees.

Taking the path from the house to the Doric Temple, we eventually reach the edge of the lake. At this point there are fine views down to the south end of the lake, and it is from here that the Big House is missed most. The landscape here is almost the equal of Blenheim, but there the marriage of Vanbrugh's architecture and Brown's landscape has a splendour that is not matched here by Brown's work and the remnant of an Adam house.

Further into the woods we find the Hermit's Cave, a charming romantic feature, probably added by Charles Hamilton, owner of the celebrated gardens at Painshill. The route leads along a narrow path where tree roots above head level grasp at rocks that project dramatically from the banks. Natural as it all looks, it was no doubt 'helped' by Hamilton and his rockwork specialist, Josiah Lane of Tisbury, Wiltshire.

But Hamilton's *tour de force* at Bowood is the cascade, a magnificent creation, with perfectly positioned ferns, ivy and craggy rocks. Of course on closer inspection it is very contrived – particularly the way the water mysteriously appears from nowhere – but seen from the stepping stones across the stream below it does looks impressive. The cascade and adjoining complex rockwork steps and paths are now being carefully restored and strengthened to cope with the increasing number of visitors – 100,000 in 1984. The standard of maintenance is high; there is no doubt at Bowood of the real dedication of the owner to his estate.

Broadlands

HENRY Temple, the first Viscount Palmerston, bought Broadlands in 1730. He told his son in a letter how he had begun to remove the formal gardens, 'giving away all the fine pyramid greens to those that will fetch them, of which many cartloads are gone already.'

His son, who inherited the title in 1757 at the age of eighteen, travelled widely throughout Britain and Europe collecting paintings, sculptures and furniture, and after returning from the first of his three visits to Italy he commissioned Brown to alter and extend the existing sixteenth- and seventeenth-century house. He was a distant cousin of Lord Temple of Stowe, where he may have met Brown, and in 1760 he had visited Newnham Paddox in Warwickshire, where Brown had made improvements to the grounds and built a new façade to the house. Palmerston must have been an ideal client; in 1767 he wrote that he had 'only settled the plans with Brown, and have left everything in the execution of them to him.'

By 1771 the splendid west front facing the river was complete. Brown reserved the impressive pedimented portico for the best landscape setting, which is at the back of the house, rather than for the entrance front.

The house is of white brick, now mellowed to a pale yellow. Lord Palmerston had admired the pale bricks that had been used at Holkham. The corners have quoin-stones which were added in the 1850s. The giant columns are rendered to look like stone and these have now weathered to a pleasant pinkish colour. These pale colours and smooth surfaces are of course the ideal foil to the colours and dense textures of mature deciduous trees, as Brown well knew. (Red brick is not nearly so good. Repton reported that Brown had once remarked that 'a red house sets a whole valley in a fever.') While Brown was altering the house at Broadlands he was also building Redgrave House in Suffolk. Both of these were simpler designs than Croome Court, lacking the corner towers. Redgrave (demolished in the 1950s) did not have the excellently proportioned projection of the Broadlands portico; it was also more severely plain, with no pediments over the windows.

The south front is also pedimented over the central three bays, but there are no columns. Here there is some likeness to Brown's design for Newnham Paddox (demolished 1952) and to the wings of Beechwood, Hertfordshire. It might be thought that the similarity of these designs shows a lack of originality; however, it should be borne in mind that designers of this time were not trying to be original; they were seeking conformity with an ideal, or, as Pope put it, 'what oft was thought, but ne'er so well express'd', that is, established ideas expressed with greater refinement.

The entrance front on the east side is Holland's work of 1789. It has four double-storey Ionic columns in the centre with a recessed loggia. This acts as a full-height screen across the old courtyard, which still exists as a light-well in the centre of the building. The third storey was added in the 1850s by T. L. Donaldson. Many of the interiors were altered or reworked by Holland in 1788-90.

Entering the house we find ourselves first in the octagonal vestibule, which is by Holland. As it is only of single-storey height with a skylight, all the upper rooms can look out into the light-well above. This leads to Brown's sculpture hall, with its Roman Doric screen. Created out of the old two-storey great hall, this is the least altered of Brown's rooms. Beyond the sculpture hall is the saloon, the central room on the west side which overlooks the River Test; this room and several others have good plasterwork ceilings thought to be by John Rose. The wall decorations probably belong to the 1788-90 alterations by Holland. Rose, like John Hobcroft the joiner, had earlier been associated with Brown at Croome Court and Newnham Paddox.

One can catch a brief glimpse of the house from Middle Bridge in Romsey (at the end of Middlebridge Street), and the entrance nearby was originally the main one. Approaching from this way we look along the delightful River Test and see the house perfectly positioned overlooking the river, separated from it only by a grass lawn. But with Brown's usual skill the road leads us up into the park and makes a wide loop round the 'offices' (which are screened with tree planting) before taking us on to the entrance front.

Before Brown's time there was a double avenue on the entrance side, and the house was approached axially.[1] Today the entrance front, on the east side, looks out across rather flat parkland, but there are now so many specimens dotted about that a long view is impossible. Selective removal of these trees would enable visitors to appreciate better the size and scale of the park. Some of them are commemorative trees, of which 250 have been planted by famous visitors since 1950, but the lack of an overall planting plan has inevitably meant that some of these trees are in the wrong place.

A long view can still be seen, however, from the south side of the house (the Orangery side). There was obviously meant to be a view down to the river from the Orangery. As at Moor Park and Luton Hoo, Brown clearly envisaged a view parallel with the one from the porticoed west front; and, just as at those two parks, the intended view has been obscured by later planting, such as commemorative copper beeches.

The apparently artless outlook from the west front was not achieved without some difficulty. A simple lawn slopes down to the river, a mere hundred yards away, and to the left the river makes an attractive curve, and whether it is natural or helped by Brown no one can say. But under the lawn in front of the house lies a culverted stream, which disappears under a shrubby mound on the north side and reappears in the

Pleasure Grounds on the south-west side. No doubt it could have been diverted to join the river higher up, but it was retained to give added interest to the Pleasure Grounds.

Looking out from the house across the river, pasture land gives way to some more distant arable fields, beyond which is wooded and slightly hilly ground. Again, careful selective thinning could produce longer views. A stiff row of poplars strikes an un-Brownian note. Brown planted in groups, never in rows.

The Pleasure Grounds have recently been cleared of undergrowth and old and unhealthy trees, and it is planned to undertake some replanting shortly, mainly at shrub level. It seems likely that this will be done in an authentic manner and will not just be another horticultural collection.

Brown's 'out of door works' for Lord Palmerston also included a new kitchen garden, 'Stores, Dairy etc; lodges, (and) repairs to Spursholt Farm.' The two Southampton lodges have gone, replaced by charming if totally different neo-Tudor ones by Eden Nesfield. Brown's Dairy, which overlooks the canalized stream, with its tiny falls, has Gothick hood-moulds and glazing bars, and shows some resemblance to the cottage at Roche Abbey. It has shallow vaulted ceilings, and was obviously intended for the aristocracy to play the rural life, and not as a practical working dairy.

NOTE

1   Hampshire Record Office, 27M60 Map 6.

Burghley

BURGHLEY House, says Nikolaus Pevsner, is 'the grandest of all Elizabethan mansions':

> With its turrets and innumerable chimney-stacks, Burghley is the most improbable apparition in the gentle landscaped grounds outside Stamford. In size and in swagger it can compete with any contemporary palace this side of the Alps.

In 1754, Brownlow Cecil succeeded as ninth Earl of Exeter, and at once consulted Lancelot Brown to help him put the estate in order. This proved to be a virtually continuous relationship, which ceased only with Brown's death in 1783. When Brown was staying at Burghley in 1778, he wrote to another client, Lord Harcourt of Nuneham Courtenay:

> This is a great place, where I have had twenty five years' pleasure in restoring the monument of a great minister to a great queen.[1]

Brown began advising the Earl of Exeter about the grounds, but he was soon involved in alterations and additions to the house itself. An early proposal was characteristically drastic: there could be no appreciation of the landscape from the house while a large service wing on the north-west side of the house remained. Lord Exeter duly agreed to its demolition.

South of the house Brown made a long sinuous lake, curving the sides gently in his inimitable manner. To the south-east it widens out to make a big loop which turns back towards the house, when it suddenly becomes quite narrow, in contrast with the larger area of water nearby. The dam is discreetly hidden by evergreen planting in Brown's customary skilful way. The overall impression is one of effortless elegance: there are no harsh shapes or jagged breaks, but only smooth curves and easy lines. The contours are gentle and graceful, and everywhere the planting is marvellously mature. Access to the lakeside area near the house is restricted, but the deer park, on the north and west sides of the house, is almost always open; and if the gate on the bridge is open one can walk right round the western end of the lake (with a little difficulty near the Jubilee Plantation).

Twenty years after Brown had first started work at Burghley, the three-arched classical bridge which crosses the lake some distance from the western end was begun. It took nearly three years to build, and in 1777 four 'lyons' were supplied by Mrs Eleanor Coade for the ends of the parapet, at a cost of £115. From the bridge there are fine views of the lake in both directions: to the east is the house, with the lake in the foreground, while in the other direction are the various colours of ash trees, willows and Wellingtonias around the end of the lake.

The contours are such that the belts of mature trees that encircle most of the estate are scarcely apparent from the house. On the south side they are on the far side of the hill; on the north side they are hidden by various other plantings. There are, perhaps, too many enormous trees: selective thinning to open up some longer views might be no bad thing.

Another of Brown's clients, Lord Dacre of Belhus in Essex, wrote to his friend Sanderson Miller in 1756:

Brown tells me that he has the alteration of Burghley, and that not only of the park, but of the house, which, wherever it is gothick he intends to preserve in that style: and whatever new ornaments he adds are to be so. ... He says he would give the world you should see his designs: having the highest opinion of your skill in this way. I asked him why he did not send them to you ... but his answer was that the drawings were so large it was impossible.[2]

Several of Brown's drawings have survived, including a plan of the ground floor of the house, and elevations of the north and south fronts. He enlarged many of the windows on the south front and gave Gothic arches to the sash-window frames, and he seems also to have suggested a battlemented parapet as an option to his client, since one half of his elevation shows a balustraded parapet and the other shows crenellations. But although the central section of the south front was raised, to regularize it, the original balustrade was apparently put back. Inside the house, Brown did some work in the chapel, where he is thought to have introduced the Coade stone virgins which act as lamp-holders. In the billiard room the Gothick ceiling dates from Brown's time, and so do the pedimented bookcases in the library. Much later on, in 1781-2, Brown made plans for the new staircase and hall which gave improved access to the so-called George Rooms, the state rooms on the first floor of the south front. A discreet touch was needed here, so as not to conflict with the wall paintings by Verrio and others.

On the north side of the house he built the two-storey stable block around a courtyard, with Gothic windows, a crenellated parapet and a hipped roof. More interesting is the charming greenhouse which now serves as the tea-room for visitors. Its position, was designed to square up the lines of some of the old buildings which were at an odd angle to the main block. It faces south and has eleven large windows of Georgian proportions, but with shallow Gothic arches at the top, and three delicate arches in the frames. There are four turrets like miniature versions of those in the main house, and the roof is hipped, with a crenellated parapet. The stonework between the tops of the windows and the string-course is carved into narrow Gothic arcading. Surprisingly for such a long, low building, the Gothic detailing (which is supposed to give a vertical emphasis) is remarkably effective.

Beside the lake is Brown's delightful Bath House, which is neo-Jacobean and therefore closer to the house in style than his other building work. It has a 'fantastick' parapet like a kind of open fretwork, and extraordinary pinnacles at the corners. Built at a time when even Gothic-revival was relatively new (and when Sir William Chambers was advocating the Chinese style), Brown's little Bath House must be one of the earliest attempts at neo-Jacobean, and it makes a charming and light-hearted garden ornament.

Notes

1   E. W. Harcourt, *Harcourt Papers*, vol. VIII p 266, quoted by Stroud.
2   *An Eighteenth-Century Correspondence*, ed. L. Dickens and M. Stanton, 1910, quoted by Stroud.

Castle Ashby

CASTLE Ashby is set in rolling Midland country, and the park has a wide, expansive feeling. 'Castle' is a misnomer: it is a large Elizabethan house, not especially attractive in appearance, the outstanding feature of which is the Palladian 'insertion' in the south front, which is thought to be by Inigo Jones.

Capability Brown started work here in 1761, for Charles, seventh Earl of Northampton. But two years later both the Earl and his wife died of consumption, and work continued for Spencer, the eighth Earl, until he ran into grave financial difficulties in 1774. This left unexecuted the largest feature of Brown's design, which was to have been an enormous lake to the north, near Grendon village. A small part of this lake was made, about fifty years later, but in a slightly different position. These are the Grendon and Scotland Ponds, which can be seen in the distance from the terrace on the north side of the house, though not as clearly as one would like because so many trees have now grown up in front of them. The tower of Grendon Church can also be seen from the terrace, and was clearly used as an 'available' eye-catcher.

A survey prepared immediately before Brown started work at Castle Ashby shows that a chain of small ponds already existed to the east of the house. Brown greatly enlarged these to form the Park Pond and the lower Menagerie Pond. These are fed by the smaller Warren Ponds, which act as silt traps. The Menagerie Pond and the Menagerie itself, beyond the lake, can be seen from the terrace of the house, but the Park Pond is not quite so clearly visible, owing to the size of some of the trees.

On the south side of the house (the Inigo Jones side) there is an immense avenue of trees which existed before Brown's time and which he retained. The avenue was extended in the nineteenth century to a length of three and a half miles. Like many such avenues it looks tremendous on plan, dwarfing the nearby villages, but owing to the lie of the land only a small section can be seen from the house at ground level.

Around the house are some intrusive Victorian terraces, designed by Matthew Digby Wyatt, which have destroyed Brown's original conception of lawns sweeping right up to the house. The complicated carpet bedding of these terraces has itself been destroyed since then, being too labour intensive. The terraces have elaborate balustrades with writing in enormous capital letters as balusters: 'Consider the lilies of the field' is the message. The worst effect of these absurd balustrades is that they interrupt the line of sight, making a large part of the parkland invisible unless you stand immediately behind them.

If Brown's plan had been completed it would have provided a circular walk around the north side of the estate of the greatest variety, giving a succession of views of the house and the lakes from different angles. Today one can trace a route similar to the one planned. On the east and west sides of the house Brown created walks, slightly raised, and separated from the park by a ha-ha. This part of the estate is now described as a nature trail and a guide is available – an intelligent idea which could usefully be extended to include the whole circuit, round to the Dairy Walk.

Starting on the circuit we first pass the church, scarcely noticeable amongst the trees, though not as much screened as the one at Stowe. The planting area through which we now pass is also designed to screen the kitchen garden of Brown's time, which is now an Italian garden with an orangery by M. D. Wyatt. The layout of the Italian Garden has been drastically simplified, but it is still surrounded by *bosco* as all good Italian gardens should be. In the nineteenth century an arboretum was established near the Warren Ponds, an idea which works well as it cannot be seen from the rest of the park, and so any extraneous plantings do not disturb the overall picture. Reaching the Terracotta Bridge we get our first real sight of the lake, obscured till now by the many enormous mature trees in the park.

A further raised walk, still separated from the park by a ha-ha, gives us ever-better views back to the lake. A walk such as this was intended to give a series of pictures, each slightly different as the foreground alters and the prospect gradually changes, a concept explained by W. Burgh in his commentary on William Mason's poem *The English Garden*:

A path is a series of foregrounds; and to adapt each part of this to the various combinations of the distant objects which always result from change of place or aspect, is the proper business of art.

Emerging at the far end, beyond the so-called Knucklebone Arbour, we suddenly get a marvellous view back to the house. It is the classic Brownian view: a cedar in the foreground, the house in the background framed by trees, and the lake in the middle distance with great grass swards stretching before and behind. Only the messy appearance of the terraces immediately in front of the house spoils the clarity of this splendid scene.

Moving round towards the Menagerie we catch further glimpses of the house through the forest of mature trees between the house and the lake; the lawn on this side is less cluttered and more as Brown intended. The view back along the lake is very attractive, with good contouring, especially as seen from the dam between the two lakes. Brown's Menagerie was carefully placed to give the most flattering view of the house, which seen from here, on the diagonal, looks much larger than it really is. The lower Menagerie

Pond is in the middle distance, but regrettably it is now obscured by some alders, which could well be removed.

We continue our circuit with some difficulty. It is to be hoped that a 'trail' will be formed here in due course. We·follow the Park Road, crossing the great sward on the north side which sweeps down to the Scotland and Grendon Ponds, and eventually we reach the Dairy Walk. This is another raised walk with a ha-ha, badly overgrown with nettles and brambles; and when we reach the charming Dairy we find that it now looks onto a dilapidated tennis court.

Part of Castle Ashby village was originally on this side of the house and is shown dotted on Brown's 'Great General Plan', but as it obscured the views across the park it was duly removed.

Brown's foreman at Castle Ashby was John Midgely. An undated letter from him to Brown has survived, and reveals the care with which grading and thinning of planted areas was undertaken:

> I have taken down both the elms, as I could not bring the ground very well together without; and I have shortened the spinny and taken down some of the limes and trimmed some up, so as to let your eye through, without making an avenue, which, when the wall is taken away will make a fine opening ... You'll let me have twenty pounds against next Saturday night to pay the men.

Chillington

———

THE world as seen from Chillington is in all directions a gentle, pastoral and harmonious place; its green lawns and spreading trees seem the result of nature's work rather than of the improver's. Only a lurking pylon or two over the tops of distant trees serve to remind us that we have not stepped back in time and the modern world does still exist. But as we approach the lake we soon have another reminder: the M54 is completely invisible from almost every part of the estate, but its noise has destroyed the peace of the lake area and all the southern part of the estate. To stand beside the lake is a strangely disparate experience: seeing the cool, tranquil peaceful scene, and hearing the constant hum of traffic, rising sometimes to a roar, that drowns the sound of water lapping, the noise of the wind in the branches overhead and the cries of water-birds across the lake.

The house has a perfect setting on slightly rising ground, backed by mature oaks and beech trees. The main front is simple but effective, in red brick with a central full-height stone portico of unfluted Ionic columns, which are slightly blackened with age. It was designed by Soane, but is surprisingly similar to Brown's own work elsewhere, probably owing to the influence of Henry Holland, in whose office Soane worked until about

1777. The end bays are heightened (like Croome, and also Stowe before later alterations), a clever device used by Soane to link the new front with the earlier south front.
There is little in the way of a garden near the house: the main front is still surrounded
by lawns, and a small unobtrusive formal rose garden exists on the south side, designed
by Inigo Triggs[1] in 1911.

The mile-long avenue of oaks to the north-east was planted in 1725 and preserved by
Brown. A path leading diagonally south-east from the house leads to a narrow winding
canal, and on into Old Park Wood. The canal disappears then reappears, still only the
width of a river, backed by gently sloping contours topped by groups of Scots pine. The
water is still and dark, like a black mirror. From this side the beeches lean out across
the canal and on the far side willows and reeds encroach on the water. The woodland
on the left is dense with *Rhododendron ponticum*, yew and holly, which conceal any awkward contours. Across the canal some of Brown's 'clumps' still look elegant on the
sloping fields. In dense woodland the canal turns, and we see Paine's Bridge in the
distance, a simple, one-arched classical design in pinkish stone. Immediately beyond the
bridge the enormous lake appears, bright and reflective after the shady canal. It is
bordered by dense tree-planting, broken here and there by fields.

The path at first follows the water's edge, but soon it turns into the wood. Sadly, the
tall Gothick Temple that stood here has recently been demolished because it had been
allowed to become unsafe.

Soon we come to the Ionic Temple, possibly by Robert Adam, and here the wood-
lands open to a new view of the lake, with the three-arched Sham Bridge (by Brown)[2]
in the far distance, while closer on the opposite side is the almost ruined Grecian
Temple. Behind the Ionic Temple the M54 lies hidden. Further exploration of the park
yields varying views of the lake, and a backward glance reveals another view of Paine's
Bridge. After crossing a bridge over a creek, the route leads to the Sham Bridge and
eventually takes us back across lawns to the house.

NOTES

1 H. Inigo Triggs, architect, garden-designer and writer, 1876–1923. As his *Formal Garden in England* (1892) shows, his
approach was strongly eclectic.
2 James Paine, *Plans of Noblemen's and Gentlemen's Houses* (1767), according to Stroud.

Claremont

W HEN Robert Clive came back from India in 1767, successful and immensely rich,
he bought several properties, one of which was Claremont, near Esher in Surrey.
It was already an important landscape garden, described in 1727 by Stephen Switzer
as 'the noblest of any in Europe' – though perhaps that was going too far.

Sir John Vanbrugh had bought the estate for his own use in 1708, 'the situation being singularly romantic', he said. He built himself a small house with walled gardens covering seven acres, which still exist in part. Three years later he sold the property to the Duke of Newcastle, who later became Prime Minister. He was also Earl of Clare, and this, together with the mount near the house, gave the estate its name. The Duke commissioned Vanbrugh to enlarge the house and design the Belvedere which still stands on the mount: it is a kind of sham castle, rather like a brick keep with a tall turret on each corner. The grounds were landscaped by Bridgeman and a plan from *Vitruvius Britannicus*, 1725, shows a mostly formal layout with a wide avenue of trees, four abreast on each side, stretching out in front of the house, and a longer avenue of the same design running parallel with the principal front. The most interesting part of the grounds, however, then and now, is beyond the mount, not visible from the house, nor even connected to it visually. Here Bridgeman made a circular lake and the famous turf amphitheatre, which has recently been restored by the National Trust.

After Vanbrugh's death the Duke employed William Kent to alter the garden, and two surviving plans by John Rocque, of 1738 and 1750, record how Bridgeman's immense avenues were removed by degrees, in favour of scattered clumps like those Kent had planted at Euston. Kent also changed Bridgeman's circular pool into a larger informal lake with an island, on which he built an elegant pavilion. At the southern end the lake was fed by a cascade with three stone arches, similar to his work at Stowe and Rousham.

When Lord Clive bought the estate from the Duke of Newcastle's widow in 1768, he decided that Vanbrugh's house was too damp and inconvenient, and, money being no object, proceeded to pull it down. Sir William Chambers, who was already rebuilding Clive's house in Shropshire, was asked to provide plans for the new house. Brown was also asked and his design was eventually chosen, much to Chambers' annoyance. Seven of Brown's contract drawings survive, marked 'referred to by us in our agreement' and signed by both him and his client.

Brown's alterations to the landscape seem to have been limited, his main contribution being to move the Portsmouth road further away from the house. At some stage the cascade beside the lake was altered to a grotto, and this awaits renovation by the National Trust. The Kent gardens with the lake and amphitheatre are now owned by the Trust, but the house and Belevedere belong to Claremont School. Although the general impression of the landscape on the side surrounding the school is pleasant enough, there have been inevitable compromises as the school has outgrown its original size. The siting of the swimming pool and tennis courts is unhappy, and the impact of the school buildings as one approaches the main house is more unfortunate. They form a motley collection, displaying every nuance of style of the 1960s and '70s. Brown's solution, I suppose, would be to plant a thick band of evergreens between them and the drive to screen them from view on the south-east side. Of all these new buildings the booby prize must go to the headmaster's house, a dreary suburban bungalow looking quite lost in a corner of a Brown landscape. A large part of the park had already been lost, however, before the school moved in, for in about 1930 the estate was sold off in lots, and large areas were used for residential development and now form part of the 'stockbroker belt'.

In contrast to Vanbrugh's wide-spreading, turreted house, Brown's is compact, neat and plain. Such simplicity of style and planning represented not only good taste but also value for money. The 'offices' are all in the basement, thus preserving the purity of the isolated, square shape of the building, which has a 'fair face' on all four sides, almost like a garden ornament. There are no rambling subsidiary courtyards: instead, the stables and some servants' accommodation were placed some distance away, beside Vanbrugh's walled kitchen garden. But more accommodation was required than could be squeezed into the basement, and Brown's solution to this was characteristically ingenious. An additional area for 'offices' and storage rooms was built at basement level around a small circular courtyard on the east side. The ground level was then raised to cover it, leaving only the circular courtyard open to the sky. It was approached and linked to the house by an arched tunnel, which had the added advantage of discreetly hiding the tradesmen's entrance, an arrangement reminiscent of his double entrance drive for George III at Richmond Park. The gentle mound that resulted was then covered with planting so that the opening above the courtyard was completely hidden, and remains so today. An elderly drawing in the house shows the basement-level plan, and indicates clearly an elaborate drainage system, presumably dating from Brown's time.

The house is built of smooth white bricks with Portland stone to the window surrounds, cornice and roof-level balustrade. About a million and a half bricks were made in the park during a two-year period, after which six acres of ground had to be made good, at a cost of £100.[1] The main elevations are of nine bays each, and there are seven to each of the sides. It is thus almost square in its overall shape, compared with Brown's earlier Croome Court, which forms a longer and thinner rectangle: this eliminated any need for corner turrets, and served to further simplify the design. The main, south front has a giant portico of four detached Corinthian columns, with a wide flight of twenty-two steps up to the principal storey. The back has a pediment and Corinthian pilasters (with only a token projection) and two curving staircases with elegant iron balustrades lead up to the piano nobile. The Corinthian capitals, according to the records, were carved by a certain Henry Wood, at a cost of £14 each, and the matching pilasters cost £4 10s. The six lions' heads in the friezes cost 20s. each, while three masks of satyrs cost 36s. altogether. Under the cornice, the 294 projecting modillions which support it were 4s 6d. each. The size of the commission made it necessary for Brown to look for help, and many of the details were done with the assistance of Henry Holland, his partner and later his son-in-law.

The interior of the house is well preserved and in spite of its use as part of a school has the air of being loved and lived in. Most impressive is the Entrance Hall, with its red scagliola columns (imitation marble made from plaster and marble chips). The floor pattern and recessed ceiling are oval, counterpointed against the square shape of the room itself. This design was later claimed by Sir John Soane, who worked for Henry Holland from 1772 onwards, but as he was only nineteen at the time, he probably worked under Brown's or Holland's direction. There are decorative relief panels on the walls, and other notable features include the plaster ceiling and fireplace with caryatids in the Great Drawing Room, and the centrally placed, top-lit staircase.

Altogether Clive is reputed to have spent £100,000 on his house and gardens at Claremont, but his riches did not bring him happiness and he did not live long to enjoy them. If the windows rattled he is supposed to have wedged them with sovereigns, which he would forget to remove; the housemaids, it is said, used to pray for a south-westerly gale.

NOTE

1 This and other information from *The Story of Claremont*, 1983, by Phyllis M. Cooper, the Claremont Guide.

Coombe Abbey

———

Tᴴᴇ Coombe Abbey estate has not yet recovered from the fifty years of neglect that followed the death of the young Earl Craven in 1921. It was acquired by Coventry City Council and is now run as a Country Park serving the West Midlands. It is clear that the management see it as an accessible slice of countryside where people from nearby urban areas can relax in green surroundings, and where parties of school-children, reared amongst tarmac and concrete, can learn about the natural environment. The size of the car parks gives some indication of the enormous numbers who come to Coombe Abbey on a summer week-end. This puts great pressure on the park, and explains the number of iron railings and concrete litter bins. But there is a definite conflict of intentions here between the recreational needs of city-dwellers, the conservation of wildlife and the countryside, and the preservation of a historic landscape. On the conservation side, nettles make good breeding grounds for butterflies, for instance, and the denser the vegetation the better the habitat for a wide variety of wildlife. One of the islands that Brown created in the lake is now the site of the largest heronry in the West Midlands, and great crested grebes, coots and many other species of water birds abound. But Coombe Abbey is not a piece of wild country and was never the special habitat of anything in particular: it was created artificially out of agricultural land, as a work of art.

Estates such as this must be managed: they cannot just be left, or they will cease to exist. The lake is not a natural feature, and without careful maintenance silt soon builds up and banks are liable to collapse (the problem of stagnant water was noticed as early as 1789 by the traveller and diarist Lord Torrington, who refused to be impressed by the park). It is to the Council's credit that one of the first tasks it undertook was to clear the lake of reeds, which by that time covered three-quarters of the water area. Extensive and costly stonework repairs are due to begin shortly on the main façade of the house, which is falling around the ears of the visitors. Brown's Menagerie building is being renovated and its domed lead-covered roof has been almost entirely rebuilt following the discovery of dry rot. This should be followed by some tree-felling so that this feature at the far end of the lake can be seen to greater advantage.

A woodland management scheme is badly needed at present. There are large areas where old trees which are past their best are being killed off by young sycamores, with brambles, nettles and sycamore seedlings making a ten-foot-high jungle. A scene like this has none of the attractiveness of natural woodland, much less the beauty of park-land.

The lake is the largest artifical water in Warwickshire, covering nearly eighty acres, and was not one of Brown's easiest projects. The ground is rather flat, and although this enabled him to make a very large lake, it is also a very shallow one. Nowhere is it more than four and a half feet deep. Silting seems to have been a problem from the start, mostly because of the nature of the sub-soil. The shallow contours of the land also make the angle between the viewer and the lake very low, so that the slightest undulation of the ground can block the view of the lake entirely. No doubt it was for this reason that the material dug out to form the lake was concentrated in one place to form a mound on the north side of the house. Later Nesfield cut down Brown's trees on the mound and planted a great number of Wellingtonias.

Brown's work at Coombe Abbey was undertaken for the sixth Baron Craven, who owned about 7,000 acres, and the work probably began in 1770. The house is now a hotch-potch of various styles and periods. Originally there was a Cistercian abbey on the site and a few fragments remain. There is an Elizabethan wing with ogee gables, and next to this, in a rather uncomfortable juxtaposition, is the classical west front with its central pediment, built in 1684. An engraving by Kip, of 1707, shows extensive formal gardens, but there is some doubt as to its accuracy since the house is not drawn correctly. After Brown's time a Victorian wing in French château style was built by Eden Nesfield, but this was later demolished, except for the ground floor. The present entrance with its wide avenue must have made more sense when this wing was standing; today the building makes a weak and confused impression at the end of the vista. Brown's entrance was from the West Lodge, a classical triumphal arch which dates from Brown's time and is probably by him. The drive from there has now disappeared under agricultural land, but when adjoining land is purchased by the Council, consideration will be given to reopening this access, which would be much more effective. From this angle the first sight of the building would have been of the classical west façade, with glimpses of the lake to the left. The area round the house itself is rather tatty, and has the municipal atmosphere of a city park.

Originally Brown's lake was some way from the house and a smooth lawn stretched from the water to the west front, as can be seen in sketches done by Maria Johnson in 1796-7, now held by the Herbert Art Gallery in Coventry. However, when the Victorian additions were made to the house the lake was extended towards the house and a moat was created on the south side. At the same time formal gardens with clipped box hedges were added in front of the west façade, which still remain, although the box has now grown too big.

Seen from the house today, the lake makes surprisingly little impact considering its enormous extent. This is mainly because the banks are now overgrown with willows that overhang the water and reduce its apparent size. Brown's usual approach was to leave the banks of his lakes rather bare, the smooth grass dotted with specimen trees sweeping down to the water, and this was his design for Coombe, as is shown on a plan prepared for Lord Craven in 1778 by Matthias Baker. Study of this plan yields several other points of interest.

As though it had been formed from the Smite Brook, Brown placed the lake further south than the original line of the brook, so that it would lie more or less centrally on the axis of the west front. It then sweeps round in a gentle curve to the north, where it originally disappeared past specimen trees into thicker planting. Seen from the house it looks vast, even though less than half of it is visible from this end. Just where it begins to curve out of view Brown created an island (now the heronry) and also brought the trees forward from the boundary, both to confuse the eye and soften the effect. At this point, looking back up the lake, there should be a splendid view of the house, but the present undergrowth of willows and sycamores makes it impossible.

The effect of endlessness is increased by an enormous hook-shaped curve at the western end of the lake. The raised bank which forms the dam is hidden in the belt of trees which also screens the park completely from the nearby Coventry road. This end of the lake is the most attractive part today, although officially it is open only to fishermen. At one point the circular weir outlet and arched overflow can be seen, although a new and slightly obtrusive concrete weir has now been constructed by the water engineers, who see the lake as a reservoir. At the other end, near the Top Pool (now the children's boating lake), the lake has been reduced by silting to the size of a stream.

The nearby stable block and various other buildings on the site may well be by Brown, including the Gothic East Lodge. The sham Gothic castle which used to house the dog kennels was unfortunately demolished in 1860. Brown also undertook some minor internal alterations to the house.

Dodington

—

DODINGTON Park is on the edge of the Cotswolds, set just below the escarpment, a most unusual situation for a Brown park. The land slopes down quite steeply from the Bath road to Dodington village, and is divided into several valleys. Alexander Pope remarked that the situation was 'pretty enough, romantic, covered with woody hills, stumbling upon one another confusedly.'

Brown's park was to surround a gabled Elizabethan house, on an H plan, owned by Sir William Codrington. According to his account book he received £1,368 for work done at Dodington between 1764 and 1767. There is no trace now of the previous garden, which Pope described as having mounts and waterfalls. About 1795 a later member of the Codrington family demolished the house, and a new one was built on the same site by James Wyatt.

The approach to the house starts high on the escarpment at the Bath Lodge, which is a charming classical rotunda, with a colonnade and a dome. The road plunges into dense woodland, mostly of indigenous beech, and winds through various open spaces between the trees before reaching the valley, where many fine trees are scattered in groups. Eventually we see the house, and Brown's upper lake, which runs north-south. Usually Brown tried to bring at least part of the lake to a position parallel with the front of the house: at Sandbeck, for example, he extended a creek from the main body of the lake to do this. But at Dodington, where the house is set in quite a narrow valley, the lake is seen end-on, leading up to the house, instead of lying across the line of sight in Brown's usual manner.

The remarkable thing about the upper lake is the way it has been preserved with the banks clear of planting, as Brown intended, to reveal the excellent contouring of the ground. Immediately above it is another very small lake, no doubt intended to act as a silt-trap. Planting is clustered around the dam at the end of the upper lake, with ilex

Right: The Park Pond at Castle Ashby, Northamptonshire.

Below: Plan of Coombe Abbey, Warwickshire, 1778. The original line of the stream is marked. Brown's entrance drive from the south-west is also shown.

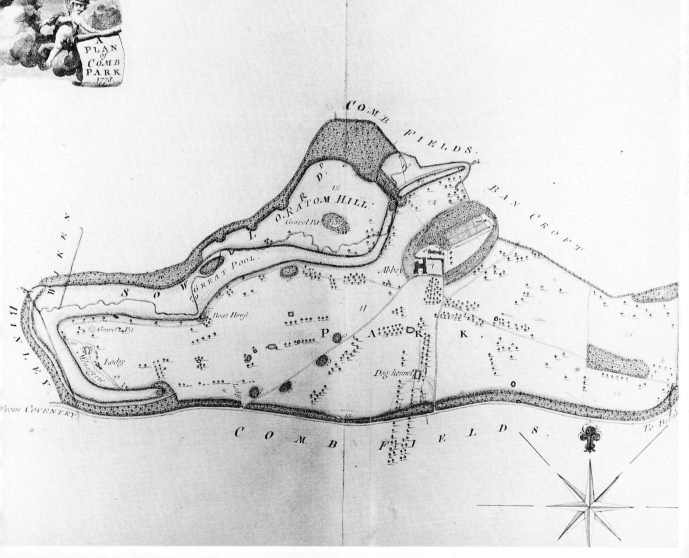

Dodington Park, Avon, a watercolour showing the later house by James Wyatt, with one of the Brown lakes on the right-hand side.

Brown's design for a rustic bridge at Rothley was not carried out, but the roadway between the lakes at Grimsthorpe is somewhat similar.

The ruins of Roche Abbey. Trees grow amongst the ruins, and there is ivy on the walls, in a romantic manner.

Sandbeck House from Malpas Hill. This view of the Brown landscape shows the lawns sweeping uninterruptedly up to the house.

Trentham Park, Staffordshire. The tree-covered islands have been carefully positioned to mask the extent of the lake.

The elevation of Trentham House, as altered by Brown and Henry Holland for the second Lord Gower. Demolished in the mid-nineteenth century.

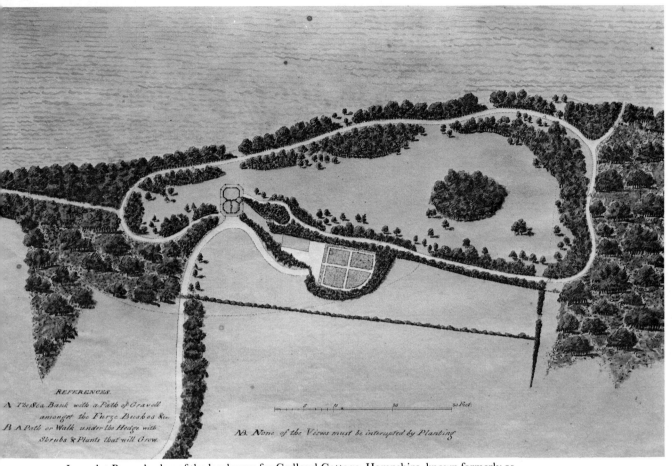

REFERENCES.

A The Sea Bank with a Path of Gravell amongst the Furze Bushes &c.
B A Path or Walk under the Hedge with Shrubs & Plants that will Grow.

NB. None of the Views must be interupted by Planting

Lancelot Brown's plan of the landscape for Cadland Cottage, Hampshire, known formerly as Boarn Hill.

Claremont House, Surrey, from the east. One of Brown's finest essays in the English Palladian manner.

A view of the landscape from Harewood House, from a drawing by Lady Sheffield (née Harriet Lascelles), made about 1825.

A sketch showing an unexecuted bridge at Harewood. The subtle planting shown in these early sketches no longer exists; nor does the temple by Paine.

The village of Milton Abbas, laid out to a plan which Brown made *c*1774. Seen across the lake the houses form a picturesque cluster in the landscape.

Undergrowth and weeds at Milton. This area was once part of the lake. Sadly, many of Brown's landscapes are now in this kind of derelict condition, and good maintenance is the exception.

The lake at Patshull, Staffordshire.

Tong Castle seen across the lake. Today the M54 motorway runs across the site of the house.

trees and beeches underplanted with many evergreens such as box, Portuguese laurels and aucubas.

The difference in level between the two lakes has been exploited by making a cascade in a castellated Gothic surround, fed by a curving aqueduct from above. It is not certain whether this is by Brown or by Wyatt. A few steps lead to the end of the upper lake, and there is a fine view looking up the valley towards the escarpment, where the hills are topped with woods. Beyond the cascade is a matching Gothic icehouse with a turret, and from here also there are good views of the house and of both lakes. Another good vantage point is the top of the terrace steps which lead down from the small formal garden on the south-east side (the front that faces the approach road).

The tall planting at the far end of the lower lake acts as a buffer to contain the narrow valley, preventing a possible 'corridor' effect, and on the north-west side it serves to hide Dodington village. The trees around the lake include a fern-leaved beech (*Fagus sylvaticum heterophylla*), a Lucombe oak, a weeping ash and two large walnut trees. At the far end of the lake is a classical garden building in a slightly decayed state, with unusual fluted columns, which was positioned to give a flattering view of the house looking back up the lake.

The grounds are in a good condition, carefully maintained (the only jarring note being a number of wooden fences which interrupt the sweeping lines of the landscape) and the park provides a fine impression of Brown's work, virtually unspoilt by later additions.

Grimsthorpe

Aɴ excellent example of a Brown landscape can be seen at Grimsthorpe in Lincolnshire. Few traces remain of the earlier landscape, nor is there any intrusion of a later one. The pale colour of the castle contrasts beautifully with the green lawns that surround it, sweeping down to the lake. There is no other feature; the castle is enough. The whole landscape is like an immense, shallow saucer, and on the skyline irregular belts of trees form the horizon. The lake is large enough for the landscape, and what is so miraculously preserved is the wide, smooth surface of the lawns, perfectly contoured and not cluttered with trees, and meeting the edges of the lake as neatly as Brown intended. It is true that the smaller, upper lake is a little overgrown, and the far side of the main lake has its share of nettles, but the general effect is still magnificent. The only regret is that the sham bridge is rather overgrown and cannot be seen to advantage.

While parts of the castle date from the thirteenth century, the main part of the house was built in the reign of Henry VIII, with sympathetic alterations in matching style made during the nineteenth century. The most interesting part architecturally is quite different: this is the Vanbrugh wing, on the north-west side of the house, looking out on the extensive North Avenue of trees which pre-dates Brown's work. On the south side of the house are 'The Groves', a wooded area with paths that look out across the park; this is the remains of Stephen Switzer's work, also done before Brown's time.

Brown's client at Grimsthorpe was the Duke of Ancaster, who was one of the Lords who had signed the petition for Brown's royal appointment. It appears that Brown had already done some work at Ancaster House at Richmond upon Thames. His first recorded visit to Grimsthorpe was in 1771. Afterwards a survey was prepared by Samuel Lapidge, and in 1772 Brown sent the Duke several drawings, including one for 'Water in the Bottom' and one for 'a Sham Bridge to be placed at the head of that water the road to Grimsthorpe goes over'.[1] This was to have eleven arches, spanning three hundred and fifty feet in all, but was never built. Instead there is a series of rockwork arches, rather similar to the bridge proposed at Rothley (but also never built). Brown's charges for the drawings amounted to £105. It seems that the work was carried out by the Duke's estate staff, but the dam was made by an engineer called John Grundy before Brown arrived on the scene.

The most impressive approach to the castle is from the village on the south side of the park, past an imposing entrance lodge and along the Four Mile Drive, through what was once the deer park. As we emerge from some plantations, a view of the lake and the castle beyond lies suddenly before us. In Arthur Young's words:

... the house appears at first view (as well as afterwards as you proceed) extremely magnificent; being admirably situated on a hill, with some very fine woods stretching away to each side ...[1]

NOTE

1   Arthur Young, *Six Months' Tour through the North of England* (1770).

Petworth

PETWORTH is perhaps the most perfectly preserved of all Brown's parks. The wonderfully smooth lawns sweep away in every direction, kept in order by the resident deer herd. As originally intended, the placing of the sunk fences allows the deer to come right to the windows, and not even a gravel drive separates the lawns from the house.

With Brown's usual precision, the lake can just be seen from the ground floor windows of the house; he did not waste his clients' money on excessive excavation. When we step out onto the grass, about fifteen inches lower, it is no longer visible. On the right looking out from the house is one of Brown's famous knolls, exquisitely contoured, and crowned with trees, leaving the lower slopes exposed. In front of us the park stretches out, and to the left is a glimpse of sympathetic Sussex countryside. As we walk towards the lake we see an 'eye-catcher' on a distant ridge; this is the Monument, designed by Sir John Soane about 1812, a castle-like affair. (A keeper's lodge with towers had been shown by Brown on his original plan in 1752.)

Turning round, we can look back at the great façade of Petworth House. It is perhaps rather featureless against the smooth landscape: the tough architecture of Blenheim or Grimsthorpe makes a better foil to a Brown park. At one time there was a dome (there are records of payment to the slater for the 'sircular roofe'); but this feature, which probably would have made the house more arresting, was removed in the 1770s.

Brown first went to Petworth in 1751, when he was still living at Stowe, and his plan, which is on display at Petworth, shows several features reminiscent of Stowe: a grotto at the far end of the lake, a sham bridge at the southern end, nearer the house, and, in the Pleasure Grounds, a Rotunda, similar to Vanbrugh's at Stowe. This last feature was the only one to materialize. The plan has various annotations, such as 'Fine undulated hill, adorned with groups of cedars and pines', and 'plantations of shrubs and plants of low growth that will not prevent the prospects'. One of Brown's last tasks at Petworth was to move the road on the western boundary further away from the house, which allowed more parkland between the lake and the boundary.

The Pleasure Grounds are on the north side of the house and are a particularly fine example of their kind, containing magnificent sweet chestnuts and a fine collection of plants of many kinds, some added in the late nineteenth century. Before Brown's time this area consisted of straight walks through a birch plantation. Some of these he retained, but others he replaced with winding gravel paths. The Doric Temple was moved from 'the Terass' to its present position, and the Rotunda was added on a ridge at the far end, giving wide views which contrast with the enclosed feeling in the Pleasure Grounds.

It is astonishing that from the park there is no hint of Petworth town: it is only when we are further back from the house that the church can be seen over the roof. In fact the house is very awkwardly placed, squashed against the little town, and the approach on that side is to the nondescript east front, which has none of the magnificence of the west front. But there is no hint of any of this from the park: nothing exists, it seems, but this marvellous unspoilt landscape and the great west front framed by magnificent trees; and the proximity of Petworth town was not the only difficulty Brown had to contend with, making Petworth far from the ideal site. The house does not sit on 'rising' ground, as at Berrington or Kimberley, and so does not face 'the greater landscape' of Sussex, as it might have done if Brown had started from scratch. Moreover the parkland does not lie stretched out in front of the house in the ideal way; Grimsthorpe is the perfect example of this, where the vast horizon, like a rim, surrounds the park with distant tree-planting. At Petworth the landscape falls away awkwardly in several directions, with a bony ridge running down the centre, which fortunately is slightly to the right when seen from the house.

There are two landscapes at Petworth. One, centred on the Upper Pond, features the house, and is fairly well contained, apart from the glimpse already mentioned of distant country. Beyond the lake lies an open valley, which takes us round the ridge of high ground into a second, wider landscape. This is like a great amphitheatre, backed by another ridge on the north-west side of the park, on which the Monument stands. Large groups of specimen trees spill down from this ridge, while on the eastern boundary the Lower Pond is just a small feature in the large landscape. The ridge that divides the two is planted with a few clumps, and from here we see the 'borrowed landscape' of Sussex.

This is a truly three-dimensional landscape, to be appreciated from every angle. In early Renaissance gardens the view is best seen from fixed points; French gardens were a little more linear; while in the English garden it became *de rigeur* to lead the observer along the curving line of a serpentine, gravel path (the classic example survives today at Stourhead), along which all the designed views are displayed. But Brown goes a step further: such is the quality of his parks that they can be viewed from any position.

The carefulness of the contouring shows up to greater advantage at Petworth than almost any other of Brown's parks because of the high standard of maintenance, which has kept the edges of the lakes clear of trees, nettles and undergrowth.

Recently new areas of planting have been added, some of which will help protect the park from traffic noise. Some are large circular clumps in the Brownian manner, of which there are already several good examples here.

Sandbeck Park and Roche Abbey

THE splendid house was built by James Paine for the fourth Earl of Scarbrough in 1765. The garden front is particularly good, with its projecting portico of two-storey Corinthian columns supported on three rusticated arches. There is a fine view of the park from here. This house is more sculptural, more heavily modelled, than Brown's own work, which is more severe with plain surfaces. The whole setting forms a perfectly coherent picture, being unspoilt by later additions. It seems that the landscape around the house was created at the same time as the building, in the 1760s; the work at Roche Abbey, however, was done later, from 1764.

Although there are coal mines and mining towns within a few miles of Sandbeck, there is no trace of them from here: looking from the garden front the view is bounded by a ridge called Malpas Hill on the right-hand side, which until recently was densely planted with beech trees. Following a recent summer drought about a thousand trees died of beech-bark disease, leaving a rather thin layer of trees along this horizon. They have been replanted, but will of course take many years to mature.

The contours at Sandbeck allowed for a lake quite close to the house, which is always advantageous in that the lake does not have to be so large to look impressive. Looking from the garden front the main part of the lake lies to the left, and there are two narrower 'creeks', one of which runs across parallel with the house, but is now obscured by a large number of specimen trees. The removal of one or two copper beeches dating from the Victorian period would perhaps remedy this. The water in the main part of the lake is deep, but the creeks are rather shallow, and some extensive (and expensive) dredging has recently been carried out by the present Lord Scarbrough, who has also had a simple timber bridge rebuilt.

This is another of Capability Brown's natural landscapes, which is to say there are no temples or grottoes, nor even a stone bridge. There are one or two buildings by Paine in the park, such as the Head Gardener's house and the Chaplain's house, which is now in poor repair. It is interesting that these two houses, on opposite sides of the park, both have their own landscape setting. The Chaplain's house is intended to relate to the Lower Lake, an effect which is now blurred; today the lake is virtually surrounded with willows. The Head Gardener's house also faces a small lake which is now in such a poor state that it is scarcely visible behind undergrowth.

On this side of the house, the entrance side, an avenue leads down to Roche Abbey. However, the contours prevent one seeing very far down this avenue from the house. The abbey is still owned by Lord Scarbrough, though it is in the care of English Heritage (the Department of the Environment) as an Ancient Monument, and the fabric is kept in good repair. It seems that although the ruins were some distance from the new house they were too good an opportunity to miss. There was no need here for sham castles like the ones at Wimpole or Coombe Abbey; here was the genuine thing, only awaiting the right setting.

In 1774 a contract was drawn up between Lord Scarbrough and Brown for various improvements:

Then an Agreement made between the Earl of Scarbrough on the one Part and Lancelot Brown on the other, for the underwritten Articles of Works to be Performed at Sandbeck in the County of York – (To Wit)

Article the 1st – To compleat the Sunk Fence which seperates the Park from the Farm and to Build a Wall in it, as also to make a proper Drain at the bottom of the Sunk Fence to keep it Dry.

Article the 2nd – To demolish all the old Ponds which are in the Lawn, and to Level and Drain all the Ground where they are.

Article the 3rd – To Drain and Level all the ground which is between the above mentioned Sunk Fence and the old Canals mentioned in the Second Article. To plant whatever Trees may be thought necessary for Ornament in that Space discribed in this Article and to sow with Grass seeds and Dutch clover the whole of the Ground wherever the Turff has been broke up or disturbed by Drains, Leveling, or by making the Sunk Fence.

Article the 4th – To make good and keep up a Pond for the use of the Stables.

Article the 5th – To finish all the Valley of Roach Abbey in all its Parts, According to the Ideas fixed on with Lord Scarbrough (with Poet's feeling and with Painter's Eye) beginning at the Head of the Hammer Pond, and continuing up the Valley towards Loton (also Loughton) in the Morn as far as Lord Scarbrough's Ground goes, and to continue the Water and Dress the Valley up by the Present Farm House until it comes to the seperation fixed for the Boundary of the New Farm. N.B. The Paths in the Wood are included in this Discription and every thing but the Buildings.

The said Lancelot Brown does Promise for himself, His Heirs, Executors and Administrators, to perform or cause to be Performed in the the Best manner in His or Their Power between the Date hereof and December One Thousand Seven Hundred and Seventy Seven, the above written five Articles.

For the Due Performance of the above written five Articles The Earl of Scarbrough does Promise for himself, His Heirs Administrators and Executors to Pay or cause to be Paid at the underwritten Times of Payment Two Thousand Seven hundred Pounds of Lawful money of England and three Hundred Pounds in consideration of and for the Plans and trouble Brown has had for his Lordship at Sandbeck previous to this Agreement.

Lord Scarbrough to find Rough Timber, four able Horses, Carts and Harness for them, wheelbarrows and Planks as also Trees and Shrubs.

The reference to 'Poet's feeling and Painter's Eye' comes from William Mason's *The English Garden*, published 1772. The implication seems to be that a lot was to be left to Brown's taste and judgement in the course of the work. Levels and contours are hard to work out in advance, and many decisions have to be left until the operation is actually in progress.

At Blenheim Brown raised the level of the water under Vanbrugh's existing Grand Bridge; but here at Roche he raised the level of the ground by several feet. The effect was to hide all the low-level ruins and emphasize the taller remains; as William Gilpin put it, 'The ruin stands now on a neat bowling green'. But this effect has now disappeared, because at the end of the nineteenth century, interest in history having overtaken appreciation of picturesque scenery, the bases and fragments were all excavated again. The antiquarians also removed the ivy from the walls and cleared the trees which Brown had left growing amongst the ruins. A contemporary drawing shows the original scene, a highly romantic conception, demonstrating clearly that Brown's work was not all, 'shaven' and bland, as his later critics complained.

Today the abbey can still be seen in the valley adjoining the Maltby to Oldcoates road. The long narrow lake which Brown created in the valley has sadly disappeared, and so too have some of the large mature trees on the slopes (but it is hoped to replace these shortly). It is altogether a most romantic setting, with limestone cliffs projecting from the valley sides here and there in a manner worthy of Salvator Rosa. Brown probably also designed the simple Gothic cottage near the entrance, with its own lawn stretching across to the ruins.

More could be made of the various attractive cascades which still remain on the River Ryton, one of which betrays the existence of the larger, upper lake nowadays hidden by trees. To reach this we must turn right just beyond the old ruined gateway and follow the track. It is regrettable that this lake is now in poor condition; the view across it to the ruins must have been enchanting. Even when the project was scarcely complete William Gilpin wrote, with a note of criticism, that Brown had

formed a very beautiful scene. But I fear that is too magnificent ... it is possible that this lake may in some future time become its situation; when the marks of the spade and the pick-axe are removed, when osiers flourish, and its naked banks become fringed and covered with wood.

Today the wheel has turned full circle and Gilpin's wishes have come true: the valley sides of the upper lake are so densely wooded that one cannot see anything for the trees. From the stepping stones by the cascade some of the lower ruins can be seen, but many trees need felling, and one can see neither the lake from the path in the valley nor the intended views across the lake to the ruins.

Sherborne

THE finest approach to Sherborne is from the northern entrance to the park, near Pinford, which unfortunately is not open to the public. The drive descends steeply, with the deer park on Jerusalem Hill facing us, while to the right some planting hides the lake until we reach the Robert Adam bridge. From here a splendid romantic view appears, with a surprise effect equal to the one at Blenheim. If the Blenheim view is astonishingly wide, this is a long vista, looking down the length of the lake, which is nearly a mile long and covers sixty acres. The romantic outline of the house can be seen in the distance, nestling amongst trees and poised beside the lake. The part of the lake in the foreground is unfortunately badly silted up and overgrown with reeds, and nineteenth-century maps show that this has been the case for many decades. The main part of the lake is in excellent condition, however, having been dredged in about 1977. The restoration of this end of the lake would be well worthwhile if only for the sake of the exceptional view.

The other entrance drive, the normal approach, is also good. Passing the dignified stable buildings we come suddenly almost to the edge of the lake, but from here its great length is not apparent because of its curved shape. On the far side of the lake is the house with its extraordinary clusters of turrets and chimneys, and to the left the medieval castle, framed by gaunt cedars and looking even more picturesque.

The house was built in 1594 for Sir Walter Ralegh. Viewed from this approach it lacks the classic lawn sweeping down to the water – which was impossible owing to the cluster of subsidiary buildings around the house – but instead the trees are clustered round it, as if the building itself was a picturesque ruin.

It is the north front which has a grassy slope down to the lake, and here the house faces the old castle. The ancient cedars which frame it are now past their best: they used to lean out across the water, but having been pruned over-zealously for safety they look extraordinarily long-legged.

The edges of the lake are clear of planting and the intended effect of well contoured, exposed ground surfaces has been maintained. The planted area between the drive and the old castle has been cleared of undergrowth during the last few years and a sensible policy of gradual renewal is being undertaken. This planting, which was designed to screen the stables and kitchen garden area, seems to have been mainly beech originally, with an underplanting of yew and holly.

A pleasant walk along the east side of the lake leads to Sir Walter Ralegh's seat, near the old castle. Gradually the view widens out until we can see right down the length of the lake, and beyond the house to Jerusalem Hill and the tree-clad slopes of the distant deer park. Near the stream and cascade is Pope's Seat, from which the view is particularly good. A romantic ruined tower, covered in ivy, stands nearby.

From the south side of the house, there is a view over a long tree-covered ridge which runs roughly parallel with the main body of the lake. This is particularly attractive at the far end, where the whole outline of planting is softened by scatterings of specimen trees spilling down the slopes. Nearer the house, unfortunately, there is some intrusion by farmland, and the geometrical division of fields partly spoils the effect.

Trentham

Just south of the scarred industrial landscape of the Potteries lies an astonishing contrast: the lush romantic scenery of Trentham Park. A good vantage point is the lakeside balustrade in the later Italian garden, from which there is a long view, with wooded slopes on the right-hand side, various wooded islands on the lake and the Monument at the far end on Tittensor Hill.[1]

Brown's lake, which is about three-quarters of a mile long, was formed from a smaller existing pool; he had no difficulties with water supply, since the River Trent provides an ample source. His plan, prepared in 1759, shows the river flowing through the lake, but today it flows parallel with the lake, mostly hidden by planting and banks. It is possible, however, that it has always been the way it is now, as Brown did not always stick rigidly to plan with regard to his lakes.

A few years later Brown (in partnership by then with Henry Holland) redesigned the house for Lord Gower. The new front was fifteen bays wide and three storeys high, with a pediment over the three end bays on each side. He also designed a pair of lodges in the south-west corner of the estate, near Tittensor, which once marked the main entrance, but are nowadays stranded in a remote corner of the park. John Byng (Lord Torrington) later wrote that the house was 'wonderfully altered from the grand to the modern', and in the park, 'my old friend L. Brown is to be traced at every turn: he certainly was a grand planner and leveller of ground – and a judicious former of water; the lake, here, is very fine ...'[2] Brown's plan contains a clear example of 'waving line' planting, but the subtlety of this effect is virtually lost because the planting has now become almost continuous along the water's edge. However, occasional clearings and the undulating edge of the lake give some slight impression of the original effect.

Family fortunes rapidly increased, and the inheritance of immense wealth enabled the owner of 1833, the Duke of Sutherland, to remodel and greatly extend the house, creating a vast Italianate palace, to designs by Sir Charles Barry (architect of the Houses of Parliament). The sight of this great rambling building with its tower at the head of the lake must have been most dramatic. Between the building and the lake, a suitably large 'Italianate' (ie French) formal garden was laid out by Barry and W. Nesfield. Brown's great lake was big enough to take all this, and the Barry *palazzo* was probably a better match for the grandeur of the landscape than the earlier house.

By 1905, however, the River Trent was so badly polluted that the smell forced the Duke to move out and most of the house was demolished. Today the site is owned by Trentham Gardens Limited. The formal beds are well kept, and the lake is in good condition; the woodland is in a semi-natural state.

A marvellous mixture of cedars, yews and mature deciduous trees grows on the right-hand side of the Italian garden, looking towards the lake. It is only later that one discovers that it hides a permanent fun-fair, and that a miniature railway runs down one side of the lake. But the most offensive intrusion is the new Exhibition Hall, for which planning permission should never have been granted. Looking like an industrial packing shed, it stands in full view beside the Italian garden, and even from the far end of the lake on a misty autumn day it forms an all too clearly visible backdrop to the statue of Perseus. There are other eyesores, such as a derelict swimming pool, some rowing club huts, a slope for water-skiers, and a caravan park (fortunately not visible from the lake), but none to match the Exhibition Hall.

It is a pity that Trentham has not been maintained with more imagination and taste, for it remains, despite everything, a very beautiful lake, apparently so natural and mature that it has to be pointed out that it is a landscape that was created artificially as a work of art.

———

NOTES

1 The Monument was added in 1836, in honour of the first Duke of Sutherland.
2 The Torrington Diaries, vol III, ed. C. Bruyn Andrews.

Castle Ashby, Northamptonshire. At the end of one of the 'close walks' this view back to the castle suddenly appears: the classic ensemble of the house, grass, trees and water.

Petworth, West Sussex. One of the most perfectly preserved of all Brown's landscapes, it is threatened by plans for a by-pass.

Harewood from the south-east, by J. M. W. Turner.

The lake at Tong, Shropshire, with the church tower used as an eye-catcher. Although it looks so tranquil, the noisy M54 is only a few yards from this spot.

Notes on Further Brown Parks

―――――

Berrington

―――――

BERRINGTON Hall is a pleasant Palladian house built by Henry Holland from 1778 onwards. It is approached through parkland full of innumerable mature specimen trees, and is surrounded by beautiful unspoilt Herefordshire countryside. The house is built of brownish-pink sandstone, and has a portico of four unfluted Ionic columns, with matching service buildings to the rear.

Brown was consulted as early as 1775, in particular about the siting of the house, and his account-book shows that work continued until 1782, at a cost of £1,600. It looks south-west to distant views of the Brecon Beacons, while further to the west are the Black Mountains and the Skirrid. The ground slopes down diagonally from the façade to a fourteen-acre lake. Unfortunately, all this land is let by the National Trust as farmland, so there is no public access to the lake or the woodland beyond it, nor to the woodland to the west. The lake itself is badly silted up and overgrown, with only a few inches of water in many places. The island is joined to the banks by reeds and the whole lake is surrounded by swampy ground and undergrowth, except on the house side which only has nettles. There is also a heronry on the lake, which no one wants to disturb.

The Trust has concentrated instead on the garden areas around the house, which do not intrude on the landscape, where there is much of horticultural interest. But as the Trust has many gardens of horticultural interest and not many Capability Brown landscapes, it is to be hoped that soon it will find a way of restoring the lake and the surrounding parkland, including the woods to the west of the house, which now obscure the views to the Brecon mountains.

Cadland Cottage

———

Tʜᴇ landscape of the ornamental cottage at Cadland is of interest for three reasons: firstly, and uniquely among Brown's surviving landscapes, it is by the sea, and demonstrates again how Brown varied his approach according to the situation; secondly, it covers only a very small area – about eight acres; and thirdly, it is currently being restored by enthusiastic owners.

The present building dates from the 1930s, but on the site there was originally a *cottage orné* which would have been used for outings from the main house, which Brown and Henry Holland built for Brown's banker Robert Drummond between 1775 and 1779. The main house was on Southampton Water, on land now covered by Fawley oil refinery, but the cottage is on the Solent, with quite a different outlook.

A plan of the landscape survives, which is unusual in being delicately coloured. The scheme consists of a circular walk, which at first appears to lead away from the sea, but then swings round to a path set midway up the slope between shore level and the lawn, and there are occasional views across the Solent, which seem to have been angled towards particular features on the Isle of Wight opposite. The shoreline is generously planted, which gives protection from sea winds, but because of the low level of the path the lawn, which is seen from the house, is not visible from here. Eventually the path turns away from the shore into a densely wooded area, arched over with laurels, before leading back towards the house. As it rises gradually to the level of the lawn the planting breaks to reveal both the lawn and a new view of the sea. The lawn area is of a loose, flowing shape, and the clump of trees towards the far end of the lawn has the same visual purpose as an island at the end of a lake: it masks the end of the lawn, blurring its edges and leading the eye on. On a miniature scale, therefore, Brown has managed to provide a circuit-walk with several quite contrasting moods.

An extensive programme of restoration is being undertaken by the owners, with professional assistance, and partly funded by grants from Hampshire County Council. This has included not only tree-felling and the remaking of paths, but also the underplanting of some areas with shrubs and ground-cover plants that were in common use at the end of the eighteenth century. There is also a walled kitchen garden which now contains borders of mixed planting: in this way the 'modern' plants have been kept separate from the Brown landscape.

Harewood

HAREWOOD House was built for Edwin Lascelles, and it was he who employed Brown to improve the grounds and create the thirty-acre lake. In 1753 Lascelles inherited his father's fortune (made in the infamous sugar plantations of the West Indies) and took control of the Yorkshire estates.

The house was designed by John Carr with some amendments and interiors by Robert Adam, and is built of a local millstone grit of an unusual brownish colour. The portico to the Carr house, shown in a painting by Turner, was removed when Sir Charles Barry altered the house in 1843, which has given the south front of the house, facing the lake, a rather severe appearance. Barry also created the terraces which now separate the house from the park, but they are sufficiently low for the view of the lake not to be entirely obscured by the balustrading.

The remains of the old Gawthorpe Hall, where the Lascelles' ancestors lived before the new house was built, are now hidden beneath the lake; but Brown refers to Harewood as 'Gawthorpe' in all his records. It seems that he had some trouble with the lake, which leaked through a hole which Lascelles' steward claimed was 'large enough to bury a horse in'. Eventually a surveyor called John Hudson was called in, who charged Lascelles £1,000 to mend it. The lake (still in excellent condition) is skilfully shaped around the kitchen garden, which is screened by trees and is quite invisible from the house, even though the house is on higher ground. But the wide view from the top of the terraces can no longer be described as a Capability Brown landscape. The lake itself is backed by trees, and beyond it there is an expansive area of hilly parkland; but today the planting on this area is best described as 'lumpy', in that it consists of a mixture of blocks of tree-planting and fields of fairly stiff outline.

A good impression of the original appearance of the landscape beyond the lake is given by several illustrations of the park on view in the excellent exhibition room. In particular, a coloured drawing shows a bridge across the lake (which was never built); beyond which the early planting can be seen, consisting of long belts which mostly follow the contours, a few Brownian clumps, and a scattering of specimen trees: altogether a softer, subtler picture than what exists today. Another drawing, made about 1825 by Lady Sheffield, *née* Harriet Lascelles, shows a similar view, with the planting a little more mature, and the temple designed by John Carr (since destroyed) on the skyline. An old and rather misty photograph taken from the Barry terraces in about 1850 shows the same effect.

The part of the park open to the public is a woodland area planted in the Surrey style with rhododendrons and ornamental trees. The Brown landscape itself is not accessible and the public are not able to look back at the house across the lake as Turner, Girtin and many other artists did. The path through the Pleasure Grounds winds round to a timber bridge across a charming cascade, which gives a fine view of the lake with many mature trees along the nearer banks. The cascade is seen to advantage from some stepping stones further downstream. Unfortunately, the horticultural planting intrudes in several places: dwarf pointed conifers of a bluish tinge and some small purple-leafed trees are the worst offenders. At some stage, presumably the Victorian era, the dam at the end of the lake was turned into a rock garden, which was another error, as Brown's solution would have been to hide the dam with dense planting. In fact a mature yew beside the timber bridge probably survives from the Brown period; yew, left untrimmed, forms a big 'skirt' which is particularly useful for this purpose. Brown's aim was Improved Nature, not a garden; and the modern garden plants like *Juniperus* 'Skyrocket' are out of place here. Nearby, a specimen of *Nothofagus antarctica* shows that it is quite possible to plant things which are horticulturally interesting and yet perfectly in keeping with the Brownian scheme.

Himley

BROWN was consulted by Viscount Dudley and Ward in 1774 about work at Himley, and Spyers spent about fourteen days making a survey. Various payments were made to Brown in 1780 and 1781, amounting to £1,200.

Today the park is owned by Wolverhampton Metropolitan Borough; the house is used by Wolverhampton Polytechnic, and is unspoilt externally. It has a large portico on one elevation, and the older front looks across a grass lawn to the Great Pool, a pleasant lake now used for yachting. There are many good trees and the woodland on the slopes to the north is particularly good.

Two more lakes lie behind the house, but sadly the Rock Pool is empty and the cascade there is not working. A rocky or cliff-like area exists here. South of the Rock Pool is now unfortunately a golf course, divided off from the rest of the park by a chain-link fence. Further on is the Island Pool, now used by fishermen. Despite its municipal air, some impression of a Brown landscape can still be gained.

Kimberley

THE house at Kimberley was designed by William Talman in 1712, with the end turrets added a little later. It is a perfect period piece of soft pink brick; the central bay is pedimented and the turrets on the end bays are reminiscent of Croome Court.

Brown's plan of the grounds is dated 1763, and the work cost £3,000.

The house overlooks a twenty-eight-acre lake, which could be beautiful, but it is in such a poor condition that it is hard to get a clear impression of it. The banks on the far side are overgrown with dogwood so that the intended views, such as the one shown in Morris's *Country Seats of Great Britain*, are almost impossible. The edge of the lake is so overgrown that it is hard even to see the water except from the pastures in front of the house. Clumps of trees, including some Scots pine, frame the house when viewed (with difficulty) from the lake. On the left-hand side, as seen from the house, the lake narrows to river size, but it is a mass of reeds, rushes and willows. On the other side, but hard to see among the nettles, is a charming cascade.

This dereliction is not without some benefits, however: the lake is now the haunt of innumerable water birds, some of them rare, and in autumn the colours of the chestnut trees overhanging the water are a memorable sight.

Milton Abbey

WHEN Brown first began to advise Lord Milton, in 1763, his client was living in a house formed from the remains of the old Benedictine abbey, next door to the fine abbey church which still stands. The town was close by, and although it had decayed since medieval times, it still contained a High Street, a Market Street, an inn, a school-house and over a hundred houses. At this stage Brown carried out considerable landscaping work, which amounted to more than £2,000 by 1770. But his most interesting work did not start until about 1780, when a new village was built to replace the old town, which was too close for Lord Milton's liking. This was the most ambitious of all the village-moving projects of the eighteenth century.[1]

In the early 1770s Lord Milton decided to rebuild the house in the Gothic style, and chose Sir William Chambers to design it for him. But Chambers was not sympathetic to the Gothic style: the only departure from the classical style which seems to have interested him was Chinese architecture. He was not sympathetic to Lancelot Brown either: although Brown apparently worked for Lord Milton without any upsets, Chambers called him an 'unmannerly imperious Lord, who has treated me, as he does everybody, ill . . .'[2]

The house was not a success: not only is it a different colour from the church, it is basically a horizontal composition, with incongruous and half-hearted Gothic detailing on a long, flat façade. In 1774 Chambers resigned from this 'vast, ugly house', as he called it, and it was finished off by James Wyatt.

A year earlier, however, he had prepared 'a plan and elevation of a part of the intended village', of which no record appears to have survived. Following his departure Brown was asked to prepare another plan for the village, but this too has disappeared. He charged Lord Milton £105, which suggests that there was a considerable amount of work involved, since several of his plans for landscape improvements were charged at less than £60.

The site chosen for the new village was out of sight from the house, in a narrow valley which led down to the lake on Milton's estate. The road is very slightly serpentine on plan, showing the kind of line which is the hallmark of Brown's work: on paper it is hardly noticeable but on the ground it is quite striking. Pairs of thatched white-painted cottages, set back behind a wide grass verge, follow the line of the road smoothly, with no jagged projections. Halfway along is James Wyatt's unassuming village church, which was needed because Lord Milton retained the big abbey church for his own private use. Nearby are the almshouses, which were moved from the old village and rebuilt stone by stone. The villagers, needless to say, strongly objected to their half-mile transportation. One of them was a solicitor who knew his rights, and proved to be Lord Milton's most able opponent. Milton had to wait twenty years for this Mr Harrison to die before he could complete the project.

The view down the road as it slopes towards the lake is delightful, winding first one way and then the other. But the view back to the village, seen across the lake, is even better, as the foreshortened view up the street turns the whole village into an attractive cluster of buildings. This was one of the earliest attempts at picturesque village planning: it was much more usual for cottages to be placed in neat and rather dull straight rows, as at Nuneham Courtenay in the 1760s. The planning at Milton anticipates John Nash's Blaise Hamlet of 1810 (where the cottages are much more picturesque individually), but here the group as a whole forms a scenic feature.

The lake and the whole of the surrounding landscape are still extremely attractive and among the wooded hills and spreading lawns there are many scenes of great beauty, despite the encroachments of staff houses, playing fields and a golf course. The lake has silted up at one end, forming a morass of dogwood, reeds and rushes, but early Ordnance Survey maps indicate that this happened many decades ago.

Lord Milton originally hoped to create another lake to the north of the house, but although many difficult and expensive preparations were made, the plan was never carried out. Brown's last bill was paid only a few weeks before his death: maybe with Brown's departure Lord Milton gave up the attempt.

NOTES
1   Maurice Beresford, *History on the Ground* (Alan Sutton, reprinted 1984), pp 198–203.
2   British Museum, Add. MSS.51, 136F14; quoted by Stroud.

Patshull

PATSHULL was owned by Lord Pigot, formerly Governor of Madras, who paid Brown £52 10s for 'a general plan for the Place and Journeys'.

The 'delightful serpentine expanse of water' described in *The Beauties of Staffordshire* (1813) still exists at Patshull. One of Brown's largest lakes, at sixty-five acres, it is long and winding, with various branches or creeks, and is still beautiful, despite less than perfect maintenance.

The house, built by James Gibbs about 1750, is rather severe, and is set high above the surrounding land. It is now used by the local authority as a rehabilitation centre. As we approach Patshull we see a small part of the lake from the minor road from Pattingham; turning into the park we cross the lake by a low bridge, and after a third of a mile come to the Church Pool on the left, with tall conifers, probably Victorian, behind it. Reeds are gradually invading the water. Early plans show that the right bank, nearest the house, was originally clearer of planting than it is today. Looking right from the driveway we catch another glimpse of the Great Pool, through trees which screen the dam between the two lakes. The remains of hollies can be found here, no doubt originally planted to mask the slope. The drive passes the church and after a short distance reaches the house, which is approached through a series of forecourts, the first with a pedimented gateway. On the south side of the house elaborate flights of steps lead down to the lawn, while the west elevation looks out on the Church Pool. There is extensive Victorian planting, such as Wellingtonias, around the house, but this is done so well that it does not conflict with Brown's planting of the park. On the contrary, the gloomy quality of the conifers matches the house rather well.

A detour from the drive takes us to a classical lakeside temple, which has been incorporated into a hotel and restaurant. The result is not as bad as one might imagine: the scale has been maintained and the glass behind the columns of the temple is a nice touch. But it would appear to better advantage if one or two trees were cut down to show more of the temple, and some evergreen shrubs were planted to mask the extensions and the parked cars.

The temple is excellently sited and gives the best view of the lake. Facing it is a tributary 'creek' of the lake, while to left and right there are views up and down the main part of it. The creek winds very slightly to the south at the far end, a typically Brownian touch to obscure the end of the lake. There is a distant view of the spire of Pattingham Church.[1]

Today the park is a large golf course and the lake is used for boating and fishing. Although the use of Brown's parks as golf courses is not ideal, it is better than ploughing them up for crops. The bunkers and greens inevitably disrupt the contours, but on the other hand the grass is mown to a close finish, smoother even than a deer park. If it were mown closer to the water at Patshull it would prevent nettles and weeds growing up at the water's edge. The most insensitive feature of these golf courses is the 'bitty' planting that is added (presumably as wind breaks); an example of the way such intrusions destroy the landscape can be seen at Brown's Moor Park near Rickmansworth. The lake at Patshull would benefit if it were cleared of silt and rushes in places. On the far side of the lake there is now too much waterside planting: early maps show that the east bank opposite the house was quite open.

NOTE

1 In fact the spire is younger than the park, being nineteenth century, by Sir George Gilbert Scott; the tower itself is fourteenth century.

Tong

———

THIS is one of the lost landscapes. The M54 runs through almost on top of the site of the demolished mansion, but miraculously the lake remains, with its picturesque view of Tong church at the end. Its outline is simple and pleasantly curved, with relatively steep sides for a Brown lake. Today it is used by an angling club, and also by swans, coots and moorhens.

Brown made several journeys to Tong in 1765 and supplied 'various plans and elevations for Tong Castle' for a certain George Durant, who had made a fortune in Havana. Whether the house was built to Brown's plan or not is uncertain, since its appearance was unlike anything he did anywhere else. There are few buildings quite like this strange design, which was not very accurately described fifty years later as 'a mixture of Gothic and Moorish architecture'. Perhaps the nearest equivalent to Tong Castle is Milton Abbey, which was designed by Sir William Chambers and completed by Wyatt. They are both rectangular Palladian blocks with a veneer of Gothick details, but those of Tong are more chunky than the timid Gothick at Milton Abbey. If Brown was involved at Tong, perhaps the source of the details was James Gibbs's Gothic Temple at Stowe.

Ugbrooke

———

'TIS yours, My Lord, with unaffected ease,
   To draw from Nature's stores and make them please:
With taste refined to dress the rural seat,
And add new honours to your own retreat.

So wrote Joseph Reeve, addressing the fourth Lord Clifford, owner of Ugbrooke Park near Chudleigh in Devon. Father Reeve was tutor to Lord Clifford's children, and the chaplain to the family. He continues:

To shade the hill, to scoop or swell the green
To break with wild diversities the scene,
To model with the Genius of the place
Each artless feature, each spontaneous grace.
For, as you work, the Genius still presides,

The wooded glen at Downton, part of the estate owned by Richard Payne Knight. A romantic piece of natural countryside which the devotees of the Picturesque could admire. Drawing by Thomas Hearne, *c*1790.

Two engravings by Thomas Hearne published with Payne Knight's *The Landscape*. A parody of a Brown landscape (*above*) with an excessively serpentine river, complete lack of waterside planting and large areas of 'shaven' lawn. *Below*, the estate altered to conform with Payne Knight's preference for the picturesque qualities of rough textures and unkempt nature. Bracken, rocks, weeds and dead branches strew the foreground.

'Before and after' sketches by Repton of Lord Sidmouth's house in Richmond Park. Repton disapproved of deer coming right up to the house, and shows them here peering in at the windows. Repton's proposals for Lord Sidmouth were quite alien to anything Brown ever did. This scheme is an early example of the 'Gardenesque' – an attempt to give scope to the increasing interest in horticulture.

Opposite: The approach to Woburn Abbey, a landscape designed by Humphry Repton (1752–1818) following closely the Brown manner.

Above: One of the most famous of the *jardins anglais* was Ermenonville, owned by the Marquis de Girardin, author of *De la Composition des Paysages*.

Below: A scheme by J. C. Loudon for a suburban villa. His attempt to combine the landscape garden with horticultural display is not wholly successful, as the oddly shaped island beds show.

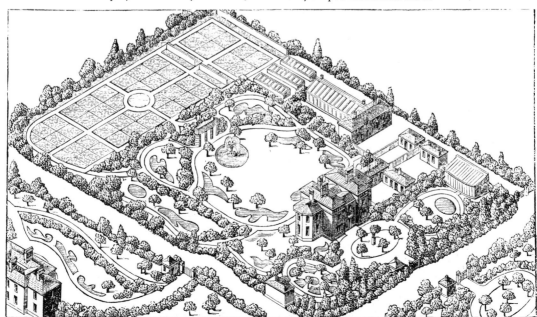

One of Brown's most ambitious schemes was at Fisherwick, where he designed both the Palladian house and the grounds. Virtually nothing remains today of this 'profusion of embellishment ... this earthly paradise ...' (*History of Staffordshire*). Watercolour by John Spyers, 1786.

Overleaf: Brown's landscape at Longleat has now reached maturity.

Directs each stroke and each improvement guides.
Hence thro' the whole irregularly great,
Nature and Art the wond'rous work complete;
In all so true, so unperceived the skill,
That Nature modified is Nature still.

Today Ugbrooke Park still appears as a natural scene. A cynic might say all the Brown parks that have not been ploughed up or built over can be divided into two kinds: those which have been treated as gardens (and have become a repository of all kinds of horticultural treasures) and those which have been treated as wild nature (and have reverted to native woodland). Ugbrooke tends towards the second category, but the mature oaks with bracken beneath them, the dark lakes, the narrowness of the valley, the Gothick house, the glimpses of the Devon landscape and the distant outlines of Dartmoor make this unique amongst Brown landscapes.

Just who designed the house is not entirely certain. Humphry Repton attributed it to Brown, and it appears that Brown did submit plans for a house in 1761. These drawings are now lost, but Robert Adam also submitted schemes, and drawings apparently by him survive.[1] It seems most likely that in the end Lord Clifford adopted a cost-cutting scheme: the house is in the Gothic style, but it is a weak Georgian Gothick of very little charm; its regularity and symmetry are incongruous with its Gothicism, and its symmetry lacks a central dominating feature.

Magnificent evergreen oaks, chestnuts and cedars form a fine background for the house, however, which faces west down a sloping lawn. At present too many wooden fences destroy the parkland atmosphere and interrupt the flow of the contours. The ground slopes down towards the valley and to the Middle Pond, which runs slightly on the diagonal to the south-west. But the view of the lake is obscured by a large number of bushes along the water's edge. The fields on the right hand side as we look down to the lake have lost their Brownian touch. Originally, as can be seen on early Ordnance maps, the perimeter planting of the estate ran along the skyline around the so-called Danish encampment (marked Castle Dyke Camp on the maps). From here the parkland swept down to the outer dyke where there were groups of specimen trees, and down again right to the edge of the Middle Pond, with more scatterings of specimen trees nearer the lake. Today, alders run almost continuously along the edge of the lake, obscuring the view of specimen plane trees behind. The fields higher up have been divided, and kale is grown below the outer dyke.

The views from the encampment and the dyke are splendid: there can hardly be another Brown park in such a windswept, rugged setting. The valley is so steep one cannot see the lake from here, though this may be due partly to the trees near the water. Some of the woodland of the estate is now devoted to conifers and in one or two places this produces stiff lines which are incongruous. There are also several good groups of mature Scots pine, which seem most appropriate to their setting.

The Upper Pond is now surrounded by farm buildings, and has recently been restored to fulfil one of its functions, which is to act as a silt trap. At the base of the Middle Pond some repairs have been carried out, which look a little raw at the moment as they have not had time to mature. A timber footbridge enables one to cross the Middle Pond where the water leaves the main body of the lake and enters a shallow pool, which also acts as a ford. All is dark here in the shade of trees. From here the water falls steeply in a cascade. Originally it fell over a smooth rim to rocks below; in Joseph Reeve's words:

Spent in the windings of the skirting grove,
The lingering current scarcely seems to move,
When lo! abruptly from the rocky steep
Headlong it falls, and dashes down the deep,
From crag to crag the tumbling waters bound
And foam and fret and whirl their eddies round
Till by degrees in milder falls they play
And in soft whispers gently glide away.

This has now been altered to a more stepped cascade which, as it splashes over irregular stones, still looks quite pretty – though it cannot be seen to advantage as the woodland below is so overgrown.

Below the cascade is the Lower Pond, backed on the north side by steep woods. It is very attractive, though some thinning out on the south side would help to restore it to its original form.

———

NOTE

1   See an article by Alistair Rowan in *Country Life*, 27 July 1967.

The Landscape Garden after Brown

———

Humphry Repton once remarked of the minor figures influenced by Brown: 'Brown followed Nature: his illiterate followers copied *him*.' Much more research needs to be done before we can assess the work of men such as Richard Woods (?1716–93), William Eames (1729–1803), Thomas White (*c*1736–1811), or a certain Mr Richmond; and there were many others. Of these, it seems that Richard Woods may have been the most talented. He helped Lord Dacre implement Brown's proposals at Belhus in Essex, apparently with Brown's approval, and his plan for Alresford, of 1764, shows sensitive planting around the perimeter, but the deer park itself seems to be completely bare of trees. Woods also did some work at Wardour Castle in Wiltshire, a splendid Palladian mansion by James Paine; from the house one can see the ruins of the attractive medieval Wardour Castle, some distance away, and a guide book of 1801 remarked that, 'between this edifice and the house, the ground is broken by plantations, suggested by Mr. Wood, of Essex, the judiciousness of which Brown himself had the taste to admire'.[1]

In all of its stages the Landscape Movement produced a good deal of literature, both in verse and prose. One of the earliest writings to reflect the mature, Brownian phase of the Landscape Movement was a letter by Joseph Spence (1699–1768), Professor of Poetry at Oxford, to the Reverend Wheeler,[2] of 1751. Apparently it was a draft for a book which he never completed; it was eventually included in *Observations, Anecdotes and Characters of Books and Men* in 1820, but had been widely circulated during the eighteenth century. In 1752 Spence translated from the French a work which he called *A Particular Account of the Emperor of China's Gardens* (by J.D. Attiret, 1747), which served to supplement what had been learned of Chinese gardens from the engravings of Matteo Ripa published in Italy twenty years earlier.

William Shenstone's aptly named *Unconnected Thoughts on Gardening* were not published until the year after his death in 1764. Here we meet, perhaps for the first time, the expression 'landskip gardener' (Brown always referred to 'improvement' or 'place-making'). Although Shenstone's own garden was more associational than Brown's work, his *Thoughts* contain much that is relevant; for example, one thinks immediately of Brown's skill at contouring when Shenstone remarks that 'smoothness and easy transitions are no small ingredient in the beautiful . . .'

But it was an anonymous poem of 1767 which was to praise Brown most highly. Its lengthy title was *The Rise and Progress of the Present Taste in Planting Parks, Pleasure Grounds, Gardens, etc. from Henry the Eighth to King George the Third in a Poetic Epistle to the Right Honourable Charles Lord Viscount Irwin*, and in it the writer expresses the dissatisfaction with the garden at Stowe which was current by this date: the straight lines of Bridgeman's layout were still evident, it seems. The poet admits that Cobham had 'formed a great design', but suggests that:

Could he have dropped the dangerous Rule and Line,
Then Stowe had been with nobler wildness graced,
And shown the full result of genuine taste.
But tiresome grows each long, long, lengthening aisle
Where captive Nature never deigned to smile,
Where crowded statues, crowded structures glare,
And only serve to make the Vulgar stare.

This was the opinion in 1767 of the garden which had been considered as the acme of everything desirable in the 1740s. Just to make himself quite clear the writer remarks:

But nothing looks so miserably vile,
As a dull regularity of style.

But the most remarkable part of the poem is the praise which the poet lavishes on Lancelot Brown, and in particular his work at Temple Newsam (which had begun only two years earlier). The poet's comparison of Brown's work to that of the great painters and poets is particularly noticeable:

But your great artist, like the source of light,
Gilds every Scene with beauty and delight;
At Blenheim, Croome and Caversham we trace
Salvator's wildness, Claud's enlivening grace,
Cascades and Lakes as fine as Risdale drew
While Nature's vary'd in each charming view.
To paint his works wou'd Pousin's Powers require,
Milton's sublimity, and Dryden's fire:
For both the Sister Arts in him combin'd,
Enrich the great ideas of his mind;
And these still brighten all his vast designs,
For here the Painter, there the Poet shines!
With just contempt he scorns all former rules,
And shows true Taste is not confin'd to schools.
He barren tracts with every charm illumes,
At his command a new Creation blooms;
Born to grace Nature, and her works complete
With all that's beautiful, sublime and great!
For him each Muse enwreathes the Lawrel Crown,
And consecrates to Fame immortal Brown.

Thomas Whately's *Observations on Modern Gardening* (1770) was the most thorough treatise on the subject to be produced in Brown's time, and remains even now the best aid to the understanding of the Landscape Movement in its mature phase. He draws the distinction between the 'emblematical' approach of the earlier phase of the Landscape Movement, and the 'expressive' approach of Brown and his followers. Whereas the former might use a funerary urn to induce feelings of mournfulness, the latter rejected the use of symbols, and created the mood directly with a landscape of rocks and dark trees.

Two years later the first of the four books of William Mason's poem *The English Garden* was published. It is a mixture of intelligent observations on the subject, some general and some detailed, with passages of poetry-spinning here and there. In many ways Burgh's commentary printed with the poem is more useful than the poem itself, since he explains some obscure points. Brown himself must have been familiar with the work, as it is quoted in the contract for Sandbeck Park, and no doubt he read Mason's remarks on Addison, Kent, Southcote, and Shenstone, and on Brown himself:

Him, too, the living Leader of thy powers,
Great Nature! him the Muse shall hail in notes
Which antedate the praise true Genius claims
From just posterity: Bards yet unborn
Shall pay to Brown that tribute, fittest paid
In strains, the beauty of his scenes inspire.

But also in 1772 Sir William Chambers (joint Architect to the King with Robert Adam) published *A Dissertation on Oriental Gardening*. Between 1757 and 1763 Chambers had designed several garden buildings for Princess Augusta, widow of Frederick, Prince of Wales, at Kew, next door to the gardens at Richmond which Brown transformed from 1765 onwards. In those days it covered only nine acres. In 1772, after the death of Princess Augusta, George III purchased Kew and it was merged with the Royal Gardens at Richmond; and the smaller garden gave its name to the larger.

Contained in Chambers' *Dissertation* was a thinly-veiled attack on Brown. The contact between the two men became overtly competitive in 1769 when Lord Clive invited both of them to prepare designs for his new house at Claremont. As we have seen, it was Brown's design that was successful, and this may have prompted Chambers' remarks in his *Dissertation*. Like many descriptions of Chinese gardens, Chambers' pamphlet consisted partly of his own ideas about gardening foisted onto the Chinese. Unfortunately he did not make it clear which features of Chinese gardens he was recommending and which he was merely recording. Thus some of his remarks may be taken as criticism of the Brown manner:

In their crooked walks they carefully avoid all sudden or unnatural windings, particularly the regular serpentine curves of which our English gardeners are so fond; observing that these eternal, uniform undulating lines are, of all things, the most unnatural, the most affected and the most tiresome to pursue ...

In another place he writes:

Our virtuosi have scarcely left an acre of shade, nor three trees growing in a line, from Land's End to the Tweed ...

And according to the Chinese:

Nature affords but few materials to work with. Plants, ground and water, are her only productions: and though both the forms of these may be varied to an incredible degree, yet have they but few striking varieties, the rest being of the nature of changes rung upon bells, which though in reality different, still produce the same uniform kind of jingling; the variation being too minute to be easily perceived.

Art must therefore supply the scantness of nature ...

But how? To 'enliven' these Chinese landscapes, says Chambers,

Nothing is forgot that can either exhilarate the mind, gratify the senses, or give a spur to the imagination.

Their scenes of terror are composed of gloomy woods, deep vallies inaccessible to the sun.... The trees are ill formed, forced out of their natural directions, and seemingly torn to pieces by the violence of tempests: some are thrown down, and intercept the course of torrents ... the buildings are in ruins.... Bats, owls and vultures, and every bird of prey flutter in the groves; wolves, tigers and jackalls howl in the forests; half-famished animals wander upon the plains; gibbets, crosses, wheels, and the whole apparatus of torture, are seen from the roads; and in the most dismal recesses of the woods ... are temples dedicated to the king of vengeance ...

Soon Chambers was completely carried away by his own fantasy:

His road then lies through lofty woods ... where innumerable monkies, cats and parrots clamber upon the trees, and intimidate him as he passes; or through flowery thickets, where he is delighted with ... the harmony of flutes ... Sometimes ... the passenger finds himself ... surrounded with arbours of jessamine, vine and roses, where beauteous Tartarean damsels, in loose transparent robes, that flutter in the air, present him with rich wines, mangotans, ananas, and fruits of Quangsi; crown him with garlands of flowers, and invite him to taste the sweets of retirement on Persian carpets and beds of camusath skin down ...

It was not surprising that Chambers was not taken seriously. One of his friends told him that after reading the work twice he was still not 'able to comprehend ... your precise idea of Oriental Gardening'.[4] But the jealous references to Brown were fairly obvious, such as his remark that 'peasants emerge from the melon ground to take the periwig and turn professor', and that 'this island is abandoned to kitchen gardeners well skilled in the culture of salads'.

This was all an easy target for William Mason in his anonymous parody *An Heroic Epistle to Sir William Chambers*, which went into fourteen editions in four years. Chambers' book was translated into French, however, and no doubt it helped to contribute to the misunderstanding of *le jardin anglais* abroad.

Perhaps the most important and readable study of the Landscape Movement was Horace Walpole's *History of the Modern Taste in Gardening*. Written about 1770 but not published until 1780, Walpole's attempt to trace the history of the movement has had a great influence on all the historians who have followed him. In view of Sir William Chambers' opinions, and those of Price and Payne Knight later on, Walpole makes some pertinent observations:

Still there is a more imminent danger that threatens the present, as it has ever done all taste. I mean the pursuit of variety. A modern French writer has in a very affected phrase, given a just account of this ... He says, *L'ennui du beau amène le goût du singulier*. The noble simplicity of the Augustan age was driven out by false taste. The gigantic, the puerile, the quaint, and at last the barbarous and monkish, had each their successive admirers ... If we once loose sight of the propriety of landscape in our gardens, we shall wander into all the fantastic sharawadgis of the Chinese ...

Walpole himself attempted some landscaping work at Strawberry Hill. In fact many outstanding parks were made in this period by enthusiastic owners without professional help. Unfortunately, the owners with taste and enthusiasm were not always the ones with the money. William Shenstone had great difficulty in funding his improvements at the Leasowes, and Charles Hamilton (1704–86) was eventually forced, in 1771, to sell his famous park at Painshill in Surrey when he ran out of money. He had acquired Painshill in 1738, and began to carry out agricultural improvements as well as aesthetic ones.

In the 1750s Hamilton made a lake with several rocky islands and an outline which was more intricate than any of Brown's. He was a friend of Peter Collinson (1694–1768), who introduced many new species of plants from North America and elsewhere and who no doubt passed some on to Hamilton. When J.C. Loudon went to Painshill he reported seeing cork trees (*Quercus suber*), American oaks, tulip trees, deciduous cypresses (*Taxodium*), a tupelo (*Nyssa sylvatica*) and some of the first rhododendrons and azaleas.[5] There were extensive plantations of Scots pine and spruce, which formed a background to the park and gave to Painshill an atmosphere quite different from Capability Brown's parks.

For Horace Walpole, Painshill was a perfect example of the 'forest or savage garden', as he explained:

I mean that kind of alpine scene, composed almost wholly of pines and firs, a few birch, and such trees as assimilate with a savage and mountainous country.[6]

At Painshill, said Walpole:

All is great and foreign and rude; the walks seem not designed, but cut through the wood of pines; and the style of the whole is so grand, and conducted with so serious an air of wild and uncultivated extent, that when you look down on this seeming forest, you are amazed to find it contains a very few acres.[7]

If Lancelot Brown's parks have a Claudian air, the influence at Painshill is obviously Salvator Rosa.

The garden buildings were as original as the style of planting: there was a Gothic Tower, a Gothic Abbey, and a Gothic Temple. There were also a Roman mausoleum and a Roman bath, but the most extraordinary feature was a complicated and highly artificial-looking grotto made of tufa. It was made by Josiah Lane of Tisbury, the same man who worked with Hamilton when he altered Brown's cascade at Bowood. At another point in the park Hamilton introduced some parterres, described by Thomas Whately as being 'in the midst of a thicket'.[8] Painshill is now in a ruinous state, but it seems that Hamilton had created a highly original and romantic kind of landscape.

If Hamilton introduced 'savage' forest scenery to Surrey, Lord Lyttelton had no need to on his estate at Hagley in the rugged Clent Hills, for Nature had been there before him. George Lyttelton (1709-1773) was the nephew of Lord Cobham of Stowe, a politician, and a friend of Alexander Pope, Shenstone and James Thomson. After the death of his father, Lyttelton began to make 'improvements'. Walpole was enthusiastic:

You might draw, but I can't describe the enchanting scenes of the park ... I quite forgot my favourite Thames! Indeed, I prefer nothing to Hagley but Mount Edgecumbe. There is an extreme of taste in the park ... and there is such a pretty well in a wood, like the Samaritan woman's in a picture of Niccolo Poussin! ... I wore out my eyes with gazing, my feet with climbing and my tongue and my vocabulary with commending ...[9]

Although the park lacked water, Lyttelton contrived to produce 'a beautiful cascade falling down the rocks', and 'a grotto where the water runs'. As early as 1756 he was showing interest in the scenery of the Lake District, and a correspondent wrote, telling him how 'beauty, horror and immensity' were united at Keswick. 'To give you a complete idea of these three,' wrote Dr John Brown,[10] '... would require the united powers of Claude, Salvator and Poussin.'

It seems that the Landscape Movement opened the door to the appreciation of natural scenery. Whereas Defoe and Smollet had admired 'the country of England smiling with cultivation, ... exhibiting all the perfection of agriculture', the habit of enjoying a park for its pictorial or visual qualities quickly became a habit of looking for pictorial scenery in the countryside generally. And in this regard, it is worth remembering that it was only with the advent of Lancelot Brown that the parks were landscaped in a natural manner on a scale large enough to compare with the countryside itself. Horace Walpole seemed to foresee the whole countryside being 'improved': 'In the meantime how rich, how gay, how picturesque the face of the country! The demolition of walls laying open each improvement, every journey is made through a succession of pictures . . .'

Perhaps the most dramatically sited estate was Persfield (now Piercefield), which is a few miles north of Chepstow on a loop of the River Wye. On one side of the house the land drops suddenly in steep rocky cliffs to the Wye in a piece of natural scenery which was much admired at the time.

William Shenstone thought it was a matter of temperament whether one preferred this kind of scenery or the gentle and pastoral: 'Taste depends on temper. Some prefer Tibullus to Virgil, and Virgil to Homer – Hagley to Persfield and Persfield to the Welsh mountains.' Thomas Gray was quite clear in his preference for the mountains. He told William Mason in a letter that:

> The mountains are extatic, and ought to be visited in pilgrimage once a year ... A fig for your poets, painters, gardeners and clergymen that have not been among them: their imagination can be made up of nothing but bowling-greens, flowering shrubs, horse-ponds, Fleet-ditches and Chinée-rails.[11]

If what one was seeking in the landscape was the character of Edmund Burke's 'sublime', the parks of country houses, unless they were exceptionally situated, were certain to disappoint. But this did not stop several writers from complaining, as Chambers had done, that the parks of Capability Brown and his followers were insufficiently exciting. It was no coincidence that the two most prominent of these critics, Richard Payne Knight and Sir Uvedale Price, had estates in the wild Welsh Border country.

Richard Payne Knight (1750–1824), a collector and scholar of wide-ranging interests, published his poem *The Landscape* in 1794. In it he expounds his ideas on the Picturesque, and gives vent to his feelings about Brown landscapes, which he condemns for their lack of picturesque irregularity. Included in the slim volume were two contrasting etchings by Hearne and Pouncy which illustrate more clearly than anything Knight says just where his preference lay. One is an exaggerated view of a Brownian landscape; the other shows the same scene, but now the house is a lumpy Victorian pile, there is denser planting, in the foreground are rocks, bracken, undergrowth and fallen branches, and the bridge has become rustic. Of course the irony is that in their decayed state today very many Brown parks look more like the lower, 'picturesque' view than the upper one.

In his poem Knight pictures the improvers at their work:

> See yon fantastic band,
> With charts, pedometers, and rules in hand
> Advance triumphant, and alike lay waste
> The forms of nature, and the works of taste!
> T'improve, adorn, and polish, they profess;
> But shave the goddess, whom they come to dress;
> Level each broken bank and shaggy mound,
> And fashion all to one unvaried round;
> One even round, that ever gently flows,
> Nor forms abrupt, nor broken colours knows;
> But, wrapt all o'er in everlasting green,
> Makes one dull, vapid, smooth and tranquil scene.

Knight soon proceeds to launch a blistering attack on the 'follower' of Brown:

> Hence, hence! though haggard fiend, however call'd,
> Thin, meagre genius of the bare and bald;
> Thy spade and mattock here at length lay down,
> And follow to the tomb thy fav'rite Brown:
> Thy fav'rite Brown, whose innovating hand
> First dealt thy curses o'er this fertile land;

It was no wonder that Walpole referred to Price and Payne Knight as 'infidels', and called Knight's work an 'insolent and self-conceited poem' written by a 'trumpery prosaic poetaster'.

The way Brown placed his houses in the landscape came in for more criticism from Knight:

> Oft when I've seen some lonely mansion stand,
> Fresh from the improvers desolating hand,
> 'Midst shaven lawns, that far around it creep
> In one eternal undulating sweep ...
> Tired with th'extensive scene, so dull and bare,
> To Heav'n devoutly I've address'd my pray'r –
> Again the moss-grown terraces to raise,
> And spread the labyrinth's perplexing maze;
> Replace in even lines the ductile yew,
> And plant again the ancient avenue.
> Some features then, at least we should obtain,
> To mark this flat, insipid, waving plain;
> Some vary'd tints and forms would intervene,
> To break this uniform, eternal green.

Knight might seem an unreliable judge, however, in the light of his other tastes: he considered the Elgin marbles 'second-rate' and Michelangelo's sculptures worse than third-rate. Moreover neither he nor Price was ever faced with the practical difficulties of landscaping someone else's estate.

Uvedale Price published his *Essay on the Picturesque* in 1794, the same year as Knight's poem. He maintained that the modern improvers had overlooked 'two of the most fruitful sources of human pleasure', which he claimed were variety and intricacy:

> Intricacy in the disposition, and variety of the forms, the tints, and the lights and shadows of objects, are the great characteristics of picturesque scenery; so monotony and baldness are the greatest defects of improved places.

Many pages are devoted to trying to define 'Picturesque', a word to which Price (like Knight) attempted to give new meaning. Already William Gilpin had included it in the full title of his book, *Observations on the River Wye, and Several Parts of South Wales, etc. Relative Chiefly to Picturesque Beauty*, published in 1782, but his use of the word is the same as ours: he defined it in an earlier book,[12] as 'that kind of beauty which would look well in a picture'.

Price tried to create a new category, between Burke's 'sublime' and 'beautiful'; to him there was a quality that was pleasing to the eye which had neither the smoothness of the beautiful nor the uniformity of the sublime. After considerable discussion he says:

> I think, however, we may conclude, that where an object, or a set of objects, is without smoothness or grandeur, but from its intricacy, its sudden and irregular deviations, its

variety of forms, tints, and lights and shadows, is interesting to a cultivated eye, it is simply picturesque ...

However, exact definition was not so easy, and the two writers having set out to attack others, began to attack each other. Payne Knight claimed that Price's definition of the Picturesque would give 'a pimpled face ... the same superiority over a smooth one as a variegated tulip [has] over a plain one ...' And so the argument continued, and before long, according to Shelley, they were like 'two ill-trained beagles snarling at each other when they could not catch the hare.' Even fifty years later, when the Picturesque controversy had virtually died out, Ruskin commented that, 'probably no word in the language ... has been the subject of so frequent or so prolonged dispute; yet none more vague in their acceptance.'[13]

But, although Payne Knight and Price were convinced they had discovered something, it seems more likely that they had in fact defined a quality which is a permanent feature of certain styles and periods.[14] A more useful classification is Norberg-Schulz's 'romantic' category, which has already been discussed. In view of Price's call for variety, it is worth noting that Norberg-Schulz remarks that in a 'romantic' landscape 'the ground is rarely continuous, but it is subdivided and has varied relief; rocks and depressions, groves and glades, bushes and tufts create a rich "microstructure".'

The 1790s also saw the publication of Wordsworth's and Coleridge's *Lyrical Ballads*, in which the new attitude to nature is exemplified. Nature was now something to be reverenced, explored and experienced; it was the source of:

> ... sensations sweet,
> Felt in the blood, and felt along the heart
> And passing even into my purer mind
> With tranquil restoration:[15]

To the Romantics the idea that you could 'improve' Nature was absurd and irreverent.

It was natural scenery that took over from the landscape garden as the prime object of interest for many writers and travellers, and the kind of scenery admired at the turn of the century was of a sort impossible to transport to East Anglia or the Thames Valley, however magical the skill of the improver. But while the connoisseurs of scenery were arguing over definitions and points of detail, there still remained a good market for the landscaping of estates. One man at least was prepared to take up the mantle of Lancelot Brown.

In 1788, five years after Brown's death, Humphry Repton decided to fill the gap, and put his painting and drawing ability to good use as a landscape gardener. He set about visiting some of the outstanding parks in East Anglia, such as William Kent's landscape at Holkham and Brown's landscape at Redgrave. Later he made a special pilgrimage to Stowe and Blenheim, and Brown's son, Lance, gave him 'the maps of the greatest works in which his late father had been consulted, both in their original and improved states'; a priceless gift.

His first commissions were for local acquaintances, but his reputation spread and before long he was advising numerous landowners on the improvement of their estates. But although Repton worked hard to acquire a background knowledge of surveying and horticulture, he inevitably lacked the twenty years of experience that Brown had by the time he was thirty-six. No doubt it was for this reason that Repton always worked as a professional and never as a contractor like Brown. His technique of selling his ideas to his client was quite different from Brown's. When a client asked Brown to improve his estate he was effectively buying his taste and expertise. Even in the early days, when he was still working for Lord Cobham, his reputation at Stowe gave him a kind of seal of approval, and he was evidently so confident and spoke with such authority that clients were often willing to comply with any suggestion which funds would permit. For this reason he seldom produced any sketches (his drawing for the park walls for Woodstock is a rare exception).

Repton found that his proposals had to be demonstrated before they could be undertaken. Furthermore, an increasing number of clients were not members of the landowning aristocracy, but successful merchants, accustomed to making sure they obtained value for money. Repton's technique, which was first adopted for his fourth client, Lady Salusbury, was to prepare a Red Book (as they have become known), containing a report with sketches and watercolours. At least seventy of these have survived. Usually the watercolours had a 'slide', or overlay, which showed the unimproved scene; lifting this, one discovered the transformed scene as it would be with Repton's proposals carried out. In 1794 William Mason wrote to William Gilpin:

> Repton, a successor to Mr. Brown much in vogue, can draw in your way very freely, which Brown could not do in any way. By this means he alters places on paper and makes them so picturesque that fine folks think that all the oaks etc. he draws on paper will grow exactly in the shape and fashion in which he delineated them, so they employ him at a great price so much the better on both sides, for they might lay out their money worse and he has a numerous family of children to bring up.[16]

Repton's plans, however, lack the subtlety of Brown's and, unlike Brown's, were rarely for a whole estate; normally, they related to a small area, such as the immediate surroundings of the house. This may have been because the client was not prepared for the high cost of a complete survey, but it does illustrate Repton's piecemeal and at times cosmetic approach, compared with Brown's wider strategy.

Many of Repton's proposals were for the alteration of estates in which some improvement had already been carried out; he was called in to advise at several of the parks which Brown had laid out, or where he had prepared plans (which was only natural as Repton had assimilated so much from Brown and continued to work in a style which was recognizably derived from his). Some of the Brown parks where he worked were Brocklesby, Corsham, Crewe Hall, Ealing Park, Longleat, Moccas, Sheffield Park and Wimpole. Almost always, he retained Brown's overall scheme, and his advice was often limited to such things as additional planting or alterations near the house. Very seldom did he suggest any earth-moving or contouring on anything like the scale of Brown's works.

He was influenced to some extent by the debate on the Picturesque, and was on good terms with its protagonists until the arguments became heated. His main disagreement with Price and Payne Knight lay in his recognition of the need to provide for the utilitarian needs of the client:

> I have discovered that utility must often take the lead of beauty, and convenience be preferred to picturesque effect, in the neighbourhood of man's habitation.[17]

Farmland, Repton thought, should be accepted for what it is, and he criticized Shenstone for trying to make too much ground ornamental. He thought, moreover, some intervening terrace, garden or fenced-off space should, for practical reasons, separate the house from the park: for example, his 'before' painting of Lord Sidmouth's house at Richmond Park, shows cows and deer virtually peering through the windows of the Palladian house; the 'after' painting shows the deer banished, and replaced with gravel walks, rows of curious arched trellises, roses and bedding plants in a rather Victorian manner.

Repton also disagreed with the idea of allowing neglect and decay for the sake of their picturesque value. He wrote to one of his clients advising him to adopt principles

which are wholly different from those which the wild improvers would wish to introduce. Places are not to be laid out with a view to their appearance in a picture, but to their use and the enjoyment of them in real life.... With this in view, gravel walks and neat mown lawns, and in some situations, straight alleys, fountains, terraces, and for aught I know, parterres and cut hedges, are in perfect good taste and infinitely more comfortable ... than the docks and thistles, and litter and disorder, that may make a much better figure in a picture.[18]

Gradually, Repton became more and more interested in the area immediately around the house, in the garden rather than the landscape. Although he was no botanist, and his horticultural knowledge was limited, he was no doubt aware of the keen interest in plants, especially newly introduced ones, amongst his clients, and in many of his later schemes he introduces specific areas where these could be displayed. In 1816 he wrote, 'I have lived to reach that period when the improvement of houses and gardens is more delightful to me than that of parks or forests, landscapes or distant prospects.'

In the way he laid out these gardens he was unashamedly eclectic, copying styles from every period and nation. At Ashridge there were to be fifteen different kinds of garden, while at Woburn he proposed:

a terrace and parterre near the house; the private garden, only used by the family; the rosary, or dressed flower garden, in front of the greenhouse; the American garden, for plants of that country only; the Chinese garden, surrounding a pool; the botanic garden; the animated garden, or menagerie; and lastly the English garden, or shrubbery walk, connecting the whole ...[19]

He defended this approach against possible critics:

I will hope there is no more absurdity in collecting gardens of different styles, dates, characters, and dimensions, in the same inclosure, than in placing the works of a Raphael and a Teniers in the same cabinet or books sacred and profane in the same library.[20]

This capricious approach to style seems to anticipate the Victorian period, when the external style of a building was chosen as arbitrarily as one might choose a suit of clothes.

But gradually Repton became aware that he was receiving fewer (and smaller) commissions. He attributed this to the diminishing number of clients of 'taste', and the growing ranks of men who were

... solicitious to *increase* property rather than *enjoy* it; they endeavour to improve the *value*, rather than the *beauty* of their newly purchased estates.[21]

In such a world, he concludes, 'it is not therefore to be wondered at, that the art of landscape gardening should have slowly and gradually declined.'

As we have seen, an increasing horticulturalism – the interest in plants for plants' sake – was a contributing factor to the decline of the Landscape Movement: few arboreta and plant collections have been successful visually, and many plantsmen do not even attempt such a thing.

An increasing interest in antiquarianism, which frequently expressed itself as a wish to preserve anything old, regardless of its aesthetic merits, also played its part in the decline of 'taste'. Horace Walpole had joined the Society of Antiquaries in 1753 because of his interest in Gothic architecture. But eventually he resigned, declaring 'I have no curiosity to know how awkward or clumsy men may have been in the dawn of arts or in their decay.'[22] He had wanted to discover what was best in Gothic architecture, but felt he had made no progress: 'I endeavoured to give our antiquaries a little wrench towards taste – but it was in vain.'[23]

The degeneration of garden design in the nineteenth century can be seen in such schemes as that by J.C. Loudon, where the wayward shapes of the beds cut into grass (misapplied from Repton) and the lack of any overall concept, lead one to feel that perhaps the whole-hearted revival of the formal garden by Sir Charles Barry (1795–1860) or W.A. Nesfield, (1793–1881) is preferable to this compromised creature, the Gardenesque. But Loudon's contribution to horticulture was immense. To write his magnificent eight-volume *Arboretum et Fruticetum Britannicum* he is said to have consulted two thousand books and every botanist and great landowner in the country, and also many overseas. Under the weight of such vast knowledge it was not surprising that Taste wilted.

Abroad, the English style spread rapidly from about 1770 onwards. Horace Walpole wrote home from France in 1771 that 'English gardening gains ground here prodigiously',[24] but he was not always enthusiastic about the results. He visited the Tivoli gardens, then on the outskirts of Paris, which had been made for a financier by the name of Boutin, who, said Walpole, had:

tacked a piece of what he calls an English garden to a set of stone terraces with steps of turf. There are three or four very high hills, almost as high as, and exactly in the shape of, a tansy pudding. You squeeze between these a river, that is conducted at obtuse angles in a stone channel, and supplied by a pump; and when walnuts come in, I suppose it will be navigable.[25]

Other examples of the style are more successful, however, and the average *jardin anglais*, *englischer Garten*, or *giardino inglese* usually consisted of something rather like Stowe today: a combination of classical temples, naturalistic planting and irregular lakes. The French were the first to be enthusiastic, but the idea soon spread to Germany, Sweden, Poland, Hungary,[26] Russia and Italy, and throughout the English-speaking world.

The writer of Brown's obituary made a shrewd remark when he said that such 'was the effect of his genius that when he was the happiest man, he will be least remembered; so closely did he copy nature that his works will be mistaken.' William Whitehead, then Poet Laureate, made a similar point in his poem *The Late Improvements at Nuneham*, which appeared in 1787. At Nuneham Brown (and Nature) had created what Horace Walpole described as 'one of the most beautiful landscapes in the world'. The poem depicts Dame Nature and Brown contesting about who should get the credit for it:

Dame Nature, the Goddess, one very bright day
In strolling thro' Nuneham, met Brown in her way;
And bless me, she said, with an insolent sneer,
I wonder that fellow will dare to come here.
What more than I did has your impudence plann'd,
The lawn, wood and water are all of my hand.

But Brown replies:

> Who thinn'd, and who grouped, and who scattered those trees,
> Who bade the slopes fall with that delicate ease,
> Who cast them in shade, and who placed them in light,
> Who bade them divide, and who bade them unite?

Eventually Dame Nature concedes the point. She 'dropped him a curtsie, and blushing withdrew', but mutters to herself:

> I may have my revenge on this fellow at last
> For a lucky conjecture comes into my head,
> That, whate'er he has done, and whate'er he has said,
> The world's little malice will balk his design;
> Each fault they'll call his, and each excellence mine.

Today Dame Nature has had her revenge. Gradually the brambles and the undergrowth spread, the stonework crumbles, and reeds advance across the lakes as the silt slowly accumulates. Although some landscapes have been deliberately destroyed, most are suffering from sheer neglect; but, given the will and resources, the 'capabilities' of these landscapes for restoration still remain good in many places.

Four days after Brown died, Horace Walpole wrote to William Mason, saying he had 'made a bad epitaph for him, which ... you may recolour with any tints that remain on your pallet':

> With one Lost Paradise the name
> Of our first ancester is stained;
> Brown shall enjoy unsullied fame
> For many a Paradise regained.

If these scenes of Paradise could be restored once more, we would be able to make a fuller assessment of the work of Lancelot Brown, the man who was:

> Born to grace Nature, and her works complete,
> With all that's beautiful, sublime and great!
> For him each Muse enwreathes the Lawrel crown,
> And consecrates to fame immortal Brown.

———

NOTES

1 Revd Richard Warner, *Excursions from Bath* (1801).
2 Partly reprinted in *The Genius of the Place*, Hunt and Willis.
3 Chambers obtained this work through the influence of John Stuart, third Earl of Bute, who advised Princess Augusta at Kew. Lord Bute had a brief but unpopular stint as Prime Minister in 1762–3, and was also a keen amateur botanist who first made Kew an important botanic garden. Several of Chambers' buildings at Kew have survived, including the Pagoda, the Orangery and the Temples of Aeolus and Bellona. This seems to have been the height of his practical contribution to garden design.
4 Revd. R. Clive, according to Stroud.
5 For a detailed survey see Michael Symes, 'Charles Hamilton's plantings at Painshill', *Garden History*, vol. XI, no. 2, autumn 1983.
6 *History of the Modern Taste in Gardening.*
7 *Ibid.*
8 *Observations on Modern Gardening.* Whately gives a detailed description of Painshill.
9 Letter to Richard Bentley, 1753
10 John Brown, *A Description of the Lake at Keswick* (1771). The earlier date suggested by D. Jacques, *Georgian Gardens*.
11 *The Correspondence*, ed. Paget and Toynbee, 3 vols, Oxford 1935. Vol 2 p 899, quoted in Willis & Hunt, op. cit.

12 William Gilpin, *Essay on Prints* (1768).

13 *The Works of John Ruskin*, ed. Cook and Wedderburn, 1903-12. Vol. 8., quoted in *The English Vision* by D. Watkin.

14 When Nikolaus Pevsner gave a lecture on 'The Picturesque in Architecture' at the Royal Institute of British Architects in 1947, he illustrated it with buildings of so many different styles and dates that Sir John Summerson remarked afterwards, 'what Doctor Pevsner this evening described as picturesque architecture is simply architecture.'

15 *Tintern Abbey Revisited.*

16 Letter of 26 December 1794, Bodleian MS Eng. misc. d. 571 f. 224, quoted in *Humphry Repton, Landscape Gardener 1752-1818*, exhibition catalogue, George Carter, P. Goode and K. Laurie (1982).

17 *The Landscape Gardening and Landscape Architecture of the late Humphry Repton*, J.C. Loudon, ed. 1840. p. 99.

18 Quoted by D.C. Stuart in *Georgian Gardens.*

19 *An Inquiry into the Changes of Taste in Landscape Gardening* (1803).

20 *Fragments on the Theory and Practice of Landscape Gardening* (1810).

21 Preface to *Fragments on the Theory and Practice of Landscape Gardening* (1810).

22 Quoted by D. Jacques in *Georgian Gardens.*

23 *Ibid.*

24 Walpole to Chute, 5 August 1771. Yale Walpole xxxv pp. 125-6.

25 *Ibid.*

26 See *The Picturesque Garden*, Pevsner ed., which includes 'The English Garden in Hungary' by Anna Zador, and 'The Arrival of the English Garden in Poland and Bohemia' by Brian Knox.

Gazetteer of Brown's Works

ADDERBURY
5 m s of Banbury, Oxfordshire

Client: Duke of Buccleuch
Small-scale landscape with two, small, linked lakes. Undated plan shows proposed screening for 'offices'. House now an old people's home, owned by Oxfordshire County Council. Restoration programme currently (1985) dredging lakes, removing fallen trees and planting new ones.
  Not open.

ADDINGTON PLACE
1½ m E of Croydon

Client: James Trecothick
In 1781–2 Brown received £800 for work. Early plans show there was once a very small pond and a pinetum. House demolished, park now a golf course.

ALNWICK CASTLE
Alnwick, Northumberland

Client: Hugh Percy, 1st Duke of Northumberland
Extensive works, including damming a stream to form the 'river', from 1760; much survives in good condition. See Willis, *Capability Brown in Northumberland* and *Capability Brown and the Northern Landscape* (Tyne and Wear County Council Museum).
  Privately owned; open regularly.

AMPTHILL PARK
8 m s of Bedford, Bedfordshire

Client: Earl of Upper Ossory
Work done to the value of almost £2,400 in 1771–2. Most of grounds now large public park owned by local council. In reasonable condition, but some facilities badly sited.
  Open to the public.

ANCASTER HOUSE
London Borough of Richmond

Client: Duke of Ancaster
Minor work carried out in 1772. House no longer stands.

ASHBURNHAM
Ashburnham, 7 m NE of Hailsham, East Sussex

Client: 1st Earl of Ashburnham
Plan prepared in 1767. House mostly demolished; extensive park once contained three curving lakes, much woodland and a cascade. See *Country Life*, Vol. 113, pp 1158, 1246, 1334.
  Not open.

ASHRIDGE
3½ m N of Berkhamsted, Hertfordshire

Client: Francis Egerton, 3rd Duke of Bridgewater
Work done 1754–68. Brown's involvement on earlier house uncertain; later rebuilt by Wyatt in Gothic style. Repton made extensive alterations to gardens around house, but elsewhere much of Brown's work remains. Part now a golf course.
  House and 90 acres privately owned; remainder (3500 acres) owned by the National Trust.
  Open occasionally.

ASKE
2m N of Richmond, North Yorkshire

Client: Sir Lawrence Dundass
Undated plans by Brown for a bridge and 'the Head of the Water'. Lake and parkland survive with good trees and Gothic folly possibly by Kent or Brown.
  Privately owned; open occasionally.

ASTROP
¾ m NE of Kings Sutton, Northamptonshire

Client: Sir John Willes
Attributed to Brown in undated poem in Methuen archives, now in Wiltshire County Record Office. Formerly a large lake with two small islands, perimeter planting and clumps. House now demolished.
  Not open.

AUDLEY END
1 m W of Saffron Walden, Essex

Client: Sir John Griffin Griffin (later 9th Baron Howard de Walden and Baron Braybrooke)

Work begun 1763; excellently maintained by English Heritage. See pp. 92–3. Sewage works recently built in park is not noticeable from house and lake.

English Heritage; open frequently.

AYNHOE
6 m SE of Banbury, Northamptonshire

Client: William Cartwright, MP

Work costing more than £1,300 done 1760–63. Gardens near house originally laid out *c*1714. Park (separately owned) now farmed, but overall impression remains. No lake. See John Antony, *Gardens of Britain*, Vol 6.

House owned by the Mutual Households Association; open regularly.

BEECHWOOD
Near Markyate, s of Luton, Bedfordshire

Client: Sir John Sebright

Plan for grounds and alteration of house done in 1754. Little remains of parkland, now farmed and under separate ownership. No lake. House now a private school. Wings each side of the house (façade 1702) almost certainly by Brown, in a restrained classical style. Many trees have been felled; a few protected cedars remain. Rough sketch of a bath-house survives, probably by Brown, marked 'This front to stand obliquely in order to show its side in perspective to the windows of the house'.

Not open.

BELHUS
Aveley, w of Grays, Essex

Client: Lord Dacre

Work on landscaping grounds started 1753; partly built over. Tudor house, which Lord Dacre restored in Gothic style, demolished in 1956. Now a municipal park.

BELMONT *see* WARNFORD PARK

BENHAM
Near Speen, w of Newbury, Berkshire

Client: William, 6th Baron Craven

Brown designed house, built from 1774 by Henry Holland. Stone, originally two storeys with central projecting portico with Ionic columns. Third storey added later, when pediment to portico removed and replaced by straight balustrade. Brown did extensive work to the grounds, beside the River Kennet (once crossed by a wooden Chinese bridge).

Privately owned; not open.

BERRINGTON
3 m N of Leominster, Herefordshire

Client: Thomas Harley

Much of Brown's landscape, done in 1781–2, remains. House by Holland. See p. 141.

Owned by the National Trust; open frequently, but most interesting parts of park not open to the public.

BLENHEIM
Woodstock, Oxfordshire

Client: George Spencer, 4th Duke of Marlborough

Most famous of all Brown's parks (and deservedly so) and probably the largest, done mostly in 1764–8. See pp. 93–105.

Open frequently.

BOWOOD
2½ m w of Calne, Wiltshire

Client: William Petty, 2nd Earl of Shelburne (later Marquess of Lansdowne)

Splendid, well-maintained landscape, done 1761–8; part of house has gone. See pp. 106–8.

Privately owned; open frequently.

BRANCHES
Near Cowlinge, 10 m SE of Bury St Edmunds, Suffolk

Client: Ambrose Dickens

In 1763–5 Brown carried out work to value of £1,500. See p. 61.

Not open.

BROADLANDS
Romsey, Hampshire

Client: Henry Temple, 2nd Viscount Palmerston

Fine landscape, done 1764–78; see pp. 108–10. Main (south) front of house and some internal work also by Brown, with later work by Holland.

Privately owned; open frequently.

BROCKLESBY
10 m w of Grimsby, Lincolnshire

Client: Charles Anderson Pelham (later 1st Baron Yarborough)

Brown submitted plan for grounds in 1771, and in 1772 made plans for ruins of Newsome Abbey. In 1773 made further plan to suit a new house, never built; instead he altered existing Jacobean house. Damaged by fire in 1898, but Brown's hall reconstructed. Large park had several lakes, extensive perimeter planting and many very large scattered clumps. Repton made some alterations *c*1794 but his Red Book is lost. Mausoleum by Wyatt; formal terraces added in C19; much of park given over to forestry.

Not open.

BURGHLEY
In Cambridgeshire, 1 m SE of Stamford, Lincolnshire

Client: Brownlow Cecil, 9th Earl of Exeter
Fine Brown landscape, made in 1754–82. See pp. 110–12.

Privately owned; open frequently.

BURTON CONSTABLE
7½ m NE of Hull, Humberside

Client: William Constable
Brown visited before 1760 and again in 1773. His plans for area immediately round house and for a Gothic screen to some park buildings survive. Early maps show a long 22-acre lake with a bridge, a menagerie, and dotted, 'clumped' and perimeter planting.

Privately owned; open regularly.

BURTON PARK
3 m S of Petworth, West Sussex

Client: Richard Biddulph
Brown's involvement here has recently been identified by Dr Peter Willis following his study of Brown's bank account: he received £200 from Biddulph in 1758. Several lakes. House now St Michael's School.

Not open.

BURTON PYNSENT
Curry Rivel, Somerset

Client: William Pitt, 1st Earl of Chatham
Brown built a pillar here in 1765, in memory of Chatham's benefactor, from whom he unexpectedly inherited the property.

CADLAND
Fawley, Hampshire

Client: Robert Drummond
House of creamy-white bricks by Brown and Holland 1775–9 has gone; site is used by Fawley Refinery. Front was of five bays, with a minimal projection to three centre bays and a low pediment. See *The Destruction of the Country House*. Brown also did the extensive grounds. Because of maturity of existing planting the Reverend William Gilpin reported in his *Remarks on Forest Scenery* (1791) that Brown said 'It was the oldest new place he knew in England!'

For Cadland Cottage, once the site of a *cottage orné* on the Solent, see p. 142.

Privately owned; not open to the public.

CARDIFF CASTLE
Cardiff, South Glamorgan

Client: John Stuart, Lord Mountstewart (later 4th Earl of Bute)
Brown's first visit was probably in 1775 and Spyers did a survey in 1777. Mainly an architectural commission, undertaken with Henry Holland, to re-model and modernize interiors of medieval (and later) buildings. Landscape work included a new drive, turfing and tree-planting around the keep. Little of Brown's work can be seen today. William Burges transformed the castle in 1875.

Open to the public.

CASTLE ASHBY
6 m E of Northampton, Northamptonshire

Client: Charles Compton, 7th Earl of Northampton and Spencer Compton, 8th Earl
Interesting large-scale landscape, begun 1761, with several lakes and garden buildings. Terraces added near the house in C19. See pp. 112–14.

Privately owned; open frequently.

CAVERSHAM
NE Reading, Berkshire

Client: Charles, 2nd Baron Cadogan
Probably begun 1764. Once famous; mostly built over since 1960. House altered for the worse in C19. See p. 79.

Not open.

CHALFONT HOUSE
Chalfont St Peter, E of Beaconsfield, Buckinghamshire

Client: Charles Churchill
Brown's bank account shows payment of £35 from Churchill in 1760. Repton worked here later, but produced no Red Book.

Not open.

CHARLECOTE
5 m E of Stratford-upon-Avon, Warwickshire

Client: George Lucy
Brown's work, begun 1757, survives as deer park, well maintained by National Trust. Contains a small lake and wilderness, cedars and an attractive Jacobean house.

Open frequently.

CHARLTON
2 m NE of Malmesbury, Wiltshire

Client: ?Howard, 12th Earl of Suffolk
Brown did kitchen garden and two cottages, but his 'plans and elevations for alterations of the [Jacobean] house' and 'sketches for water to be made near the house' were not adopted. Large park with no lake.

Not open.

CHATSWORTH
4 m E of Bakewell, Derbyshire

Client: William Cavendish, 4th Duke of Devonshire
Little documentary evidence for Brown's presence: work is attributed on basis of references by contemporary writers such as Horace Walpole, who noted in August 1761 that the owner was 'making vast plantations, widening and raising the river ... and levelling a great deal of ground to show the river, under the direction of Brown' (*Journals of Visits to Country Seats*). Very large park with a complex history and features of special interest both pre-Brown and post-Brown. See John Antony, *Gardens of Britain Vol 6* and 'The Capability Brown Lawn and its Management' in *Landscape Design*, December 1983.

Privately owned; open frequently.

CHILHAM CASTLE
6 m W of Canterbury, Kent

Client: Thomas Heron
Brown made plan in 1777, and later supplied drawings for a greenhouse, offices, stables, lodges and gates. House is mostly Jacobean. Brick terraces and steps apparently pre-Brown; intricate shape of lake makes attribution to Brown doubtful. Some of his building work was carried out but removed during the Victorian period.

Privately owned; open frequently.

CHILLINGTON
8 m NW of Wolverhampton, West Midlands

Client: Thomas Giffard
Splendid park, with large lake and several interesting features, now spoilt by noise of nearby M54. Work carried out, perhaps by owner, before 1762. See pp. 114-15.

Privately owned; open regularly.

CLANDON
3 m of Guildford, Surrey

Client: George, 1st Earl of Onslow
Massive brick house of 1730, with only 8 acres, owned by the National Trust; park owned by Onslow's descendants. Brown's plan dated 1781 now lost. Small lake, just visible from the house.

House is open frequently; park is not open.

CLAREMONT
Esher, Surrey

Client: Robert, Lord Clive
Fine Palladian house, 1769, was Brown's first collaboration with Holland, see pp. 115-17. Brown also did work in grounds. Bridgeman/Kent landscape recently restored by National Trust. House now a private school.

House and grounds open regularly, but access to each is separate.

CLIVEDEN *see* TAPLOW

COLE GREEN
2 m E of Welwyn Garden City, Hertfordshire

Client: William, 2nd Earl Cowper
Brown received payments totalling over £400 in 1756-61 for landscape work. In 1799 Repton did work here and at nearby Tewinwater estate and made series of lakes. House was demolished in 1801 and estate merged with adjoining Panshanger Park. New house (Panshanger) built 1806-9, demolished 1953. Park now a gravel pit. Tewinwater survives.

COMPTON VERNEY
2 m NE of Kineton, Warwickshire

Client: John Peyto Verney, 6th Baron Willoughby de Broke
Once fine landscape now deteriorating, and house empty. Cedars are past their best and stonework of fine classical bridge in disrepair. Work started before 1768 and cost over £2,800. House and one lake can be glimpsed from Stratford/Kineton road; larger lake, on opposite side of road, is used for fishing. Chapel and possibly orangery also by Brown.

Privately owned; not open.

COOMBE ABBEY
5 m E of Coventry, West Midlands

Client: William, 6th Baron Craven
Begun 1771. Brown's enormous lake best viewed from fishermen's entrance; rest of landscape not in good repair. Formal garden added in C19. See pp. 118-20. Owned by Coventry City Council, now a country park.

Open very frequently.

CORSHAM COURT
4 m W of Chippenham, Wiltshire

Client: Paul Methuen

Brown did extensive work to house from 1760, including doubling width of Elizabethan wings on south side. In park made a ha-ha and proposed a lake (made by Repton). Left several avenues intact but removed one on east side to create extensive views. Also removed walled garden on north side and brought park right up to house. Built charming Gothic bath house north-west of house, and made North Walk through trees with views across park. See John Sales, *West Country Gardens* (1980).

Privately owned; open regularly.

COWDRAY
½ m NE of Midhurst, West Sussex

Client: Anthony Joseph Browne, 7th Viscount Montagu

Elizabethan house in ruins, but grounds, according to Ian Nairn (*Buildings of England: Sussex*), kept in good condition by the Cowdray Estate. Brown records payments totalling £850 from 1772-4.

Not open.

CROOME
4 m W of Pershore, Hereford and Worcester

Client: George William, 6th Earl of Coventry

Brown's first major commission, begun *c*1750. He built splendid mansion and made large landscape, now in poor state. Also built his only church here in 1758. House and about 40 acres have recently changed hands. Rest of the park separately owned and farmed.

Parts of the park open very occasionally.

CUFFNELLS
E of Lyndhurst, Hampshire

Client: Sir Thomas Tancred

Brown did work at an unknown date and received £165. Reverend William Gilpin mentions it in his *Forest Scenery*, 1791. Early maps show no lake, except a small round pond south-west of house. House demolished; park now farmed, but many fine trees remain; other areas full of overgrown rhododendrons and brambles.

DACRE HOUSE
Lee, London Borough of Lewisham

Client: Sir Samuel Fludyer

Brown advised in 1767. House demolished *c*1900 and site built over. See *Two Old Lee Houses* by E. and J. Birchenough.

DENHAM PLACE
6 m NE of Uxbridge, Buckinghamshire

Client: Benjamin Way

Brown was paid £600 in September 1773. Early maps show no particular features and no lake. House now used as offices.

DIGSWELL
N Welwyn Garden City, Hertfordshire

Client: John Willes

Work amounting to over £1,100 done in 1771-3. Early maps show small park with small serpentine lake near River Mimram; also path through trees called Monk's Walk. House remains, with only 4 acres; rest now built over. The lake survives, now separated from house by a road.

Not open.

DITCHLEY
4 m NW of Woodstock, Oxfordshire

Client: 3rd Earl of Lichfield

The house is by James Gibbs, 1722. Brown probably altered existing fishpond, and did some contouring around house before 1777. J. C. Loudon worked here *c*1807, and Geoffrey Jellicoe in 1930s. Now owned by the Anglo-American Ditchley Foundation.

Open regularly.

DITTON
2 m SE of Slough, Buckinghamshire

Client: Edward Hussey Montague, Baron Beaulieu

£3,450 was spent on landscape works, 1762-74.

Not open.

DODDINGTON
10 m S of Crewe, Cheshire

Client: Sir Thomas Broughton

Brown prepared plans for new house *c*1770, and perhaps advised on enlarging lake, tree-planting etc. Lake once had domed rotunda on an island. House now a private school, Goudhurst College, leased from descendants of Brown's client. Park in fair condition, but large areas recently sold off and now farmed.

Not open.

DODINGTON
10 m NE of Bristol, Avon

Client: Sir William Codrington

Attractive landscape survives. Work began in 1764.

See pp. 120–29. Sold very recently by Codrington's descendants.

Privately owned; not open.

DYNEVOR CASTLE
3 m W of Llandeilo, Dyfed

Known in Brown's time as Newton Castle. He submitted plans in 1775. Walk to medieval castle (Dynevor Castle) known as 'Brown's Walk'. C18 house now almost a ruin, recently acquired by local authority. Land farmed but retains some parkland atmosphere.

Privately owned; not open.

EATON
3 m S of Chester, Cheshire

Client: Richard, Baron Grosvenor (later 1st Earl of Grosvenor)

Brown began work before 1761 and received £800. His changes can be seen by comparing 1738 estate plan, 1758 views and 1798 estate plan (see Ian Laurie's 'Landscape Gardeners at Eaton Park, Chester' *Garden History*, 12.1, spring 1984). Lakes probably made later by John Webb in Brownian manner. Part of house demolished 1961. Park in good condition; conservation plan for restoration has been commissioned.

Privately owned; not open.

EDGBASTON
Edgbaston, SW Birmingham, West Midlands

Client: Sir Henry Gough

Brown prepared plans in 1776. Part of park now a golf course. Lake, Edgbaston Pool, designated Site of Special Scientific Interest.

Privately owned.

ELVEDEN
5 m SW of Thetford, Suffolk

Client: General George Keppel, 3rd Earl of Albemarle

Brown was paid over £1,400 for work done 1765–9. Part of estate still parkland, with small pond. Sometimes referred to as Eldon.

Privately owned; not open.

EUSTON
3 m SE of Thetford, Suffolk

Client: Augustus Henry Fitzroy, 3rd Duke of Grafton

Brown was paid £900 for work in 1767–9 in park landscaped earlier by William Kent.

Privately owned; open regularly.

FAWLEY COURT
1 m N of Henley-on-Thames, Oxfordshire

Client: Sambrooke Freeman

Now Divine Mercy College and Museum. Brown received over £340, created lawn to link house with River Thames. Temple by Wyatt on island in river. C19 planting has spoilt relationship of house with river. See 'The Freemans of Fawley and their Buildings' by G. Tyack in *Records of Buckinghamshire*, Vol. XXIV, pp. 130–43.

Open very frequently.

FAWSLEY
S of Daventry, Northamptonshire

Client: Lucy Knightley

Brown received £388 for work done 1763–6. Early maps show large interesting lakes on three sides of house and church. Now under split ownership.

Not open.

FINMERE RECTORY
5 m W of Buckingham, Buckinghamshire

Client: Richard Grenville

Brown landscaped garden here while working at Stowe. House rebuilt in 1830s and landscape no longer exists. Roundell Palmer, in *Memorials, Family and Personal* (1896), says it was 'all so disposed as to produce the effect of a long perspective and considerable space where there was really little'.

FISHERWICK
4 m E of Lichfield, Staffordshire

Client: Arthur Chichester, 5th Earl of Donegall

One of Brown's most ambitious schemes, begun 1768; payments continued until 1782. Large Palladian house and 'offices' by Brown, and large-scale landscape with lake, cascade and 100,000 trees. House demolished and landscape destroyed 40 years later when sold in 42 lots. A few plantings and outbuildings remain, but large part of park now being used to extract gravel.

FLAMBARDS
Harrow, Middlesex

Client: Francis Herne

Also known as Flamberts. Small-scale landscape with sinuous lake backed by trees survives as part of Harrow School. Brown did extensive work 1756–70 on house and grounds; house since rebuilt.

Not open.

GARRICK'S SHAKESPEARE TEMPLE
Hampton, London Borough of Richmond

Client: David Garrick
Octagonal temple, built 1756 or 7 with Ionic portico and domed roof beside River Thames, to house Roubiliac's bust of Shakespeare of 1758. Site formerly belonged to Garrick's Hampton House on other side of the road and is connected to it by a tunnel under Hampton Court Road, probably by Brown. Now owned by the London Borough of Richmond.

   Interior open frequently.

GAWTHORPE *see* HAREWOOD
GATTON
2 m N of Redhill, Surrey

Client: Sir George Colebrook
Brown worked here 1762-8. Early plans show temple and several lakes, one large, with two islands and river-like section, and a long, narrow and winding piece of water called The Serpentine, with a waterfall into Engine Pond. Also made plan for a 'great water menagerie'. House now Royal Alexander and Albert School. Brown also worked at Upper Gatton, q.v.

   Not open.

GLYMPTON
8 m SE of Chipping Norton, Oxfordshire.

Small park attributed to Brown by Laurence Whistler. Early plans show Brownian lake.

   Not open.

GRIMSTHORPE
4 m NW of Bourne, Lincolnshire

Client: Duke of Ancaster.
Brown received £105 for extensive set of drawings in 1772. Work probably carried out by estate staff. Fine landscape still exists. See pp. 129-30.

   Privately owned; open regularly.

HALLINGBURY
Great Hallingbury, near Bishop's Stortford, Essex

Client: Jacob Houblon
Brown received payments in 1758 and 1778 for general plan and plans for lodges. House (reminiscent of Osterley) demolished 1922. *Country Life* article of 1914 illustrates extensive gardens in Lutyens style, done by Messrs Wallace. Lake still exists. Outbuildings now houses. Land under split ownership and ploughed.

   Not open.

HAREWOOD
7 m S of Harrogate, West Yorkshire

Client: Edwin Lascelles
Large-scale landscape with fine lake begun after 1772. See pp. 143-4. Formerly known as Gawthorpe.

   Open frequently.

HEVENINGHAM
12 W of Southwold, Suffolk

Client: Sir Gerald Vanneck
Many of Brown's plans survive for this late work, begun 1781. Present owner is renovating fine house by Sir Robert Taylor and it is to be hoped will continue into interesting park.

   Not open at present, but house and lake can be seen from road.

HEWELL GRANGE
Tardebigge, Hereford and Worcester

Client: Lewis Windsor, 4th Earl of Plymouth
Brown received £345 for work in 1768. Repton did a Red Book in 1812. In 1880s house rebuilt and elaborate garden made in 'early Jacobean English Renaissance' style, now gone. House now a reform school.

   Not open.

HIGHCLERE
In Hampshire, 4 m S of Newbury, Berkshire

Client: Henry Herbert
In 1770 Brown made several plans for grounds, and for alteration of house and offices. House later rebuilt by Sir Charles Barry. Landscape work probably carried out by estate staff. Large, attractive park with two lakes, one overlooked by a temple. New motorway will soon cut into park and run close to one lake.

   Privately owned; open regularly.

HIGHCLIFFE
Near Christchurch, Dorset

Client: John Stuart, 3rd Earl of Bute (of Luton Hoo)
Repton attributes a 'bathing place' to Brown; Gilpin mentioned park in *Forest Scenery* (1791). House rebuilt in 1830s and partly demolished in 1970.

   Not open.

HILL PARK
1 m W of Westerham, Kent

Client: Earl of Hillsborough
Brown received £1,200 for work in 1772-5. Early maps show a medium-size park with no large lake,

a pond near house and a cascade in woods to the east. Later known as Valons or Valence. House demolished; Valence School for the Handicapped now stands on site.

Not open.

HILL'S PLACE
w *edge of Horsham, East Sussex*

Client: Charles Ingram, 9th Viscount Irwin
Brown mentions visits in 1769 and 1771, but no drawings or accounts are known. House largely demolished and ground split up in 1816; now built over. Name survives in Hill's Cemetery.

HILTON
E *of Fenstanton, Cambridgeshire*

Client: Mr Pigot (later General Pigot)
Brown made plan after 1777.

Not open.

HIMLEY
6m s of Wolverhampton, West Midlands

Client: John Ward, 2nd Viscount Dudley and Ward
Late project, 1780–82. See p. 144. Owned by Wolverhampton Borough.

Open daily.

HOLKHAM
2m w of Wells-next-the-Sea, Norfolk

Client: Margaret, widow of Earl of Leicester
Brown visited in 1762; extent of his work uncertain.

Open frequently.

THE HOO
Kimpton, Hertfordshire

Client: Thomas Brand
Brown did drawing for bridge over lake and received £150 in 1758. Bridge was not built, but early maps suggest other proposals were. House demolished in 1958. Outbuildings now a chicken farm. Some parkland remains, but lake has gone.

Not open.

ICKWORTH
3m sw of Bury St Edmunds, Suffolk

Client: George William Hervey, 2nd Earl of Bristol
Brown worked on grounds from 1769; in 1781 made plans for new house (not built). Present house built 1794. Extent of surviving Brown work uncertain.

National Trust; open frequently.

INGESTRE
4m e of Stafford, Staffordshire

Client: John, 2nd Viscount Chetwynd
Brown's plan for area north of house survives, dated 1756, and shows several Kent-like features, eg Sham Bridge to small rounded pond (like arched cascades at Rousham). Also Triumphal Arch and other features, probably not built. Existing 'reservoir enlarged and made oval' and obelisk in octagonal pond are surprisingly formal elements, showing influence of Bridgeman and Stowe. Now used by Sandwell Metropolitan Borough Council Education Department as an outdoor pursuits centre.

KELSTON
3m nw of Bath, Avon

Client: Caesar Hawkins
Brown received £500 for work done in 1767–8. House (on ridge overlooking River Avon) and 6 acres now leased to Methodist Association of Youth Clubs; land farmed, but some impression of park landscape remains.

Not open.

KEW *see* RICHMOND PARK

KIDDINGTON
Over Kiddington, 15m nw of Oxford, Oxfordshire

Client: Sir Charles Browne
Brown is thought to have worked here as an employee in *c*1740 before going on to Stowe. Early maps show River Glyme as narrow stream widening into a winding river and a curvaceous lake with island. Formal gardens added by Barry *c*1850.

Privately owned; open occasionally for National Gardens Scheme.

KIMBERLEY
Carleton Forehoe, Norfolk

Client: Sir Armine Wodehouse
Interesting landscape with large lake, now rather decayed. Brown did work totalling £3,000 from 1763. See pp. 144–5.

Privately owned; not open.

KING'S WESTON
nw *edge of Bristol, Avon*

Client: Edward Southwell
Brown charged £84 for plan for alterations around house (by Vanbrugh) and terrace. House now police training college, with 23 acres. Several interesting

garden buildings, one restored. Dramatic site on ridge overlooking Severn Valley (now dominated by industrial Avonmouth and housing estates).

Not open.

KIRKHARLE
20 m N of Newcastle upon Tyne, Tyne and Wear

Client: Sir William Loraine
Brown's first employment, 1732–9. House mostly demolished *c*1836, remains now called Kirkharle Farm. Few traces of parkland remain today. A plan by Brown survives, but probably dates from 1760s (see P. Willis, *Capability Brown in Northumberland*).

Privately owned; not open.

KIRTLINGTON
11 m N of Oxford, Oxfordshire

Client: Sir James Dashwood
An early project, 1751–7. Several drawings still exist; early maps suggest work was carried out. Two lakes survive some distance from house.

Park now under split ownership; not open.

KNOWSLEY PARK
Between Liverpool and St Helens, Merseyside

Client: Earl of Derby
Brown prepared plans 1775–6. Very large park with several lakes, one of great size; much planting with many large clumps. House partly demolished in 1953.

Privately owned; not open.

LACOCK ABBEY
Lacock, 3 m S of Chippenham, Wiltshire

Client: John Talbot
Brown did work in 1755–6. Lake now silted up.
National Trust; open regularly.

LALEHAM
1½ m S of Staines, Surrey

Client: Sir James Lowther
Brown made plans some time after 1763. Now a municipal park with football pitches.

LANGLEY
George Green, Buckinghamshire

Client: Duke of Marlborough
Work to value of £2,800 carried out in 1760s. Early maps show large park with much planting, sizeable lake and a monumental column north-east of house.

Privately owned; Not open.

LANGLEY
12 m SE of Norwich, Norfolk

Client: Sir T. Proctor Beauchamp
Brown's plan of 1765 survives. His proposals for several large lakes and a bridge were not carried out, but ha-ha and planting were done to plan; now added to by Victorian planting, including sequoias and rhododendrons. House now a school, with 57 acres.

Privately owned; not open.

LEEDS CASTLE
4 m E of Maidstone, Kent

Client: John Calcroft
Brown did work at 'Leeds Abbey' in 1771–2 to value of £2,000.

Open frequently.

LITTLEGROVE
East Barnet, London Borough of Barnet

Client: Edward Willis
In 1768 Brown received £700 for work here, now built over.

LLEWENI
NE of Denbigh, Clwyd

Client: Thomas Fitzmaurice
Brown prepared plan costing £100 in 1781. House demolished.

Privately owned; not open.

LONDON: 73, South Audley Street

An architectural commission undertaken with Henry Holland in early 1770s at a cost of £3,700. Soane did some work on the details. Now altered.

LONGFORD CASTLE
Bodenham, S of Salisbury, Wiltshire

Client: Lord Folkestone (later Lord Radnor)
Brown visited twice in 1777 and Spyers made a survey in 1778, at a cost of £50. Early maps show extensive park, with Pleasaunce and statue of Flora, around Elizabethan castle beside River Avon. Gardens altered 1832, simplified after 1945.

Privately owned; not open.

LONGLEAT
4 m SW of Warminster, Wiltshire

Client: Thomas Thynne, 3rd Viscount Weymouth (later 1st Marquess of Bath)
Splendid park made by Brown from 1757. Repton

advised, and further work done in C20, but overall effect is still largely result of Brown's work. See John Sales, *West Country Gardens*.

Privately owned; open daily.

LOWTHER
4 m s of Penrith, Cumbria

Client: Sir James Lowther
Brown drew up plan in 1763; payments continued until 1781. Very large park. House, then Palladian, replaced in 1806 with 'castle', by Smirke, now a ruin (illustrated in *The Destruction of the Country House*).

Not open.

LUTON HOO
Luton, Bedfordshire

Client: John Stuart, 3rd Earl of Bute
Fragment of Brown's plan survives in Metropolitan Museum, New York. Very large park with long serpentine lakes. Most of original planting felled in C19. Luton Airport buildings obtrusive near park entrance.

Privately owned; house and gardens open regularly; park not open, but lakes partly visible from drive.

MADINGLEY
4 m w of Cambridge, Cambridgeshire

Client: Sir John Hynde Cotton
Brown's improvements began in 1756: village houses that blocked view were removed and road lowered to make it less obtrusive. Small lake still exists but other views into former park from house now obscured by planting. House now Cambridge University's Department of Extra-Mural Studies. Formal gardens added in 1910.

Not open, but visible from road.

MAMHEAD
2 m w of Starcross, Devon

Client: 3rd Viscount Lisburne (later 1st Earl of Lisburne)
Brown made structural survey and gave advice about grounds in 1773. House burnt down in 1828, rebuilt by Anthony Salvin. Old maps of park show no water, but indicate an obelisk and an orangery. Packenham correspondence suggests some of Brown's advice on grounds was followed. House now Dawlish College.

Not open.

MELTON CONSTABLE
6 m s of Holt, Norfolk

Client: Sir Edward Astley
Brown's plan dated 1763; scheme cost almost £2,500 and took five years to complete. Also provided drawings for a temple, aviary and Gothic summer-house. C19 maps show lake of irregular shape, but not typically serpentine. Terraces added in C19.

Not open.

MILTON ABBEY and MILTON ABBAS
9 m sw of Blandford Forum, Dorset

Client: Joseph Damer, 1st Baron Milton (later Earl of Dorchester)
Brown started work in 1763 and probably laid out Milton Abbas village when original town behind abbey church was removed. House now a school. Attractive park survives, see pp. 145–6.

Open regularly in summer.

MOCCAS
13 m w of Hereford, Hereford and Worcester

Client: Sir George Cornewall
Brown's plan dated 1778 (now mislaid) appears to have been carried out at least in part. Repton also advised, his Red Book also lost. See R. Sidwell, *West Midland Gardens*.

Privately owned; open regularly.

MOOR PARK
1 m se of Rickmansworth, Hertfordshire

Client: Admiral George Anson, Baron Anson
Brown's work began in 1753 and cost £6,000. C17 gardens described by Sir William Temple in *The Gardens of Epicurus* (1692) destroyed by previous owner. Thomas Whately described landscape in *Observations on Modern Gardening* (1770). Beside a small pool stood a Temple of the Winds, demolished in 1936 after tree-damage. Park now a golf course and much spoilt by insensitive planting. Perimeter has been built on.

Open regularly.

MOUNT CLARE
Roehampton, London Borough of Wandsworth

Client: George Clive
House built 1772–3, probably by Brown and Holland. Enlarged and altered by Colombani in 1780. Park survived until 1930, complete with farm.

NAVESTOCK
1 m s of Ongar, Essex

Client: John, 3rd Earl Waldegrave
Brown began work in 1763 and payments totalling
£4,550 continued for ten years. In 1811 house was
demolished and park became farmland, but some
woods and a lake remain.

NEWNHAM PADDOX
NE of Monks Kirby, Warwickshire

Client: 5th Earl of Denbigh
Brown consulted in 1745 (while still working at
Stowe) when some formal canals were converted
into a serpentine lake. In 1754 designed new façade
for house (drawing survives in Bodleian Library; see
article by A. C. Wood in *Warwickshire History*, Vol.
I., No. I). House altered to French château style in
1875, demolished 1952 (illustrated in *The Destruction
of the Country House*). Little remains of landscape.

NEWTON CASTLE *see* DYNEVOR CASTLE

NEWTON PARK
Newton St Loe, Avon

Client: William Gore Langton
Before 1761. Attributed to Brown by Repton and
George Lucy of Charlecote. Early maps show large
curvy fish pond and remains of 'St Lo's Castle'. Now
a wildlife park.
   Open regularly.

NORTH CRAY PLACE
s of Bexley village, London Borough of Bexley

Client: Thomas Coventry
Brown carried out work amounting to £1,300.
House demolished in 1945.

NORTH STONEHAM
N of Southampton, Hampshire

Client: John Fleming
Brown did work in 1775-8 for £1,400. Early maps
show Brownian 'Park Pond' with an island and two
other lakes, probably earlier fishponds. House demolished in 1939.

NUNEHAM COURTENAY
7 m SE of Oxford, Oxfordshire

Client: 2nd Earl Harcourt
Large park of great interest, c1778; little impression
of Brownian landscape remains. William Mason's

famous flower garden, now derelict, was not far from
house. Brown also did extensive work to the house,
altered again in 1830s by Smirke. Carfax Conduit
acts as eye-catcher to south-west. Small lake along-
side entrance drive. Estate now belongs to Oxford
University; house leased for use as conference centre.
   Open occasionally.

PACKINGTON
Great Packington, West Midlands

Client: Lord Guernsey (later 3rd Earl of Aylesford)
Brown visited c1750, and made plan and drawings
for garden buildings in 1751. Early maps show extensive park with three large lakes, at least one with
Brownian outline. House re-cased in 1766 by Matthew Brettingham. Deer park still exists, part is golf
course.
   Not open.

PATSHULL
In Staffordshire, 7 m W of Wolverhampton, West Midlands

Client: Lord Pigot
Attractive Great Pool still exists though park is now
a golf course, see pp. 146-7.
   Privately owned; open.

PAULTONS
4 m SW of Romsey, Hampshire

Client: Hans Sloane
Brown's work in 1772-4 amounted to £640. Unusual U-shaped lake was on three sides of house
(demolished in 1955). Lake has been badly restored
with no regard for contouring: most interesting part
is a board-walk through a swamp, the silted remains
of part of the lake. Now a wildlife park.
   Privately owned; open frequently.

PEPER HAROW
2 m W of Godalming, Surrey

Client: George Brodrick, 3rd Viscount Midleton
Brown did landscaping work in 1757-8 but his design for new house not accepted. Probably improved
line of river running through grounds.
   Not open.

PETERBOROUGH HOUSE
*Peterborough Road, London Borough of Hammersmith and
Fulham*

Client: Charles Mordaunt, 4th Earl of Peterborough
Spyers made survey in 1774; work continued

until 1778, totalling over £1,200. House demolished in 1798 and a new one built in slightly different position, near an 'ancient maze'. Estate changed hands several times during the C19, losing land every time; most development took place c1897. Now completely built over.

PETWORTH
5½ m E of Midhurst, West Sussex

Client: Charles Wyndham, 2nd Earl Egremont
Large park with two lakes, begun 1751, which gives an excellent impression of an unspoilt Brown landscape, see pp. 130–32.

National Trust; open frequently.

PISHIOBURY
1 m S of Sawbridgeworth, Hertfordshire

Client: Mr Mills
Attributed by Pevsner. Long narrow S-shaped lake looks like Brown's work, but straight axial approach and Oak Walk do not. Lake now overgrown; some encroachment on park by housing. Owned by County Council.

Not open.

PRIOR PARK
Combe Down, SE Bath, Avon

Client: Ralph Allen
Famous landscape for which Brown received payment in 1760. Palladian house is dramatically sited; ground falls steeply to lake with Palladian Bridge (possibly by Brown), as at Stowe and Wilton. House is now a college.

Not normally open, but permission usually given on request.

RADLEY
2 m E of Abingdon, Oxfordshire

Client: Sir William Stonhouse
Brown received £672 for work in 1770–71. House became school in mid C19, retaining 110 acres. Part now golf course with small lake. Recent housing nearby is intrusive.

RANELAGH HOUSE
Fulham, London Borough of Hammersmith and Fulham

Client: Philip Stephens
House, built in 1764, had 21 acres attached, with a further 55 acres by 1775. Brown did work in 1774–8 to value of £1,200, possibly including work to surviving Hurlingham Park (which has a lake).

House demolished 1892 and built over.

REDGRAVE
In Suffolk, 4 m W of Diss, Norfolk

Client: Rowland Holt
Brown began work in 1763; lake dates from 1766. In 1768 made designs for casing red-brick Tudor/Jacobean house with white bricks in the Palladian style, with Ionic portico, executed by Henry Holland the Elder with Hobcraft as joiner. House burnt down in 1945, demolished 1960 (illustrated in *The Destruction of the County House*), but orangery and lake survive.

Not open.

RICHMOND (HILL STREET)
London Borough of Richmond

Client: Mr Frederick Nicolay
Brown's advice sought in 1770.

RICHMOND PARK (Kew Gardens and Old Deer Park)
London Borough of Richmond

Client: George III
When Brown became Master Gardener in 1764 he began to transform this area (no connection with today's Richmond Park). Much smaller gardens of Kew were merged with Richmond Park in 1772. See p. 64. Rhododendron Dell and Mount Pleasant (remains of earlier mount) were Brown's attempt to provide interest in flat riverside site. Planting now transformed.

RISE
5 m SW of Hornsea, Humberside

Client: William Bethell
Brown prepared plan in 1775. Early maps show medium-sized park with two irregular lakes and much planting in Rise Wood. House now a convent.

ROTHLEY
5 m NE of Kirkharle, Northumberland

Client: Sir Walter Calverley Blackett (of Wallington Hall)
Brown was consulted in 1765. Two detailed plans of the lakes survive, and drawings show proposed banqueting house, and rustic arched dam between two lakes (neither was built). Lakes still exist, but with more planting than planned by Brown. See Peter Willis, *Capability Brown in Northumberland*.

National Trust; open all year.

RYCOTE
3 m E of Thame, Oxfordshire

Client: Willoughby Bertie, 4th Earl of Abingdon
Brown did extensive work totalling over £2,400.

Large part of house demolished in early C19, but C19 maps still show park with quite large curving lake and some perimeter planting.

St John's College
Cambridge, Cambridgeshire

Client: Master and Fellows
In 1772 Brown was asked to repair bank of River Cam. In 1773 made plans to alter formal area known as the Walks at cost of £800 (now known as the Wilderness). Received gift of a piece of silver plate valued at £52 for his trouble.

Sandbeck and Roche Abbey
1½ m SE of Maltby, South Yorkshire

Client: Richard Lumley, 4th Earl of Scarborough
Brown worked here 1765-6. Good landscape survives, see pp. 132-4. Roche Abbey and immediate surroundings (but not the badly overgrown lakes nearby) leased to English Heritage.
 Sandbeck is privately owned and not open to the public.
 Roche Abbey is open frequently.

Sandleford Priory
2 m S of Newbury, Berkshire

Client: Mrs Elizabeth Montagu
Brown visited in 1781. Priory is now St Gabriel's School, and land is much reduced, but 'Brown's Pond' remains, together with specimen cedars and other tree-planting. Formal gardens added in C19.
 Not open.

Scampston
6 m NE of Norton, North Yorkshire

Client: Sir William St Quintin
Brown prepared plan in 1772; estate staff did the work. In 1773 designed timber building with Ionic columns to screen end of lake, referred to on early maps as the 'Palladium Bridge'. Maps also show series of three lakes of curved outline, with island, waterfall and bridge.
 Privately owned.

Sheffield Park
5 m NW of Uckfield, East Sussex

Client: John Baker Holroyd
Brown visited in 1776 and Spyers made survey. It is thought that Brown made lower lakes, called 'Woman's Way Ponds' on C19 maps. Repton worked here in 1789 but produced no Red Book. Two other lakes made by James Pulham towards end of C19. Garden is now of great horticultural importance; planting was started after 1909.
 National Trust owns gardens; house is privately owned; both are open regularly.

Sherborne
Sherborne, Dorset

Client: Lord Digby
Attractive landscape with a large lake, see pp. 134-5. Brown started work in 1775 at a cost of £1,250.
 Privately owned; open regularly.

Shortgrove
SW of Saffron Walden, Essex

Client: Percy Wyndham O'Brien (later Earl of Thomond)
Work included a three-arched classical bridge over the River Cam. House was burnt down in 1968, shell remains.
 Not open.

Sledmere
8 m NW of Driffield, Humberside

Client: Christopher Sykes
Brown's plan of 1777 is on display in the house. Fine park with good examples of very large, rounded clumps. Village was moved. See K. Lemmon, *Gardens of Britain*, Vol. 5.
 Privately owned; open frequently.

Southill
5 m W of Biggleswade, Bedfordshire

Client: John Byng, Viscount Torrington
Brown received £500 for plans and visits in 1777. House was sold in 1795, after which Henry Holland remodelled it and did work to grounds. There is a 'round basin' on early maps but otherwise no lake.
 Gardens are open occasionally, but not the park.

South Stoneham
2 m N of Southampton, Hampshire

Client: Hans Sloane
Small park with fishponds and salmon pool, now mostly built over. Brown was paid £1,050 for work done in 1772-80. House now a Hall of Residence for Southampton University.

Spring Hill
3 m SE of Broadway, Worcestershire

Client: Lord Coventry (of Croome Court)
House originally by Brown. Both house and landscape drastically altered in C19.

STANSTED

7 m NW of Chichester, West Sussex

Client: Richard Barwell

Brown visited twice in 1781 and made plans for house, stables etc. Spyers made survey. Mentioned by Horace Walpole in *Essay on Modern Gardening*. Several impressive avenues cut through woods. House rebuilt *c*1900.

Open occasionally.

STOKE PARK

Stokes Poges, Buckinghamshire

Client: Lady Cobham (of Stowe)

Brown made plan for park, but 'Mr Richmond' completed his proposals by making series of long serpentine lakes from five existing 'quadrilateral' ones. House (known originally as Stoke House) rebuilt in 1790s. Repton did work here *c*1792 (his plan is in the British Museum) and suggested three-arched bridge across lake. See p. 67, note 12.

STOKE PLACE

Stoke Green, Buckinghamshire

Client: General Sir George Howard

In 1771 Brown made an elegantly shaped lake, with island, immediately south of the house.

STOWE

3 m N of Buckingham, Buckinghamshire

Client: Richard Temple, Viscount Cobham

Brown employed here as head gardener, 1740–51; extent of his influence at the time is hard to determine, since Lord Cobham had strong ideas. However the gardens today are Brownian rather than Bridgemanian. House is now a school. Condition of gardens, once the most famous in the country, is disappointing: not only are there nettles and undergrowth, but also tennis courts beside the Palladian Bridge, a golf course and a motley collection of school buildings. Some original buildings have been restored. See pp. 55–7.

Open frequently.

STRATFIELD SAYE

7 m NE of Basingstoke, Hampshire

Client: Penelope Pitt

Payments totalling £3,900 recorded in Brown's bank account. Narrow River Loddon widened to form long winding lake. Part of estate now a country park.

Open frequently.

SWYNNERTON

3 m W of Stone, Staffordshire

Client: Thomas Fitzherbert

Undated plan for 'Swinerton', apparently an early Brown drawing, survives. Proposed lake (the fish pond enlarged) was not made, but perimeter planting probably was.

Not open.

SYON HOUSE

London Borough of Hounslow

Client: Hugh Percy, 1st Duke of Northumberland

Brown probably began work here, on north bank of Thames opposite George III's Richmond Park, *c*1759. He made two river-like lakes which still exist.

Privately owned; house and immediate surroundings open to the public, but not the park.

TAPLOW

2 m NE of Maidenhead, Berkshire

Client: Morrough O'Bryen

Brown worked here in 1770s. O'Bryen also inherited Cliveden, and this estate may be the area known as Taplow Court Woods, now part of Cliveden estate (National Trust). Repton did a Red Book for Taplow before 1796.

Cliveden is open frequently.

TEMPLE NEWSAM

SE Leeds, West Yorkshire

Client: Charles Ingram, 9th Viscount Irwin

Brown began work in 1760 and continued through decade. Extraordinary view from terrace of Jacobean house: to left, wooded parkland, to right, industrial landscape of open cast mining. Whether this destroyed any of Brown's lakes is uncertain; three linked lakes survive – less water than on his plan. Much good planting remains, including Brownian clumps on south side, but the owners, Leeds City Council, have treated many areas horticulturally and planted small pointed conifers and rhododendrons around the lakes. Recent intrusive car park. Recreational needs put added pressure on landscape.

Open daily.

THAME

Thame, Oxfordshire

Client: Philip, 6th Viscount Wenman

Recent discovery of payments of £300 in 1758–9 confirms tradition that Brown worked here, and made large serpentine lake.

Not open.

THORNDON
2 m SE of Brentwood, Essex

Client: Baron Petre
Brown received over £5,000 for work done in 1766–72. Spyers did a survey in 1778, and Repton did an early watercolour but gave no advice. Lake remains, but most of park is now a golf course. House, by James Paine, burnt down in 1878, but shell remains.

TIXALL
Tixall, Staffordshire

Client: Thomas Clifford
Brown visited in 1773 and later made plans for altering house, eventually given a new front with Doric portico. Demolished 1927. Brown made a flower garden, removed outbuildings which blocked the view, screened a churchyard and added a stone bridge. After his death, William Eames advised. See *Description of the Parish of Tixall* (1827) by Thomas and Arthur Clifford.
  The gatehouse (1575) is open by arrangement.

TONG
9 m NE of Wolverhampton, West Midlands

Client: George Durant
Unusual Gothick house probably designed by Brown: he supplied plans and elevations for 'Tong Castle' in 1765. Details resemble Gibbs' Gothic Temple at Stowe, and overall form recalls Chambers' Milton Abbey. Estate was sold in 1855, abandoned in 1914, and requisitioned during Second World War. M54 now runs over the house, fragments of which remain on each side. Pleasant lake survives and is easily accessible from the A41. See p. 148.

TOTTENHAM
5 m SE of Marlborough, Wiltshire

Client: Thomas, 2nd Baron Bruce (later Earl of Ailesbury)
Brown first visited c1763. Work included removal of forecourt and rectangular pools, making walled kitchen garden and flower garden, and improving views of extensive park on north-west and southeast. See p. 83. House rebuilt 1825, now a school.
  Open by appointment.

TRENTHAM
3 m s of Stoke-on-Trent, Staffordshire

Client: Granville Leveson-Gower, 2nd Earl Gower (later 1st Marquess of Stafford)
Splendid lake in large-scale wooded setting. Brown

began work c1759. Formal gardens added in mid C19 by Charles Barry. See pp. 135–6.
  Open frequently.

UGBROOKE
Near Chudleigh, 4 m NE of Newton Abbot, Devon

Client: Baron Clifford
Landscape of great interest set in romantic Devon combe. Brown's plan is dated 1761. See pp. 148–58.
  Open regularly.

UPPER GATTON
1 W of Merstham, Surrey

Client: Reverend Tattershall
Brown visited in 1765, 1766 and 1774 and did a general plan and sketches of the lodges, for payment of £52. Early plans show fairly small park with extensive planting but no water.
  Not open.

WAKEFIELD
1½ m SW of Potterspury, Northamptonshire

Client: 2nd Duke of Grafton
Brown is said to have completed Kent's work on house and grounds c1748, when still at Stowe. Thomas and Arthur Clifford, in *A Description of the Parish of Tixall* (1827) remark that 'it was the good taste which Brown evinced, while employed by the Duke of Grafton, to whom he was recommended by Lord Cobham, that laid the foundation of his future fame and fortune.'
  Not open.

WARNFORD PARK
Warnford, Hampshire

Client: Earl of Clanricarde
Brown made survey at unknown date. Early maps show long sinuous lake with island at far end, in Brown manner. House demolished 1956, but traces of parkland still visible. Known in Brown's time as Belmont.

WARWICK CASTLE
Warwick, Warwickshire

Client: Francis Greville, Lord Brooke (later 1st Earl of Warwick)
Brown did extensive work to castle and grounds c1749–51. See David Jacques, 'Capability Brown at Warwick Castle', *Country Life*, 22 February 1979, and articles by Marcus Binney in December 1982.
  Warwick Castle and immediate surroundings are open very frequently, but the park (on the other side of the river) is not.

WESTON PARK
7 m E of Oakengates, Staffordshire

Client: Sir Henry Bridgeman (later Baron Bradford)
Attractive landscape, generally in good condition.
Two contracts survive from 1765 and 1766 which
relate mainly to levelling of ground and making
sunk fences. Brown is also thought to have made
some of the lakes. Park Pool is particularly Brownian, but pointed conifers here are out of place, and
connection between house (1671) and lake is spoilt
by too many fences.
  Open frequently.

WIDDICOMBE
On Devon coast near Slapton

Client: Mr Holdsworth
Brown charged £113 for work thought to have been
done in 1750s.
  Not open.

WILTON
2½ m W of Salisbury, Wiltshire

Client: Earl of Pembroke
Brown did survey in 1779, followed by plan for alterations. Palladian Bridge had been built in the
1730s. Kent also worked here, and Chambers built
a classical pavilion beyond the river. Formal gardens added in late C19, and further work done in
1970s.
  Open frequently.

WIMBLEDON HOUSE
Near Parkside Gardens, London Borough of Merton

Client: Sir Ellis Cunliffe
In 1767 Brown did work to value of £450. House
was south-west of Wimbledon Park; site built over
in late C19.

WIMBLEDON PARK
London Boroughs of Wandsworth and Merton

Client: 1st Earl Spencer
Payments totalling £5,800 are recorded. Park covered 1200 acres, house (demolished c1940) stood
near junction of Arthur Road and Home Park
Road. Survey of park by Thomas Richardson in
1768 has survived. Most of park sold for development in 1870s. Lake remains, between golf course
and recreation ground.

WIMPOLE
7 m SW of Cambridge, Cambridgeshire

Client: Philip Yorke, 1st Earl of Hardwicke
Large-scale landscape of great interest. Brown received £3,300 for work done in 1767-72. Palatial
house (by Gibbs) originally had a Bridgeman landscape and several of his avenues remain unaltered,
including vast one on south side (currently being
replanted). Brown's plan on display in house.
Gothic folly, designed by Sanderson Miller, built by
Brown on hill opposite house. This and bridge over
lakes now restored, but lakes have not and are completely obscured by undergrowth. The Trust has de-
vised a Park Walk following route similar to circular
ride originally planned by Brown, giving good
impression of immense scale of his work. See *Country
Life* articles by Gervase Jackson-Stops, 6 September
1979, and Dorothy Stroud, 13 September 1979.
  Owned by National Trust; open frequently.

WOTTON
10 m W of Aylesbury, Buckinghamshire

Client: Richard Grenville (later Earl Temple)
Most important early landscape, described by
Thomas Whately in *Observations on Modern Gardening*
(1770). Brown worked here in 1742-6, when still at
Stowe. Grounds are at present overgrown, but some
restoration has begun, and present owner has saved
house from demolition and restored it. Two lakes,
one of which, The Warrells, appears once to have
had geometric outline, later softened. Two classical
pavilions and a five-arched rustic bridge (under restoration) which cleverly hides change in water level.
Several other garden buildings in ruined state, including a Turkish temple and a building, not visible,
on Grotto Island.
  Open occasionally.

WREST
Silsoe, 10 m N of Luton, Bedfordshire

Client: Jemima, Marchioness de Grey (wife of Philip
Yorke, 1st Earl of Hardwicke)
Brown retained earlier formal gardens (and pavilion
by Archer), tactfully adding serpentine Broad Water
on south and east sides. House was then Jacobean
with a late C17 façade, rebuilt in 1834. According
to Walpole, Brown did Bath House (near later
Orangery) as two-roomed 'ruin'.
  Owned by English Heritage; open regularly.

WROTHAM
1 m s of Potters Bar, Hertfordshire

Client: George Byng

Brown visited *c*1765, and his surveyor, Samuel Lapidge, did a survey in same year. Smaller than average park with lakes and perimeter planting. Extent of Brown's contribution uncertain. Fine Palladian house dates from 1754.

Not open.

WYCOMBE ABBEY
High Wycombe, Buckinghamshire

Client: Lord Shelburne (of Bowood)

Brown did considerable planting *c*1762, but otherwise extent of his work doubtful. Early plans show much woodland and long narrow lake called The Dyke. Repton worked here later.

Not open.

WYNNSTAY
Near Ruabon, Clwyd

Client: Sir Watkin Williams-Wynne

Brown started to advise *c*1769, but estate does not appear in account book until 1777, when he prepared plans for house (not accepted), grounds and a new dairy. Work to the grounds done by owner's staff. House now Lindisfarne College; lakes said to be in poor condition.

Not open.

YOUNGSBURY
2 m N of Ware, Hertfordshire

Client: Daniel Giles

Brown's plan undated. His lake, made from little River Rib, has narrowed owing to silting, but original outline can be detected.

Garden open, park now farmed.

⚜

Projects not carried out or doubtfully attributed

ALLERTON MAULEVERER
See under Lord Stourton, p. 194

ALTHORP
5 m NW of Northampton, Northamptonshire
Client: John, 1st Earl Spencer
Brown is said to have advised in 1780 but work was carried out by Henry Holland the Younger in Brown's style. See J. Anthony, *Gardens of Britain*, Vol 6.
 Privately owned; open regularly.

APPULDURCOMBE
Between Ventnor and Wroxall, Isle of Wight
Client: Sir Richard Worsley
On a visit in 1779, Brown made plan for alterations for which he charged £52. Judging from C19 maps unlikely that work was carried out. House now a ruin.

BADMINTON
11 m N of Bath, Avon
Client: Duke of Beaufort
Brown prepared plan for alterations to house, but work not carried out. May have altered grounds, but there is no documentary evidence or record of payments. Kent built Worcester Lodge at far end of immense avenue north of house.
 Privately owned; only open for the annual Horse Trials.

BASILDON
7 m NW of Reading, Berkshire
Client: Francis Sykes
In c1778 Brown was consulted about kitchen gardens (now car park). May have offered suggestions, but there is no evidence that he made any plans or carried out work.
 National Trust; open frequently.

BATTLE ABBEY
Battle, East Sussex
Client: Anthony Joseph Browne, 7th Viscount Montague (of Cowdray Park)

Recently identified by Peter Willis from Brown's bank account as possible work. £850 was paid into Brown's account in 1772–4.

BEAUDESERT
5 m NW of Lichfield, Staffordshire
Attributed uncertainly by Adelaide Drummond in her *Memoirs*, 1915. William Eames also said to have done some work. Repton prepared a Red Book in 1814 (possibly the book to which Adelaide Drummond refers) but his work not carried out. C16 house was demolished in the 1930s. Site now a scout camp.

BELVOIR CASTLE
7 m SW of Grantham, Leicestershire
Client: Duke of Rutland
Brown visited in 1779, and Spyers made a survey. Walpole thought Brown's proposals for house and grounds 'showed judgement and would be magnificent'. No work was carried out.

BENWELL TOWER
outskirts of Newcastle upon Tyne, Tyne and Wear
Client: Robert Shafto
It appears Brown was employee here, not adviser or contractor. His impact on park is uncertain and little remains of estate. Some drawings in the County Record Office, according to Peter Willis, could possibly be by Brown.

BOARSTALL
10 m SE of Bicester, Buckinghamshire
Client: John Aubery
Brown made two undated journeys here, and charged 15 guineas. No further details are known. Whether the property he visited is the same as that now owned by the National Trust is uncertain.

BRENTFORD
London Borough of Ealing
Client: Edward Stratford, Earl of Aldborough
In 1773 Brown provided plans and elevations of a

house at Brentford, Middlesex, but it was never built.

BUCKINGHAM HOUSE, London *see* ST JAMES'S PARK

BYRAM

1½ m N of Knottingley, West Yorkshire

Client: Sir John Ramsden
Brown visited in 1782 and Spyers made a survey. One of Brown's last projects. Early maps show large park with much planting criss-crossed with rides and avenues, clumps, etc. Lake is more intricate in shape than typical and it remains uncertain whether work was carried out to Brown's plan. House now demolished.
   Not open.

CAMBRIDGE: The Backs

Client: University Synod
In 1779 Brown presented Cambridge University with ambitious plan (now in the University Library) for riverside area between Peterhouse and Magdalene. This takes King's College as its centrepiece (the 'big house'), and other colleges are screened with trees, like 'offices'. Brown proposed doubling width of River Cam, and creating circular walk. But as plan proposed streamlining plots separately owned by various colleges, the dons admired it but set it on one side, and plan was not adopted. Brown's efforts were rewarded with a silver tray worth £50.

CAPHEATON

s of Kirkharle, Northumberland

Client: Swinburne family
Brown is said to have laid out area near house and was possibly involved with Capheaton Lake, but there is no firm evidence. See Willis, 'Capability Brown in Northumberland' in *Garden History*.
   Not open.

CHUTE LODGE

11 m NE of Amesbury, Wiltshire

Park offered for sale in 1795, and advertised as having plantations 'in the best taste, by Brown and Emes'. No other evidence exists. No lake and the obviousness of semicircular plan of ha-ha and placing of two large circular clumps make attribution doubtful.
   Not open.

COMPTON WYNYATES

5 m E of Shipston-on-Stour, Warwickshire

Client: Earl of Northampton
Spyers made survey 1765-71. In 1767 Brown wrote to the Earl, 'My man is going on with the map of Compton etc, but there is a monstrous quantity of it ...' Unlikely any work undertaken because of Earl's financial problems.
   Open frequently.

COOPERSALE

1½ m SE of Epping, Essex

Client: John Archer
Brown made plan of 1774 and was paid £35 5s. Whether any work in accordance with the plan was carried out is unknown. House *c*1700.
   Not open.

COPT HALL

2 m W of Epping, Essex

Client: John Conyers
Brown was paid £31 10s. for visits and survey at unknown date. Whether any work was carried out is unknown. House demolished *c*1920.

CREWE HALL

E of Crewe, Cheshire

Client: John Crewe
Park attributed by Lord Verulam in his *Tour* (1768), but no record in account book or bank account. Repton, who produced a Red Book in 1791 (now lost), altered lake and made new approaches. House rebuilt in 1866. See *The Destruction of the Country House*. Lake now drained and planted with poplars and conifers. Recent additional buildings very intrusive. Owned by Duchy of Lancaster.

DANSON

Welling, London Borough of Bexley

Client: John Boyd
Interesting plan held by London Borough of Bexley thought to be by 'Mr Richmond'. Drawing technique owes much to Brown and planting is sensitively handled, but treatment of lakes is almost a caricature of Brown's style. Early maps indicate that plan was not carried out.

DORNFORD

See under John Weyland, p. 194.

EALING PARK

London Borough of Ealing

Client: ? Sir Francis Dashwood
Attributed to Brown by Repton in his *Fragments on*

the Theory and Practice of Landscape Gardening (1816). Repton thinned perimeter belt. House now a school, grounds mostly built over.

EYWOOD
Between Kington and Presteigne, Herefordshire

Client: 3rd Earl of Oxford
Brown visited in 1775, but little else is known. House demolished 1954 (see *The Destruction of the Country House*, plate 122), when site was sold to a timber merchant, who felled many trees. Land is farmed but has not been ploughed up, and retains parkland character. Formal gardens added in C19.

FORNHAM ST GENEVIEVE
3 m N of Bury St Edmunds, Suffolk

Client: Charles Kent
Brown made plans for altering house and rebuilding church in 1782, but they were not carried out.

GAYHURST
2 m NW of Newport Pagnell, Buckinghamshire

Client: ? George Wright
Attributed to Brown by Walpole but only Brownian feature on early plans is by Repton who worked here before 1793. Fish Ponds show no sign of Brown's touch. An avenue remains on north side, and solid planting blocks view on south side.
   Not open.

GIBSIDE
6 m SW of Gateshead, Tyne and Wear

Client: George Bowes
Brown wrote to the owner, George Bowes (d. 1760) in 1750 when he was still at Stowe, about a column, but there is no other evidence of his being involved here.
   Chapel and avenue owned by National Trust and open regularly.

HAINTON
10 m W of Louth, Lincolnshire

Client: George Heneage
Attributed to Brown on basis of unsigned pencil sketch for some perimeter tree planting (also shown on C19 plans). However, a straight-sided canal shows no sign of being 'improved'. Part of house demolished.
   Not open.

HAMPTON COURT
London Borough of Richmond

Client: George III
Brown made few alterations here, although as Master Gardener he was responsible for its maintenance. See p. 62. Long straight canal and radiating avenues are one of the few survivals of the Bridgemanian style.
   Open frequently.

HANWELL
N of Hanwell village, London Borough of Ealing

Client: Mr Bayly
Brown charged £8 for a visit, and Lapidge made a survey. First edition Ordnance Survey map, which shows stiff rectangular outline of site scarcely masked by dotted and perimeter planting, suggests no work was carried out. No lake. Park possibly survives as part of golf course.

HARLEYFORD
2 m SW of Marlow, Buckinghamshire

Client: Sir W. Clayton
Grounds traditionally attributed to Brown, but no evidence to support the suggestion.

HARTWELL
1 m SW of Aylesbury

Client: 1st Baron Vernon
Ascribed by Capt. W.H. Smyth in *Aedes Hartwellianae*, 1851. No other documentary evidence.

HAYNES
5 m SE of Bedford, Bedfordshire

Client: Henry Carteret
Referred to by Brown as 'Hawnes' in correspondence in 1778. Uncertain whether any of his work was carried out. There was quite a large park with perimeter planting and a curious circular pool with central circular island.

HESLEYSIDE
10 m W of Kirkharle, Northumberland

Client: ? Edward or William Charlton
Brown's name has been linked with this estate, but a 1776 plan is not by him and consists of five avenues. See Brian Hackett, 'A Formal Landscape at Hesleyside in Northumberland', *Archaeologia Aeliana*, 4th series, 38 (1960), pp. 161-7.

INGRESS ABBEY
on River Thames near Greenhithe, Kent

Client: John Calcroft
Brown did work in 1760–72 for Calcroft (owner of Leeds Abbey) who 'extended the plantations and gardens which Lord Besborough had begun', but not necessarily with Brown's help.

LATIMER
3 m E of Amersham, Buckinghamshire

Client: Lord Cavendish
Attributed by George Johnson in *History of English Gardening* (1829). Early maps show River Chess widened out into Great Water and Lower Water.
    Privately owned; not open.

MAIDEN EARLY (or Erlegh)
Earley, 1 m SE of Reading, Berkshire

Client: William Matthew Burt
Brown made plan, his assistant Cornelius Griffin made preliminary survey. Date unknown. Repton also did work, before 1795. House demolished in 1960.

OAKLEY
3 m NW of Ludlow, Shropshire

Client: Robert, Lord Clive (also owned Claremont)
Visited 1772. Appears that no proposals carried out.

PULL COURT

Client: Dowdeswell family
Attributed by Pevsner in *Worcestershire* (*Buildings of England*). Now Bredon School, which owns 47 acres of original 8,000.
    Not open.

PUTNEY HEATH
London Borough of Wandsworth

Client: Baron Tracey (later 6th Viscount Tracey of Toddington)
Exact location of house and whether any work was carried out unknown. Brown charged £26 5s. for a plan.

RAGLEY
2 m SW of Alcester, Warwickshire

Client: 1st Marquess of Hertford
Attributed by Horace Walpole, but no record in Ragley archives or Brown's accounts of his involvement. Park is extensive with a large lake. Hertford was signatory to petition for Brown's royal appointment in 1758.
    Privately owned; open frequently.

RIPLEY CASTLE
3 m N of Harrogate, North Yorkshire

Client: Joshua Ingilby
Traditionally ascribed to Brown by owner's family, but not backed by any documents. Lakes date from 1844. See Kenneth Lemmon, *Gardens of Britain*, Vol. 5.
    Open frequently.

ST JAMES'S PARK
London Borough of Westminster

Brown made Gardener at St James's in the same year that he was appointed Master Gardener at Hampton Court and Richmond. Two plans survive, one of which includes Buckingham House and part of its grounds. But it was left for John Nash, who appears to have used Brown's plan when making his own, to serpentine the straight canal at St James's.

SHARPHAM
2 m SE of Totnes, Devon

Client: John Bastard
Traditionally ascribed. House overlooks a U-shaped bend of the River Dart, which early engravings portray as a dramatic site.

SLANE CASTLE
9 m W of Drogheda, County Meath, Eire

Client: 1st Viscount Conyngham
A plan and elevation for Gothic stables are attributed to Brown by a hand-written note added to one of two drawings in National Library of Ireland, Dublin. Slane Castle is set in park of Brownian character, so he may have prepared a plan for this as well. Now a hotel.

TESTWOOD
Totton, Hampshire

Client: Peter Serle
A letter inviting Brown to stay survives. Early maps show a house near broad River Test, but no lake. House now offices.
    Not open.

THORESBY
Perlethorpe, 2 m N of Ollerton, Nottinghamshire

Client: Duke of Kingston
Attributed by Humphry Repton, who advised there in 1793 and 1801, and produced a Red Book. Extensive park with large lake and widened River Meden.
    Not open.

WALLINGTON
Cambo, 12 m w of Morpeth, Northumberland

Client: Sir Walter Calverley Blackett

In 1765 when he designed the lakes at Rothley (see p. 183) Brown may have advised about alterations to grounds of Wallington House, but no firm evidence exists.

National Trust; open frequently.

WARDOUR CASTLE
15 m w of Salisbury, Wiltshire

Client: Henry, 8th Baron Arundell

Brown made plan for which he charged £84. Proposals not carried out, but some work done by Richard Woods. Palladian house by James Paine is now a school.

Open frequently in school holidays.

WEST HILL
Putney, London Borough of Wandsworth

Client: Daniel Rucker

Attributed by William Angus in *Seats of the Nobility*

(1787). Repton worked here later, before 1806. House demolished during C19.

WHITLEY BEAUMONT
w of Grange Moor, West Yorkshire

Client: R.H. Beaumont

Brown visited in 1779, and submitted plan. Pre-Palladian house demolished in 1952. C19 maps of the estate do not look Brownian, despite perimeter planting and clumps. Doubtful that Brown's plan was carried out.

WOODCHESTER
s of Stroud, Gloucestershire

Client: Lord Ducie

Brown visited in 1782, Spyers made survey, but no evidence suggests any work carried out. Series of lakes still have steep artificial-looking dams. Now overgrown and given over to Nature Conservancy.

Public access not permitted.

ADDITIONAL CLIENTS WHOSE ESTATES HAVE NOT BEEN LOCATED

FRANCIS BURTON paid £100 into Brown's bank account in 1761.

HON. MISS CHETWYND, presumably a relative of John, 2nd Viscount Chetwynd of Ingestre, Staffordshire (q.v.), paid £187 1s. into Brown's account in 1761–2.

JOHN BULKELEY COVENTRY, brother of George William, 6th Earl of Coventry (of Croome Court), paid £1,300 to Brown in 1756–8.

WILLIAM DALEN or DALING paid Brown £1,300 in 1776.

WILLIAM FARMER paid Brown £84 in 1769.

THOMAS HERBERT paid Brown £180 in 1758. He was possibly connected with the Herberts of Highclere, for which Brown prepared plans twelve years later.

LORD STOURTON: Brown records a visit and survey by Spyers for 'Stourton House', whose location is uncertain. The Stourton estate at Allerton Mauleverer was not bought until twelve years after Brown's death.

JOHN WEYLAND paid Brown £31 for a plan in 1775. Brown names Dornford (Oxfordshire) as Weyland's seat, but the house was burned down in 1770 and estate was sold first to Thomas Southam, and later to the Duke of Marlborough. The Weyland estate was at Woodeaton, so there is some confusion.

'A FRENCH GENTLEMAN': Brown prepared a plan at the request of Reverend Thomas Dyer of Marylebone (see pp. 78–9).

A GERMAN 'PRINZ': a letter to Brown from Major Emmanuel Lutterton, in 1767, discusses a 'hereditary Prinz' who wished to lay out his park in the English manner. This was possibly the Duke of Brunswick Wolfenbuttel who had married Princess Augusta, daughter of Frederick, Prince of Wales.

Bibliography

1 Lancelot Brown

Stroud, D. *Capability Brown*, London, 1975

Tyne & Wear County Council Museums *Capability Brown and the Northern Landscape*, Newcastle upon Tyne, 1983

Willis, Peter 'Capability Brown's account with Drummonds Bank, 1753-1783' in 'Design and Practice in British Architecture: Studies in Architectural History presented to Howard Colvin'. *Architectural History*, vol. 27, 1984, pp 382-391.

Willis, Peter 'Capability Brown in Northumberland' in *Garden History* IX, No. 2, Autumn 1981, pp 157-83

2 The Eighteenth Century

Burke, Joseph *English Art, 1714-1800*, Oxford 1976

Humphreys, A. R. *The Augustan World*, London 1954

Mingay, G. E. *English Landed Society in the Eighteenth Century*, London 1963

3 The Landscape Movement

Hussey, Christopher *English Gardens and Landscapes 1700-1750*, London 1967

Hunt, J. D. and Willis, Peter, eds. *The Genius of the Place: the English Landscape Garden 1620-1820*, London 1975

Malins, Edward *English Landscaping and Literature 1660-1840*, London 1966

Walpole, Horace *History of the Modern Taste in Gardening* or *Essay on Modern Gardening*, London 1780-86 etc.

4 Other Works Cited or Referred to

Amherst, Alicia *A History of Gardening in England*, 3rd edn, London 1910

Andrews, C. Bruyn, ed. *The Torrington Diaries*, 4 vols, London 1934

Anon. *The Rise and Progress of the Present Taste in Planting Parks etc*, 1767

Antony, John *The Gardens of Britain, vol. 6: The East Midlands*, London 1979

Balderston, K. C. *Thraliana, The Diary of Mrs. Hester Lynch Thrale*, 1942

Batey, Mavis *Nuneham Courtenay Guidebook*, 1979

Beharrel, C. H. *Claremont Landscape Garden Guidebook*, 1984

Beresford, Maurice *History on the Ground, Six Studies in Maps and Landscapes*, 2nd edn, 1971

Berrall, Julia S. *The Garden, an Illustrated History from Ancient Egypt to the Present Day*, London 1966

Bilikowski, K. *Hampshire's countryside heritage: historic parks and gardens*, Hampshire Planning Department 1983

Binney, Marcus 'Warwick Castle Revisited', *Country Life*, December 1982

Bisgrove, Richard *The Gardens of Britain, vol. 3: Berkshire, Oxfordshire, Buckinghamshire, Bedfordshire and Hertfordshire*, London 1978

Boswell, James *Life of Johnson*, 1791

Bowood Guidebook, 1984

Braybrook, Lord *History of Audley End*, 1836

Brettingham, Matthew *The Plans, Elevations and Sections of Holkham in Norfolk*, 1761

Bridgeman, Sarah *A General Plan of ... Stowe ... with Several Perspective Views in the Gardens*, London 1739, 2nd edn, 1746

Brown, John *A Description of the Lake at Keswick*, 1771

Burke, Edmund *Philosophical Enquiry into the Origin of our Ideas of the Sublime and the Beautiful*, 1757

Campbell, Colen, et al. *Vitruvius Britannicus, or The British Architect*, 6 vols, London 1715-71

Carter, George, Goode, P. and Laurie, K. *Humphry Repton, Landscape Gardener, 1752-1818*, Norwich and London 1982

Castell, Robert *The Villas of the Ancients Illustrated*, London 1728

Chase, Isabel W. U. *Horace Walpole, Gardenist*, Princeton, New Jersey 1943

Chambers, William *Designs of Chinese Buildings, Furniture, etc.*, 1757

Chambers, William *A Dissertation on Oriental Gardening*, 1772

Clark, H. F. 'Eighteenth-Century Elysiums. The Role of "Association" in the Landscape Movement,' *Journal of the Warburg and Courtauld Institutes*, VI (1943) 165-89. Reprinted in *England and the Mediterranean Tradition*, London 1945

Clark, Kenneth *Landscape into Art*, London 1949

Clarke, George B. 'Lancelot Brown's Work at Stowe', *The Stoic* XXIV (December 1969), pp. 11–15

Cobham, Ralph 'Brown in Memoriam: Blenheim Park in perpetuity', *Landscape Design*, 146, 12/1983

Colvin, H. M., Crook, J. Mordaunt, et al. *The History of the Kings Works, vol V: 1660–1782*, London 1977

Cooper, Phyllis M. *The Story of Claremont*, 6th edn, Claremont 1975

Compton Estates Management Services *Capability Brown at Castle Ashby*, Exhibition Catalogue, 1983

Cornforth, John 'The Making of the Bowood Landscape', *Country Life*, 7.9.72, pp. 546–9

Country Life *Croome Court, Worcestershire* 25.4.1903

Cowell, F. R. *The Garden as a Fine Art*, London 1978

Cowper, William *The Task*, 1785

Defoe, Daniel *A Tour Thro' the Whole Island of Great Britain*, 3rd edn, 1742

Desmond, Ray *Bibliography of British Gardens*, Winchester 1984

Dickens, L., and Stanton, M. *An 18th-Century Correspondence*, London 1910

Drury, P. J. and Gow, I. R. *Audley End House Guidebook*, 1984

Dyer, John *Poems*, ed. E. Thomas, London 1903

Elwes and Robinson *Castles, Mansions ... of Western Sussex*, 1879

Feret, C. J. *Fulham Old and New*, London 1900

Ford, Boris, ed. *From Dryden to Johnson*, Harmondsworth 1957

Fulham History Society *History of Fulham*, London 1970

Gardner, P. H. B. *A Guide to Trees in Bowood Pleasure Grounds*, Bowood 1976

Gibson, M. *Capability Brown in Staffordshire*, Staffordshire County Library 1981

Gilpin, William *A Dialogue upon the Gardens ... at Stowe*, London 1748

Gilpin, William *Essays on Prints*, 1768

Gilpin, William *Observations on ... the mountains and lakes of Cumberland and Westmorland ... in the year 1772*, 3rd edn, London 1808

Gilpin, William *Observations on the River Wye ... in ... the year 1770*, London 1782

Gray, Thomas *Poems*, ed. A. L. Pool, Oxford 1917

Green, David *Blenheim Palace*, London 1951

Hadfield, Miles, Harling R., and Highton, L. *British Gardeners, A Biographical Dictionary*, London 1980

Hadfield, Miles *History of British Gardening*, London 1969

Harewood House, Yorkshire *Guidebook*, 1984

Harris, John *A Country House Index*, Isle of Wight 1970

Harvey, John H. *Early Gardening Catalogues*, London 1972

Hasted, Edward *History and topographical survey of Kent, 1778–99*

Hodgson, John *A Biographical Dictionary of Northumberland ... 1820*, unpublished. Northumberland C.R.O., N.R.O. 746

Hogarth, William *The Analysis of Beauty*, London 1753

Horsfield, T. *The History, Antiquities and Topography of ... Sussex*, Lewes 1835

Hume, David *Enquiries Concerning the Human Understanding*, 1748

Hunt, J. D. 'Emblem and Expressionism in the 18th-Century Landscape Garden', *Eighteenth-Century Studies* IV (1971)

Hunt, J. D. *The Figure in the Landscape*, Baltimore and London 1977

Hussey, Christopher *The Picturesque: Studies in a Point of View*, London and New York 1927

Iljin, M. 'Russian Parks of the 18th Century' *Architectural Review*, February 1964

Jackson-Stops, Gervase 'Broadlands, Hampshire', *Country Life* 4.12.80 and 11.12.80

Jackson-Stops Gervase 'Exquisite Contrivance: The Park and Gardens at Wimpole', *Country Life* 6.7.79

Jackson-Stops, Gervase and Beharrel, C. H. *Petworth House Guidebook* 1984

Jacques, David 'Capability Brown at Warwick Castle', *Country Life* 22.2.79

Jacques, David 'Capability Brown, the professional man', *Landscape Design*, February 1978, pp. 24–7

Jacques, David *Georgian Gardens: the Reign of Nature*, London 1983

Jarrett, David *The English Landscape Garden*, London 1978

Jellicoe, Geoffrey and Susan *The Landscape of Man*, London 1978

Jourdain, Margaret *The Work of William Kent: Artist, Painter, Designer and Landscape Gardener*, London and New York 1948

Kennedy, Carol *Harewood House: The Life and Times of an English Country House*, London 1982

Knight, Richard Payne *Analytical Enquiry into the Principles of Taste*, 1805

Knight, Richard Payne *The Landscape, a Didactic Poem*, 1794

Langley, Batty *New Principles of Gardening ...*, London 1728

Law, Ernest *History of Hampton Court Palace*, 3 vols, London 1885–91

Lemmon, Kenneth *Gardens of Britain, vol. 5: Yorkshire and Humberside*, London 1978

Loudon, John C. ed. *The Landscape Gardening and Landscape Architecture of the late Humphry Repton*, 1840

Loudon, John C. *The Suburban Gardener and Villa Companion*, London 1836

Manwaring, Elizabeth W. *Italian Landscape in 18th-Century England, 1700–1800*, London 1925

Marshall, William *On planting and rural ornament*, 3rd edn, London 1803

Martin, Peter E. 'Intimations of the New Gardening: Alexander Pope ... at Sherborne', *Garden History* vol. 4, No. 1

Mason, George *Design in Gardening*, 1768

Mason, William *The English Garden ...*, York 1783

Mason, William *An Heroic Epistle to Sir William Chambers ...*, London 1773

Mavor, William *New Description of Blenheim*, London 1793

Mitford, John *The Correspondence of Horace Walpole and William Mason*, London 1851

Moggridge, Hal 'Blenheim Park', *The Garden* (R. H. S. Journal) 108, November 1983, pp. 432–7

Moggridge, Hal 'Blenheim Park: the restoration plan', *Landscape Design* 146, 1983, pp. 9–10

Moggridge, Hal 'Cadland, Hampshire, restoration of Capability Brown's landscape for Bourn Hill Cottage', *Landscape Design* 144, 1983

Morris, Christopher *The Journeys of Celia Fiennes*, 2nd edn, London 1949

Morris, Francis, O. *A Series of Picturesque Views of Seats of Noblemen ...*, 6 vols, London 1866–80

Norberg-Schulz, Christian *Genius Loci: Towards a Phenomenology of Architecture*, London 1980

Norberg-Schulz, Christian *Meaning in Western Architecture*, London 1975

National Trust *Charlecote Park Guidebook*, 1983

National Trust *Wimpole Hall Guidebook*, 1983

Palladio, Andrea *Quattro libri dell'Architettura*, Venice 1570

Patterson, Allen *Gardens of Britain, vol. 2: Dorset, Hampshire and the Isle of Wight*, London 1978

Peake, Charles *Poetry of the Landscape and the Night*, 1967

Penn, John *History and Descriptive Account of Stoke Park*, 1813

Pevsner, Nikolaus et al *The Buildings of England*, Harmondsworth 1951 onwards

Pevsner, Nikolaus *The Englishness of English Art*, London 1956

Pevsner, Nikolaus *The Picturesque Garden and its influence outside the British Isles*, Washington D.C. 1974

Pevsner, Nikolaus *Studies on Art, Architecture and Design*, 2 vols, London 1968

Player, John *Sketches of Saffron Walden*, 1845

Plumb, J. H. *England in the Eighteenth Century*, Harmondsworth, revised edn. 1963

Pope, Alexander *Poems* (Twickenham edn), ed. J. Butt, et al, 6 vols, London 1939–54

Price, Uvedale *An Essay on the Picturesque*, 1794

Reeve, Joseph *Ugbrooke Park*, London 1776

Repton, Humphry *An Enquiry into the Changes of Taste in Landscape Gardening ...*, London 1806

Repton, Humphry *Fragments on the Theory and Practice of Landscape Gardening ...*, London 1816

Repton, Humphry *Observations on the Theory and Practice of Landscape Gardening ...*, London 1803

Reynolds, Sir Joshua *Discourses on Art*, ed. Robert R. Wark, 2nd ed, New Haven and London, 1975

Richardson, Jonathan *Theory of Painting*, 1715

Richardson, Thomas *Survey of the Royal Gardens of Kew and Richmond*, 1771

Rowan, Alistair 'The Landscape at Ugbrooke, Devon', *Country Life*, 20.7.67

Sales, John *West Country Gardens*, Gloucester 1980

Sales, Philip 'Ordered Naturalness at Bath', *Country Life*, 22.3.79

Scott, Rupert 'Arcadian Rot', *Architects' Journal* 2.3.83

Shaftesbury, Antony *The Moralists: A Philosophical Rhapsody*, London 1709

Sharp, Thomas 'The Replanning and Replanting of the College Grounds', *The Eagle* vol. LIV, 1950–51 (St John's) Cambridge

Shaw, Stebbing *History and Antiquities of Staffordshire*, 2 vols, London 1798–1801

Shenstone, William *Unconnected Thoughts on Gardening*, London 1764

Sherburn, George W., ed. *The Correspondence of Alexander Pope*, 5 vols, Oxford 1956

Sidwell, Ron *West Midland Gardens*, Gloucester, 1981

Smollett, Tobias G. *Travels through France and Italy*, 1766

Spence, Joseph *Observations, Anecdotes, and Characters of Books and Men Collected from Conversation*, 2 vols, ed. James M. Osborn, Oxford 1966

Strong, Roy; Binney, Marcus; Harris, John *The Destruction of the Country House*, London 1974

Stroud, Dorothy 'The Charm of Natural Landscape, Park and Gardens at Wimpole', *Country Life*, 13.7.79

Stuart, D. C. *Georgian Gardens*, London 1979

Summerson, John N. *Architecture in Britain 1530–1830*, 5th edn, Harmondsworth 1969

Summerson, John N. *Georgian London*, 2nd edn, London 1970

Switzer, Stephen *Ichnographia Rustica ...* 3 vols, London 1718; 2nd edn. 1742

Thacker, Christopher 'Voltaire and Rousseau: Eighteenth-Century Gardeners', *Studies on Voltaire and the Eighteenth Century* XC, 1972

Thomas, Graham Stuart *Gardens of the National Trust*, London 1979

Thomson, James *Poetical Works*, ed. J. L. Robertson, London 1908

Till, Eric 'Capability Brown at Burghley', *Country Life*, 16.10.75

Toynbee, P. J. and Whibley, L. *The Correspondence of Thomas Gray*, 3 vols, Oxford 1935

Trevelyan, G. M. *English Social History*, London 1944

Tunnard, Christopher *Gardens in the Modern Landscape*, 2nd edn, London and New York 1948

Tyack, Geoffrey 'The Freemans of Fawley', *Records of Buckinghamshire* vol. xxiv pp. 133–43

University of Cambridge *Madingley Hall Guidebook*, 1976

Walpole, Horace *Correspondence*, ed. Wilmarth S. Lewis, New Haven 1937 onwards

Walpole, Horace 'Journals of Visits to Country Seats', *Walpole Society* vol. 16, London 1928

Warner, Richard *Excursions from Bath*, Bath 1801

Watkin, David *The English Vision*, London 1982

Watts, Alan *The Way of Zen*, London and New York 1957

Webb, Geoffrey, ed. *The Complete Works of Sir John Vanbrugh*, vol. iv, The Letters, 1928

Whately, Thomas *Observations on Modern Gardening*, 1770

Whistler, L. et al. *Stowe, a Guide to the Gardens*, 3rd edn, 1974

Whitehead, William *The Late Improvements at Nuneham*, 1787

Williams, J D. *Audley End: The Restoration of 1762–1797*, Chelmsford 1966

Willis, Peter *Charles Bridgeman and the English Landscape Garden*, London 1977

Willis, Peter ed. *Furor Hortensis: essays on the history of the English landscape garden, in memory of H. F. Clark*, Edinburgh 1974

Wilson, Michael *William Kent: architect, designer, painter, gardener 1685–1748*, London 1984

Wittkower, Rudolf *Palladio and English Palladianism*, London 1974

Woodbridge, Kenneth *Landscape and Antiquity: Aspects of Culture at Stourhead 1718–1838*, Oxford 1970

Woodbridge, Kenneth 'William Kent as Landscape Gardener: a reappraisal', *Apollo* vol. c August 1974, pp. 126–37

Woodbridge, Kenneth 'William Kent's Gardening: The Rousham Letters', *Apollo* vol. c October 1974, pp. 282–29

Wright, Tom *Gardens of Britain, vol. 1: Kent, East and West Sussex*, London 1978

Young, Arthur *Six Months' Tour through the North of England*, 1770

Young, Edward *The Complaint, or Night-Thoughts*, 1742–5

Author's Acknowledgments

I would like to thank all those who have helped in various ways in the preparation of this book.

Of the many owners of estates I shall single out Mrs G. V. Drummond of Cadland, in particular, for her enthusiasm and interest; thanks are also due to Lord Scarbrough (of Sandbeck Park); and also to Mrs P. Brunner (Wotton), Mr Buxton (Kimberley), Captain T. H. Clifford (Ugbrooke), Mr A. Al Ghazzim (Heveningham) and Mr Kent (Dodington).

I would also like to express my gratitude to Dr Peter Willis, Miss Krystyna Bilikowski (Hampshire Planning Department), Mr George Clarke (Stowe), Mr A. M. Gordon-Lee (Cheshire Planning Department), Miss Jackson (Knowsley Borough Council), Moira Maclean Smithers, Mrs J. E. Neale (Southampton Museum) and Mr D. E. Randall (Berkshire Planning Department). The following administrative and estate staff were also helpful: Mr Robin Moore (Coombe Abbey), Mr P. McKay (Castle Ashby), Mr R. A. Pullin (Broadlands), Miss M. Macdonald (Sherborne); and also Mr H. Webber (Berrington), Mr J. B. Henderson (Croome), Mr V. Smith (Luton Hoo), the Secretary of Claremont School and the Headmaster of Beechwood School.

Others who took the trouble to answer correspondence, often at length, included the Marquis of Hertford, Lord Methuen, the Earl of Shelburne, Mrs A. R. Lucas; Miss H. C. Fiennes (Basildon Park), Mrs B. Fox (Trentham), Mr F. C. Jolly (Holkham), Mrs C. Lakeland (Weston Park), Mr M. A. Pearman (Chatsworth), Mr A. A. Rainbow (Gatton Park), Mr B. M. Thomas (Chilham Castle), Mr J. B. L. Watson (Ditchley Park), Mr R. J. H. Whitworth (National Trust, Northumbria Region); the following librarians, archivists and staff of County Record Offices: Miss A. J. E. Arrowsmith (Suffolk), S. J. Barnes (Oxfordshire), E. J. Butler (Co. Durham), Mrs R. Clarkson (Hammersmith and Fulham), J. F. J. Collett-White (Bedfordshire), W. J. Connor (West Yorkshire), C. R. Davey (East Sussex), M. W. Farr (Warwickshire), J. M. Farrar (Cambridgeshire), Mrs P. Gill (West Sussex), V. Gray (Essex), J. A. S. Green (Berkshire), H. A. Hanley (Buckinghamshire), J. T. Hopkins (Cheshire), Miss J. Kennedy (Norfolk), N. W. Kingsley (Gloucestershire), D. F. Lamb (Hampshire), D. Randall (Staffordshire), K. H. Rogers (Wiltshire), Mrs M. M. Rowe (Devon), Mrs J. C. Shepherd (Shropshire), Mrs C. M. Short (South Yorkshire), F. B. Stitt (Salt Library, Stafford), Miss R. Watson (Northamptonshire), P. Walne (Hertfordshire), A. M. Wherry (Hereford and Worcester), Miss P. J. White (Hampshire), Kent County Archivist, and the Librarian, St John's College, Cambridge; also Mr Peter Goodchild, Mr Roy Jackman, Lady Victoria Leatham, Mr Christopher Thacker and Mr S. Whitehouse.

In addition I would like to thank the numerous local people and others who gave information over the telephone, of whom I have space to mention only Mr Roger Pye (Eywood) and Miss Margaret Hudson (Gibside).

Special thanks to Mr Jim Reynolds, Mr Michael Dover, Miss Barbara Mellor; to my wife; and to Mrs Isabel Grindley for her enthusiastic help.

Picture Acknowledgments

The author and publishers would like to thank the following by whose kind permission the illustrations are reproduced on the pages indicated (numbers in italics refer to colour illustrations): by gracious permission of Her Majesty the Queen: 49 below; John Bethell: 48 left, 52 below, 98–99; Bodleian Library, Oxford: 27 above and below; British Architectural Library/RIBA: 75 above and below, 151 above and below, 152; Trustees of the British Museum: 48 right, 49 above, 69 above and below; the Cadland Trustees: 125 above (photo Armitage Photographers); Syndics of Cambridge University Library: 26 below, 51 below; Castle Museum and Art Gallery, Nottingham: 25 below; Trustees of the Chatsworth Settlement: 28 above, 45 below (photos Courtauld Institute of Art); Country Life: 45 above, 103 above and below, 124 below, 128 below; Trustees of the Croome Estate: *85* above; Devon Library Services (West Country Studies Library): 70 above; English Heritage: 97 below left; Essex Record Office: 52 above, 97 right; Lord Forteviot: 21 above (presently on loan to Brooks's Club, photo Thos. Agnew and Sons Ltd); Hampshire County Council, Historic Parks and Gardens Survey: *88*; Earl of Harewood: 126 above and below (photos Roy Harfield), *138–9*; A. F. Kersting: 22, 23 above and below; by kind permission of His Grace the Duke of Marlborough: 21 below (photo Jeremy Whitaker);

Mary Evans Picture Library: 104 above, 125 below; National Gallery, London: 24; National Portrait Gallery, London: 50; National Trust: *10–11* (Anglesey Abbey, photo Jeremy Whitaker), 25 above, 26 above, 28 below (Claremont), *46–7* (photo John Bethell), 74 below (Wimpole), 122 below (Wallington); Marquess of Northampton: 71 below; Royal Commission on Historical Monuments (England): 104 below; Trustees of the William Salt Library, Stafford: 154–55 (photo Peter Rogers); Earl of Scarbrough: 123 above and below (photos Jim Swinscoe); Geoffrey Shakerley/Photographic Records Limited: 102; Staffordshire County Record Office: 76 below (photo Peter Rogers); Roger Turner: *9* above and below, *12*, 27 above, 51 above, 70 below, 71 above, 72 below left and right, 73, 74 above, 76 above, *86–7*, 97 above, 101 above, 121 above, 124 above, 127 above and below, 128 above and below, *137* above and below, *140*; by courtesy of the Board of Trustees of the Victoria and Albert Museum: 149; Warwickshire County Council (Countess of Craven): 121 below; Weidenfeld and Nicolson Archive: 122 above, 150 above and below, 153 above and below, 156 (photo Kerry Dundas); Woodstock Town Council: 101 below (photo Cynthia Bradford); Marquess of Zetland: *85* below. The plans on pages 72 and 100 were drawn by the author.

Index

Estates mentioned only in the Gazetteer (which is arranged alphabetically) are not listed. Page numbers in *italic* refer to illustrations.